SMALL FIRM OWNERSHIP AND CREDIT CONSTRAINTS IN INDIA

Micro, small and medium enterprises (MSMEs) are considered the backbone of the Indian economy, but limited access to external finance can be a major constraint which hinders their growth and productivity. This barrier acts as a double-edged sword in the case of women and socially disadvantaged owners who are also subjected to discrimination in credit markets.

This book investigates the role of credit constraints in determining the performance of MSMEs in India and considers how gender- and caste-based prejudices influence and inform a firm owner's access to formal credit. Combining micro-econometric techniques with large-scale firm surveys, it offers readers new findings, which shed light on the effect of ownership characteristics on credit access and firm performance. It also examines recent credit policy initiatives aimed at weaker sections of society including Scheduled Caste (SC), Scheduled Tribe (ST) and women-owned enterprises and puts forward valuable policy recommendations.

This volume will serve as a useful reference text for students and researchers of economics, finance, business and management, entrepreneurship, credit policy, development economics, caste discrimination, gender discrimination and South Asian studies.

Rajesh Raj S.N. is Associate Professor at the Department of Economics, Sikkim University, Gangtok, India. His main research interests are in industrial economics, firm dynamics, efficiency and productivity analysis and informal labour. His publications include articles in academic journals such as *Small Business Economics*, *Journal of Comparative Economics*, *Manchester School*, *International Journal of Educational Development*, *Oxford Development Studies*, *European Journal of Development Research* and *Developing Economies*, among others, numerous chapters in edited volumes and the book *Out of the Shadows? The Informal Manufacturing in Post-Reform India*, co-authored with Kunal Sen (2016). He is a recipient of the Dr. V.K.R.V. Rao Prize in Economics for the year 2014 by the Institute for Social and Economic Change, Bangalore and Indian Council of Social Science Research (ICSSR), New Delhi, India.

Subash Sasidharan is Associate Professor at the Indian Institute of Technology, Madras, India. His research interests include economics of foreign direct investment, small firms and industrial development, innovation and technological change and international trade. His research work has been published in leading international journals including *Research Policy*, *Small Business Economics*, *World Development*, *Economic Modelling*, *Economic Systems* and *Developing Economies*. He is also an affiliated researcher with the Centre for Technology Innovation and Economic Research.

I0894785

SMALL FIRM OWNERSHIP AND CREDIT CONSTRAINTS IN INDIA

Rajesh Raj S.N. and Subash Sasidharan

Routledge
Taylor & Francis Group
LONDON AND NEW YORK

First published 2021
by Routledge
2 Park Square, Milton Park, Abingdon, Oxon OX14 4RN

and by Routledge
52 Vanderbilt Avenue, New York, NY 10017

Routledge is an imprint of the Taylor & Francis Group, an informa business

British Library Cataloguing-in-Publication Data
A catalogue record for this book is available from the British Library

Library of Congress Cataloging-in-Publication Data
Names: Rajesh Raj, S. N., author. | Sasidharan, Subash, author.
Title: Small firm ownership and credit constraints in India / Rajesh Raj S.N. and Subash Sasidharan.
Description: Milton Park, Abingdon, Oxon ; New York, NY : Routledge, 2021. | Includes bibliographical references and index. | Summary: "Micro, small and medium enterprises (MSMEs) are considered the backbone of the Indian economy, but limited access to external finance can be a major constraint which hinders their growth and productivity. This barrier acts as a double-edged sword in the case of women and socially disadvantaged owners who are also subjected to discrimination in credit markets. This book investigates the role of credit constraints in determining the performance of MSMEs in India and considers how gender- and caste-based prejudices influence and inform a firm owner's access to formal credit. Combining micro-econometric techniques with large-scale firm surveys, it offers readers new findings which shed light on the effect of ownership characteristics on credit access and firm performance. It also examines recent credit policy initiatives aimed at weaker sections of society including Scheduled Caste, Scheduled Tribe and women owned enterprises and puts forward valuable policy recommendations. This volume will serve as a useful reference text for students and researchers of economics, finance, business and management, entrepreneurship, credit policy, development economics, caste discrimination, gender discrimination and South Asian studies"—Provided by publisher.
Identifiers: LCCN 2020037512 (print) | LCCN 2020037513 (ebook) | ISBN 9780367135126 (hardback) | ISBN 9781003141310 (ebook)
Subjects: LCSH: Small business—India. | Manufacturing industries—India. | India—Economic policy—1991–
Classification: LCC HD2346.I4 R34 2021 (print) | LCC HD2346.I4 (ebook) | DDC 332.7/42—dc23
LC record available at https://lccn.loc.gov/2020037512
LC ebook record available at https://lccn.loc.gov/2020037513

ISBN: 978-0-367-13512-6 (hbk)
ISBN: 978-1-003-14131-0 (ebk)

Typeset in Sabon
by Apex CoVantage, LLC

RAJESH RAJ S.N. DEDICATES THIS BOOK
TO HIS LATE FATHER.
SUBASH SASIDHARAN DEDICATES THIS
BOOK TO ACHAN, AMMA, VAITHEGI,
ASHWIN AND ASHISH.

CONTENTS

FIGURES

TABLES

PREFACE

The novelty of this book lies in presenting evidence on the nature, extent, evolution and consequences of credit constraints for small firms in India. Who has and who doesn't have access to formal credit markets and the effect of such access on small-firm performance are issues that merit investigation. However, there is very little evidence on what explains the constraints to credit access for small firms in India, especially for firms owned by women and those from disadvantageous sections of Indian society, and also on how such difficulties influence the performance of these firms. Existing studies, though limited, are mostly descriptive in nature and have approached these issues mostly from a macroeconomic perspective. This book is a critical, meticulous and significant attempt to fill this obvious gap in the literature.

Our interest in this topic is nearly a decade old. We began our joint work on this topic in 2012 and have maintained this collaboration through a series of journal papers and several research grants from funding sources as diverse as the Asian Institute of Management (AIM) Scientific Foundation, Manila and Indian Council of Social Science Research (ICSSR). We have substantially benefitted in our work by the availability of detailed unit-record data with a rich set of information on the Micro, Small and Medium Enterprises (MSME) sector brought out by the Development Commissioner, Ministry of MSME. We are grateful to the ICSSR for partly funding this study without which this attempt would never have become a reality.

For long, we felt the need for a comprehensive study to understand the obstacles to the growth of the MSME sector in India. The issues facing the large and small firms are not the same. For small firms, lack of availability of credit has been a perennial issue. Despite the importance of MSMEs in the Indian economy, there have been very few attempts to put together the credit access issue in the form of a research monograph. We began this research way back in 2014, partly inspired by our previous work on the obstacles to the growth of India's informal sector. In this book, we tried to analyse an unexplored issue of credit market discrimination – the role of the caste and gender of the owner of the firm. Given the ongoing pandemic, the credit issues surrounding the MSME sector have come to the fore again.

And we also hope that the readers of this book will find the MSME sector in India an exciting avenue of research.

Over the years, we were fortunate to have benefitted immensely from the collaboration with Kausik Chaudhuri. We express our sincere appreciation to him for collaborating with us. We acknowledge discussions with Kunal Sen, Vinish Kathuria and Joe Thomas Karackattu on the topics covered in this book. We would also like to thank our host institutions, Department of Economics, Sikkim University and the Department of Humanities and Social Sciences, Indian Institute of Technology, Madras, for providing us with a stimulating intellectual environment for the duration of this study. We would like to thank the participants of the Singapore Economic Review conference for the excellent feedback. We also thank Arun Sudarsan, Radeef Chundakkadan and Prabin Chauhan Chhetri for the excellent research assistance. We are also grateful to the three anonymous reviewers assigned by Routledge for the constructive comments and suggestions which considerably improved the original manuscript. We are also thankful to our editor Ms Shoma Choudhury, Routledge, for her constant support. Finally, we are indebted to our families for the support and encouragement, who patiently put up with the long hours we spent writing this book.

1

INTRODUCTION

Introduction

The industrial landscape in developing countries is dominated by small firms, which account for the bulk of output and employment (Gollin, 2008). These firms tend to be significantly less productive and account for a smaller share of the productivity growth. The preponderance of small firms in developing economies is an important reason why aggregate productivity in these economies remains so low, relative to advanced market economies (Hsieh and Klenow, 2009). A recent study estimates that the failure of small firms to grow into large firms lowers productivity growth in the manufacturing sector by 25 percent in Mexico and India when compared with the United States of America (US) (Hsieh and Klenow, 2014). This absence of transition substantially lowers the productivity of small firms and limits their abilities to pass gains to the workers, which possibly explains why a large proportion of the individuals who own, manage and work in these enterprises belong to the urban working poor in these countries. For many small firms, the transition to larger firms could be a route out of poverty, as well as providing employment for a large proportion of less experienced and less educated workers belonging to the poorer households in urban and semi-urban areas.

What explains the substantial productivity differences between small firms and large firms in developing countries and why some small firms can make the transition to larger firms while others cannot? While emerging literature has attempted to address this question, we do not know enough on the factors that trigger the productivity difference between small and large firms in developing countries and what policy makers can do to enhance the growth and productivity of small firms. The determinants of small firm performance in developing countries remain less understood, with much of the earlier literature focusing on the large firms. In the case of large firms, studies highlight factors like trade costs, lower Research and Development (R&D) spending and macro factors such as taxation and regulation as constraints to firm growth (Giovanni et al., 2011; Acemoglu and Cao, 2015;

Rubini et al., 2012). Existing studies on small firms in developing countries, though scanty, stress firm capabilities, favorable location and geographical factors and robust social and physical infrastructure as potential drivers of small-firm growth. They single out lack of access to external finance as the most crucial factor impeding their growth (Schmitz, 1982; Davidsson et al., 2005; Nichter and Goldmark, 2009).

There is extensive literature on the importance of finance on firm growth, but this literature is mostly confined to the developed economies, and wherever the evidence exists for developing economies it is largely confined to the large firms in the formal sector. This is surprising given that the presence of large numbers of small firms in developing countries is often attributed to the credit constraints that prevent these firms from increasing in size (Hurst and Lusardi, 2004). A study based on cross-country panel data also highlights lack of access to financing as the most binding obstacle faced by small firms (Dinh et al., 2012). Further, there is substantial evidence to suggest that small firms are financially more constrained than large firms (Beck et al., 2008a, 2008b; Kuntchev et al., 2012). On the other hand, there are also studies which suggest that the development of the financial sector need not always be a pre-requisite for firm growth (Ferrando and Ruggieri, 2018). Therefore, to attribute any causative role to finance, it is imperative to study the impact of access to financial resources on firm growth and whether or not firms' access to external finance has really improved their performance. However, in the context of developing economies, we know very little about the role of financial constraints on the growth of small firms. Our study attempts to fill this key gap in the literature.

Recently, there is a small but growing amount of literature attempting to examine the role of demographic characteristics of the entrepreneur in influencing the ability of firms to raise external finance (Asiedu et al., 2012; Galli et al., 2020). These studies specifically examined whether the constraints that entrepreneurs face in the credit market differ across demographic groups (Cavalluzzo and Cavalluzzo, 1998; Blanchflower et al., 2003; Asiedu et al., 2012). This interest was driven by the significant evidence supporting the large differences in firm formation and ownership rates, productivity levels and financing pattern of businesses among different demographic groups (Muravyev et al., 2009). These authors probed into whether these observed differences can be attributed to unequal access to external financing and whether there exists supply-side discrimination – the Becker type or the statistical type[1] – in the provision of loans to minority entrepreneurs. The vast majority of these investigations are directed at exploring the role of race, ethnicity and gender as determinants of credit access, loan denials and other aspects of restricted access to finance. These studies do confirm significant gender, racial and ethnic differences in access to finance. Existing studies exploring this issue in a single country context are mostly confined to the experience of developed countries; most of them have very strong anti-discriminatory policies in place. Hence, the lessons drawn from these explorations might not be relevant to developing countries where caste and gender inequalities continue to be a pressing problem in the society. Given the growing prominence of developing countries in the world economy, there is essentially a need to provide evidence on the entrepreneurship among socially disadvantaged groups, the extent of discrimination they encounter in the credit market and its implications on entrepreneurship. This book is intended to address this void in the literature by investigating financial constraints faced by female entrepreneurs and entrepreneurs from socially disadvantaged communities in the context of a developing economy.

India presents an ideal context to investigate this issue for a number of reasons. First, small firms constitute a significant portion of the Indian manufacturing sector. Evidence shows that they account for about 45 percent of the manufacturing output and around 40 percent of total exports in 2009 (Ministry of MSME, 2011), and by 2010–2011 it employed 73.2 million workers spread over 31.1 million units (Deshpande and Sharma, 2013). Furthermore, from 2001 to 2009, small establishments displayed more rapid growth in the share of output, employment and exports (Ministry of MSME, 2009). However, despite the rising importance of small firms in the Indian economy, there is enough evidence to suggest that many MSMEs in India confront obstacles in raising external finance. The National Sample Survey Office (NSSO) surveys on unincorporated enterprises for 2015–2016 and the World Bank enterprise survey highlight access to finance as the major hindrance to the growth of small firms in India. Second, gender and caste inequalities still remain a persistent and pervasive phenomenon, despite fairly rapid rates of growth. According to the recent World Economic Forum (WEF) Gender Gap Report, India has slid down international rankings on gender gap amidst widening disparity in women's health and survival and economic participation (WEF, 2020). According to the Sixth Economic Census, women enterprises account for only about 14 percent of the total enterprises and 90 percent of them fall under the micro category. Further, about 79 percent use own finance and only four percent report to have received funds from government bodies and financial institutions (Mathew, 2019). There is also a vast inequality of income and wealth between and within castes, and estimates suggest that Scheduled Caste and Scheduled Tribe (SC/ST) households in India earn 21 percent and 34 percent, respectively, less than the national average (Bharti, 2018).[2] Few studies also highlight substantial differences by caste in the ownership pattern of enterprises in India, and under-representation of SC and STs in the ownership of enterprises (Iyer et al., 2013). Third, given that the majority of firms in India are smaller in size and that a significant share of socially disadvantaged and marginalised people in India are dependent on these firms for their livelihood, investigating the potential interaction between gender and caste affiliation of the firms owner and credit access has serious implications for the larger agenda of reducing poverty and achieving financial inclusion. Further, as small businesses already confront significant barriers in obtaining formal credit, the existence of discrimination in the credit market can be doubly disadvantageous to those belonging to such marginalized categories. Therefore, the explorations examining the prevalence of credit market discrimination can aid in suggesting suitable policy measures to improve access to institutional credit for small business owners, especially those belonging to marginalised groups. Fourth and foremost, there exist limited empirical investigations into the role of credit constraints on small firm growth, and also on gender and caste-based discrimination against entrepreneurs in the Indian context. The virtual absence of empirical evidence in the context of India is striking and needs to be addressed.

This study offers an in-depth understanding of the importance of finance on the growth of small firms in India. Another crucial focus of the study is to probe into the link between demographic characteristics of the entrepreneurs and their access to external finance. To be specific, the study intends to provide evidence of discrimination against female and socially disadvantaged (SC/ST) entrepreneurs in the credit market. We employ a mixed-methods approach to investigate whether female-owned businesses face more severe constraints than male-owned firms. By employing the same approach, we also analyse the extent of discrimination faced in the credit market by SC/ST entrepreneurs as compared to non-SC/ST entrepreneurs. Our focus is on formal (institutional) finance especially bank loans as this is stated to be the most important overall source of external funds for small firms in India, and the one for which firms face severe obstacles in accessing it (GOI, 2016; Allen et al., 2013). Thus, the hypothesis that formal financial institutions discriminate against female and SC/ST entrepreneurs is at the heart of our study.

A key reason that might explain the inadequate literature focusing on financial constraints faced by small firms in India is the lack of nationally representative datasets for small firms. However, the recent availability of a unique, large and rich dataset of Indian MSMEs presents an opportunity to address this important issue in the Indian context. We explore credit market discrimination against entrepreneurs using the unit-level data from the fourth round of the MSME census conducted by the Government of India (GOI) for the year 2006–2007.[3] This is a nation-wide survey covering all the states and Union Territories (UTs), and it focuses exclusively on the micro, small and medium units.[4] The survey covers firms of different ages and provides key information about the firms, such as ownership, firm performance, firm characteristics, finances and borrowings. We exploit data from a final sample of 1.3 million firms from the Fourth MSME Census for our empirical estimation. We will use the unit record data in two ways. First, we will conduct a descriptive analysis of the pattern of firm growth and stagnation based on the size classes of firms, by industry, region and different firm characteristics, as well as examining the relationship between finance, firm size and productivity along these firm characteristics. Second, we will undertake econometric analysis using the unit-level record data wherever appropriate, asking different questions based on the data to expand our knowledge of the constraints to growth for small firms.

This study contributes to the growing body of literature on ownership and firm performance and access to finance in the following ways. First, it sheds light on the issue of gender- and caste-based discrimination in the credit market outside of the developed world, which is still scarce. Second, in this study, we use a unique, large dataset of MSMEs in analysing the impact that differences in demographic characteristics have on obtaining formal finance. Third, our dataset is rich in terms of the detailed information about the caste affiliation and gender of the firm owner in the ownership and management of enterprises. Finally, we add to the strand of literature on sources of finance and firm growth (Tsai, 2004; Beck et al., 2015; Long, 2019). In order to overcome the financial constraints, firms often resort to mobilising funds from formal and informal sources of finance. Formal sources refer to borrowing from banks and other financial institutions, while informal sources consist of borrowing from friends, relatives and money lenders. Fortunately, our dataset contains information about the various sources of finance (formal and informal), which helps us to analyse the importance of formal versus informal finance in mitigating financial constraints and fostering firm growth.

In the remainder of this introductory chapter, we introduce the MSME sector in India and discuss its importance in the Indian economy. Thereafter, we present a brief discussion on the prevailing views on the presence of gender-wise and caste-wise disparities in economic opportunities. We then briefly discuss the methods and data employed in the study to address our main questions. Finally, we present the organisation of the book.

MSME sector in India

Definition

The MSME Development (MSMED) Act of 2006 passed by the Parliament of India attempts to coalesce a heterogeneous group of industries for effective policy formulation and implementation (Reserve Bank of India, 2019). The MSMED Act strives for aiding in the development of these enterprises as well as boosting their competitiveness. Recognising the contribution of the sector to the Indian economy, the scope of the MSMED Act 2006 has been broadened to include the services sector, which effectively means the concept of "enterprise" in this context comprises both manufacturing and service entities. The "enterprise" can be either registered or unregistered and can fall into one of the three tiers of enterprises, namely, micro, small and medium.

The registered manufacturing sector includes two types of enterprises – those employing 10 or more workers and using power or those employing 20 or more workers but not using power on any day of the preceding 12 months. These units are bound to register with the District Industry Centers (DIC) of the respective state/union territory governments. The unregistered manufacturing sub-sector, a complement set to the registered manufacturing sub-sector, covers all the residual units which are not covered under the registered manufacturing sector. Thus, the unregistered manufacturing sector covers all the manufacturing, processing, repair and maintenance services units employing less than 10 workers and using power or less than 20 workers and not using power. The MSMED Act classifies enterprises into MSMEs on the basis of their investment in plant and machinery and defines "medium" enterprises as those with investments in plant and machinery between Rs 50 million and Rs 100 million, "small" enterprises as those with investments ranging from over Rs 2.5 million to Rs 50 million and micro enterprises as those with investment in plant and machinery of up to Rs 2.5 million.

Importance of the MSME sector

Over the last two and half decades, the MSME sector has emerged as an extremely effervescent and vibrant component of the Indian economy (GOI, 2018). According to a recent estimate, the sector provides livelihood to over 69 million people in India, which is close to 40 percent of the country's total workforce, through 44 million enterprises (Saini, 2014). It is also estimated that the MSMEs contribute roughly twenty nine percent of India's Gross Domestic Product (GDP) and account for about 45 percent of the manufacturing output and around 40 percent of the total exports (*ibid*). Within the MSME sector, the manufacturing sector is a little larger than the services sector and represents 90 percent of the total industrial units spread across the entire country.

In spite of their significant contribution to the economy, the MSMEs in India face several challenges. These challenges are both internal and external in nature. Das (2008) cites lack of technological dynamism, infrastructure constraints and small scale product reservation laws as barriers to MSMEs. Small firms face information barriers about the current state of the art technology, machinery and equipment which contribute to the cost escalation. For improving the global competitiveness of the MSME sector, the need of the hour is the technology upgradation. In order to create a vibrant business environment, the availability of adequate infrastructure is crucial. Lack of infrastructural facilities poses a significant challenge to the survival of small firms, and they are the victims of poor infrastructure (SIDBI, 2010). Morris et al. (2001) show that power shortages, transportation, communication and even inadequate facilities for water supply negatively affect the growth of the MSME sector. Since the1960s, several products in the manufacturing sector were reserved for the small-scale industries. The logic behind small-scale reservation policy was to absorb the abundant labour supply by the small firms producing labor-intensive goods. Several studies have unambiguously shown that this policy of reservation of goods led to the poor economic performance of the manufacturing sector in India (Mohan, 2002; Morris et al., 2001; Garcia-Santana and Pijoan-Mas, 2014; Martin et al., 2017). Mukherjee (2018) adds to this list the lack of skilled manpower for manufacturing, services, marketing and raw material availability at a reasonable cost as other challenges facing the Indian MSME sector.

However, the most pressing and perennial problem facing the Indian MSME sector is the issue of serious credit shortage (Nair and Das, 2019; Singh and Wasdani, 2016; Banerjee and Duflo, 2014). The credit gap for the MSME sector is about 62 percent as estimated by the Working Subgroup of the Twelfth Five Year Plan (GOI, 2012). According to the results of the Fourth MSME Census, 87 percent of the registered enterprises and 97 percent of the unregistered enterprises have not received any external financing. When we probe into credit availability by gender or social group affiliation of the owner, the estimates reveal an even grimmer picture. The estimates from 2013 Sixth Economic Census show that only 0.52 percent of SC- and ST-owned firms received government and institutional credit as compared to 7.3 percent for the rest of the firms. In the case of women-owned MSMEs, the share of their Net Bank Credit (NBC) increased from 5.48 percent in 2005 to just 7.71 percent in 2014 (Athena Infonomics, 2015). These anecdotal evidences point to two possibilities: (a) MSMEs face significant barriers in obtaining credit; and (b) There is a possibility of the existence of discrimination against women and SC/ST entrepreneurs in the small firm credit market. The previous discussion also suggests a scarcity of available evidence on the link between financial constraints and firm growth for MSMEs in India. Also missing is evidence on credit market discrimination against entrepreneurs belonging to different demographic groups, namely, the role of borrowers' gender and caste on their access to finance. Given the significant role of MSMEs to growth and development and the participation of large numbers of women and socially disadvantaged people in this sector, the virtual absence of literature focusing on these issues is striking. Our attempt in this book is to address these obvious gaps in the literature while focusing on the manufacturing segment of the MSME sector. We focus on both the registered and unregistered firms in the manufacturing sector.

Gender and caste ownership in India

Despite the rapid economic growth witnessed by India during the two and half decades of economic liberalisation, the persistent gender inequality in all spheres has been ubiquitous (Mathew, 2019). This is reflected by the recent Global Gender Gap Index published by the WEF (2018) in which India ranks 108 out of 148 countries. Therefore, it is no surprise that the Global Female Entrepreneurship Index (FEI) ranked India 70 among 77 countries across the world (GEM, 2015). This is also further validated by the 2018 Index of Women Entrepreneurs that ranked India 52 among 58 countries (Mastercard, 2018). The low participation rates among women in India is attributed to cultural factors, unequal education and social norms (Korreck, 2019). However, in the context of developing economies like India, lack of access to formal finance is probably the biggest obstacle to women entering into entrepreneurship. Female entrepreneurs face additional hurdles in the credit market due to numerous demand and supply-side hurdles (Khera, 2018). Often, female entrepreneurs' demand for formal sources of finance is limited due to the lack of awareness about government run programmes and the social norms in the ownership and inheritance of land and property. On the supply side, to mitigate risk, banks and financial institutions insist on collateral in the form of land or property. The vast majority of the women in India do not own property or land which could be offered as collateral for capital. Therefore, as mentioned previously, women-led businesses are smaller in scale and they mostly are confined to informal sector.

The role of marginalised communities in promoting entrepreneurship has received the attention of researchers only recently. In the context of India, social group affiliation (caste) deeply influences economic outcomes (Deshpande, 2017; Munshi, 2019). Since the implementation of liberalisation policies in India, the state has tried to influence the economic outcomes of the socially disadvantaged sections (SCs and STs) through affirmative action programmes in several spheres. When it comes to the ownership of private capital, there exists a widespread disparity among the upper castes and the marginalised communities. In order to annihilate the skewness in the distribution of private capital, the state has made various attempts to help the socially disadvantaged sections to gain access to financial resources and promote entrepreneurship. Despite attempts made by the policy makers, SC/ST entrepreneurs face severe hurdles in the credit market and discrimination in the labour market due to the absence of networks and their lower position in the social hierarchy. They remain socially excluded from the mainstream due to the persistence of caste and other forms of social discrimination. Therefore, they are much more likely to face barriers to access to credit and human capital acquisition. Even though financial inclusion of the socially disadvantaged groups is strongly advocated by various policy initiatives, available field survey-based evidence points to the persistence of caste-based discrimination in formal finance allocation. Though there exist some anecdotal evidence and debate on the issue of whether entrepreneurs from socially disadvantaged groups face discrimination in accessing formal credit, a rigorous and much deeper examination of the role of caste in determining access to formal credit for small-businesses is almost non-existent in the case of India. Available literature on caste affiliation and credit access in India is mostly confined to the experience drawn from the farm and household sector (Kumar, 2013; Kumar and Venkatachalam, 2018). So far, the research surrounding Small Scale Industries (SSIs) in India revolved mainly around the area of growth barriers and firm performance (Goraya, 2019; Coad and Tamvada, 2012; Tendulkar and Bhavani, 1997). There is very little empirical research on the role of caste in obtaining institutional credit in the context of the industrial sector, especially on the relationship between caste affiliation of the firm owners and their access to formal credit. Thorat and Sadana (2009) show that SC/ST enterprises are mainly household enterprises and they are mostly confined to urban areas. The same finding is corroborated by another study (Iyer et al., 2013). Deshpande and Sharma (2013), using the Third and Fourth MSME Census, observe that SC/ST enterprises are small, more rural than urban and are mainly proprietary firms. Goraya (2019) combines the 2005 Economic census and the Third and Fourth MSME censuses to examine the role of capital misallocation and entrepreneurship. The findings of this study show that lower caste individuals, due to lack of access to credit, are less likely to enter into entrepreneurship.

Methodology

The present study is both descriptive and empirical in nature. We derived hypotheses for empirical testing following a detailed survey of literature in Chapter 2. We employed econometric tools to test our hypotheses. These include both linear and non-linear tools such as ordinary least squares (OLS), Logit model, non-linear decomposition methods, and propensity score matching estimators. The details of methods, including the justification for the use of selected methods, are presented in respective chapters.

Data source

The main source of data for this study is the Fourth Census of the MSMEs, completed by the Ministry of MSME in 2006–2007. We also used the Third All India Census of the Small Scale Industries 2001–2002 in Chapter 4 for descriptive analysis. In the third census, the enterprises were classified as small-SSIs and small-scale service and business (industry-related) enterprises (SSSBEs). However, following the MSMED Act of 2006, the Fourth Census revised the classification of units as micro, small and medium. Therefore, the revision of classification of enterprises makes it difficult to combine Third and Fourth Census to undertake empirical analysis. Data is publicly made available by the Ministry on its website (http://dcmsme.gov.in). The Fourth census collected information on permanently registered units on a complete enumeration basis (census), while in the case of unregistered MSMEs, a sample survey with stratified two-stage sampling was carried out. In the case of the registered sector, manufacturing enterprises comprised 66.67 percent, while in the case of unregistered sector, manufacturing enterprise share is 26.01 percent (Ministry of MSME, 2009). The Fourth census coverage includes 22.5 lakh registered units, out of which 6.58 lakh were not in operation. The census covers a total of 15,42,561 firms – manufacturing, repair, and maintenance and services. In the case of the unregistered sector, coverage includes information about 1.30 lakh units. This study focuses only on manufacturing firms.

Like any typical enterprise-level data from developing countries, our dataset also contains missing values and outlier observations that may bias our estimates. Therefore, we resorted to cleaning the original dataset to take care of the missing observations and outliers. We followed certain procedures while undertaking the data cleaning process. First, we omitted those firms which did not respond to one or more key questions. Second, we excluded those firms with seemingly unrealistic information such as missing, zero or negative output, missing labour and/or capital stock values. These elimination norms have reduced the number of firms in the dataset to 1,157,877 from 1,313,210 (about 12 percent of firms in our dataset were filtered out). We used suitable deflators (wholesale price indices) to make price corrections to the reported data on output, intermediate inputs, value added and fixed assets. Data related to wholesale price indices were obtained from the report on Index Number of Wholesale Prices in India, published by the Office of the Economic Advisor, Ministry of Industry, GOI.

Organisation of the book

The organisation of the book is as follows. We present an overview of the theoretical literature on credit market discrimination in Chapter 2. Our objective here is to highlight the main differences of perspectives in the literature and to understand their implication for discrimination in the small business credit market of India. In this chapter, we also review the important studies that have examined the role of gender, race, ethnicity and caste in credit market access. We present the historical account of MSME policies with a specific focus on credit policies in Chapter 3. In Chapter 4, we present some stylised facts about the firms in the MSME sector, mainly examining the evolution of firm size, growth and productivity by firm type (micro, small and medium), registration status (formal and informal) and location (rural and urban) at the all India level and at the disaggregated regional and industry level. Using descriptive analysis, this chapter also makes an attempt to understand the relationship between finance, size and productivity of MSMEs. In the next three chapters, we address three analytical issues that are important in our understanding of the MSME sector in India. In Chapter 5, we probe into the link between access to finance and firm growth for the MSME sector in India – that is, whether and how the financing obstacles faced by MSMEs affected their growth performance. In Chapter 6, we provide evidence for the gender-based discrimination in the credit market by examining the role of gender of the firm owner on credit access. In Chapter 7, we conduct empirical testing to examine the relationship between caste affiliation and access to formal credit. Chapter 8 summarises the key findings of the analysis in the book and examines their policy implications.

Notes

1 The different approaches to discrimination are discussed in detail in the second chapter.
2 Castes in India can be grouped into four categories: Scheduled Castes (SCs) and Scheduled Tribes (STs) who are considered the most socially disadvantaged group, Other Backward Classes (OBCs) are mildly disadvantaged while upper caste, predominantly Brahmins, are regarded as privileged compared to other castes.
3 In Chapter 4, where we present the characteristics and evolution of MSME firms, we have also employed the third MSME census data for the year 2002–2003.
4 We provide a detailed description of the data later in this book.

2

THEORETICAL PERSPECTIVES AND EMPIRICAL LITERATURE

Introduction

This chapter interacts with previous research so as to provide a gist of the key concepts and theories involved. There are four primary subsections within. In the first section, the relationship between access to finance and small firm growth is explored. Next section discusses the main theories of discrimination. The available evidence on credit market discrimination, especially the gender- and caste-based discrimination, is discussed in the last two subsections.

Finance and small firm growth

The growth of Small and Medium Enterprises (SMEs) is of great importance in developed and developing economies. Since SMEs contribute to employment, new firm formation and output in a significant way, they are considered to be a crucial driver of economic growth (Acs and Audretsch, 1993; Storey, 1994). In most of the developing countries, small firms are considered as a means of alleviating poverty (Snodgrass and Biggs, 1996). Despite the importance of small firms, the lack of dynamism of small firms in terms of growth is a concern for policy-makers in developing countries (Beck and Demirguc-Kunt, 2006).

Earlier theoretical models on firm growth include only one source of heterogeneity and they failed to explain firm dynamics (Huynh and Petrunia, 2010). The standard model of firm dynamics considers firm age and size as independent. Empirical studies overturned this assumption and found *size dependence* and *age dependence*. Subsequent theoretical developments in firm growth consider availability of capital as a significant driver of growth (Cooley and Quadrini, 2001; Cabral and Mata, 2003). This led to the need for introducing second heterogeneity in the form of financial frictions.

Firms can achieve superior performance in the absence of obstacles in obtaining finance. Firms can rely on internal and external finance to fund investment opportunities. Often firms in developing countries have limited access to capital markets and are credit rationed (Stiglitz and Weiss, 1981).

In many developing countries, due to the information asymmetry and underdeveloped financial markets, small firms find it extremely difficult to obtain external finance. This issue is further exacerbated by the fact that managers of SMEs may not have the requisite skill to make correct investment decisions, which may deter the lenders from providing funds (Macpherson and Holt, 2007).

Among the set of obstacles, as discussed in Chapter 1, finance is considered as the principal obstacle for small firms' growth in developing economies (Beck et al., 2015). The growth of firms is dependent on the availability and cost of finance. Having adequate finance helps the firms to survive beyond the initial year of operation (Demirgüc-Kunt et al., 2011) and to innovate (Ayyagari et al., 2011). Lack of finance hinders development of new enterprises. Therefore, access to finance is the key to firm growth. According to Claessens (2006), access to finance refers to the "availability of the supply of reasonable quality financial services at reasonable costs, where reasonable quality and reasonable cost has to be defined relative to some objectives standard with the cost reflecting all pecuniary and nonpecuniary cost". In a similar vein, World Bank (2008) define access to finance as "the absence of price and non-price barriers in the use of financial services". It is possible that firms that grow faster are more likely to pursue external funds since higher growth will have greater demand for internal cash flows, which eventually make them search for external funds. However, the direction of causality of finance on firm growth is an empirical question (Aryeetey et al., 1994).

Access to finance and small firm growth – a review of studies

A key proposition in the economic growth literature is the role of finance in enhancing growth by credit allocation to productive firms. A vast array of studies that probed the finance-growth nexus show that well-developed financial markets enhance the efficiency of resource allocation and promote economic growth. Studies have shown that even small firms with growth potential find it difficult to raise external finance and as firm size increases binding financial constraints reduce (Fazzari et al., 1988; Audretsch and Elston, 2002). In a much cited study, Rajan and Zingales (1998) show that firms in industries which seek external finance grow faster. Firms can use either internal or external funds to expand their production, investing in technology which requires finance. Due to the persistent deficiencies, the financial sector in developed countries is biased towards the large firms. However, recent years witnessed an increasing number of studies exploring this relationship from a microeconomic perspective.

Much of the initial academic literature on firm growth probed the role of internal finance in promoting firm growth and found internal finance as a significant driver of growth (Becchetti and Trovato, 2002; Carpenter and Petersen, 2002). Internal funds refer to retained earnings from profits. In the absence of internal funds, a firm can borrow or sell its equity. In the case of borrowed funds from financial institutions, firms will have to repay the loan for a fixed period. In the case of a default, the firms may be forced to go bankrupt by the lender. Previous research has shown that excessively leveraged firms are likely to fail (Johnson, 1997). Carpenter and Petersen (2002) examine the growth of small US firms and report that asset growth is indeed constrained by the availability of internal finance. Guariglia et al. (2011), using Chinese firm level data, find that private firms are constrained by the availability of cash flow. Rahaman (2011) too provides evidence that internal funds have a significant effect on employment growth using the data for a sample of United Kingdom (UK) and Irish firms.

The firm growth-finance literature that we discussed previously largely concentrates on the experience of the firms listed in the stock market. Probably, the easy availability of balance sheet information may be the reason for the dominance of such studies using listed firms. Even though some of these studies that examine the relationship between access to finance and firm growth include quoted small firms, these listed small firms are relatively large and mature compared to the small firms which are not listed. Small unlisted firms are distinct from large firms in numerous ways, and therefore there is an increasing need to probe the obstacles which prevent them from achieving optimal growth path. Even though the importance of finance is realised for the existence of business formation, many small firms suffer from financial constraints. The financing obstacles for such firms are far greater than that of large firms. In fact, financing constraint has double the impact on the growth of small firms compared to the larger ones (Kasseeah and Thoplan, 2012). Therefore, the new generation micro-econometric research focusing on the determinants of firm growth is largely based on survey data (which predominantly covers small firms) which list obstacles firms face in obtaining external funds.

Further, most of these studies were confined to the experience of developed countries. Becchetti and Trovato (2002) using a sample of Italian firms show that the availability of external financing (subsidy, leverage and financial constraints) significantly influence the firm growth. More recently, Donati (2016) attempts to study liquidity constraints on the firm growth of the Italian manufacturing and service sectors. The findings of the study reveal that liquidity constraints hindered the growth of small firms. Oliveira and Fortunato (2006) using an unbalanced panel data of Portuguese manufacturing firms find that financial constraints affect the growth of small and young firms. Using cross-country data, Beck et al. (2005) find that smaller firms in countries with less developed institutions face more asymmetric information and transaction costs. They show that financial development has a larger effect on firm growth.

Recently, numerous studies have investigated the finance-growth relationship in the context of developing countries using either cross-country or individual country firm level data. The spurt in the number of such studies is probably due to the availability of large scale firm level information from developing countries. Using firm level data across 30 African countries, Fowowe (2017) shows that the finance constraint exerts a significant negative effect on firm growth. This study also finds that firms that are credit constrained experience slower growth than firms which are not credit constrained. Regasa et al. (2019) using the Ethiopian Enterprise Survey investigate the role of access to finance in enhancing firm growth. The study uses firms' working capital and fixed capital financed from the external sources as a proxy for access to finance, while sales and employment growth to represent firm growth. Their findings reveal that firms which rely on internal financing recorded a higher growth than those enterprises with access to external finance. They attribute this finding to the misallocation of capital and often the loans are granted to firms with political connections than growth-oriented firms. A similar result was obtained by Beck et al. (2015) who report that microenterprises with hired workers and access to informal finance experienced higher sales growth in China. On the other hand, use of formal finance is not associated with higher sales growth.

Due to the difficulty in obtaining institutional credit, firms often combine finance from various sources like friends, moneylenders and relatives. Often, firms use co-funding (formal and informal credit together) which provides advantages from both sources of finance. A sub-set of studies exploring the role of financing patterns focuses on the sources of financing (formal versus informal). Most of these studies show that the costs and risks of providing finance to small firms are higher than for larger enterprises, regardless of the source of the capital. Beck et al. (2008c) attribute inadequate access to external finance for small firms to market imperfections, including high transaction costs and information asymmetries. The formal financial institutions in developing countries face several hurdles in providing finance to MSMEs. The lending institutions will have to monitor the performance of the borrower and ensure that they abide by the requirements of the contract. The monitoring of MSMEs in developing countries is challenging due to a variety of factors. MSMEs operate opaquely and experience greater volatility in terms of profitability and growth (Storey and Thompson, 1995). Due to severe information asymmetry in developing countries, lenders find it difficult to distinguish between risky projects which MSMEs undertake. Banks in developing countries are subject to interest ceilings which prevent them from fully recovering the cost, which makes them averse to lend to MSMEs (Harvie, 2011). Given these circumstances, banks use hard information to screen borrowers and resort to credit rationing (Stiglitz and Weiss, 1981).

MSMEs face significant constraints to obtaining finance from banking system leading them to exit the market. A sizeable share of MSMEs finds it difficult to obtain funds from the banks, financial markets and other institutions. Banks are considered as the single most important source of finance for MSMEs. Credit rationing by banks creates a financing gap which leads to lower survival rates among such firms. Banks are reluctant to lend to MSMEs since they perceive them as more risky, with a high probability of default and a lack of competition (Kauffmann, 2005). Small firms are constrained in terms of collateral and lack credit history which hinders the credit availability from formal sources. Therefore, compared to large firms, small firms rely more on informal sources of finance. Informal sources of finance are comprised of money lenders, friends and family and non-bank financial intermediaries (Allen and Qian, 2010; Ayyagari et al., 2010). Access to informal finance is subject to personal network, reputation and social status. Even though informal finance is easy to obtain, they are costly and lack scalability. It is found that informal finance can be efficiently monitored when the legal institutions are not efficient (Allen and Qian, 2010). The efficiency of informal finance in alleviating financial constraints is difficult to ascertain. Hence, the benefits associated with such loans remain an empirical question.

Ayyagari et al. (2010) show that informal financing channels did not enhance firm growth in the case of China. In their study on Sub-Saharan Africa (SSA), Mathenge and Nikolaidou (2018) find that firms that obtained bank financing are more productive than firms that finance a significant portion of their investments using other sources of finance. Further, the study also shows that small and medium firms with formal sources of finance are considerably more productive than firms with informal sources. On the other hand, Beck et al. (2015) show that financing from informal sources has a significant effect on microenterprise growth in China. Allen et al. (2005) too document informal financing as the driving force behind the growth of private firms in China. For Allen et al. (2013), the benefits of informal finance on firm growth depend on the source of the informal finance. In their study, they show that financial support from moneylenders endangers firm growth while informal finance from family members, friends and suppliers enhances firm growth in China.

The findings of the recent studies show that firms benefit from using both formal and informal sources of financing (Degryse et al., 2016). Girma and Vencappa (2015) demonstrate that bank and non-bank finance have a positive effect on the productivity growth of firms in India, with bank loans having the largest effect. An overriding assessment of many previous studies is the substitutability of informal finance for formal finance when it is based on information and relationship lending. However, recent studies show a complementary effect between formal and informal finance. A dominant view among such a strand of studies is the simultaneous use of both the sources optimally (Degryse et al., 2016; Madestam, 2014). The findings of the studies are rather inconclusive. Against this background and given the scant literature on the complementarity or substitutability of informal sources on firm growth in the context of India, in Chapter 5 we seek an answer to the question of whether formal and informal sources of finance affect firm growth differently.

Indian context

In one of the earliest studies, Das (1995) analysed the growth determinants in the computer hardware industry. This study reports that age has a positive effect while size is negatively associated with the growth of the firm. Shanmugam and Bhaduri (2002) report that older and younger firms grow slowly in Indian manufacturing. Coad and Tamvada (2012) using the third census of the registered small-scale firms find that young and small firms grow faster. Unlike other studies which focus solely on the conventional determinants (size and age) of firm growth, the study by Deshpande and Sharma (2013) combines the Third and Fourth MSME census to extend the firm growth analysis by including the ownership structure in terms of social affiliation and the gender of the owner. Contrary to the expectation, they find women-owned enterprises grow faster, while SC/ST- and Other Backward Class (OBC)-owned firms record slower growth.

Thus, from the previous discussion, access to credit is found to be a crucial determinant for small firm growth. However, in the context of India, studies exploring finance-firm growth nexus is thin. Studies on firm growth in India mainly test the validity of the Gibrat's (1931) law[1] without paying much attention to the role of finance and firm growth. Meyer (1998) shows that an important source of external finance for small firms is commercial banks, and SMEs tend to depend on banks for their financial resources while large firms can go to markets. Often banks are reluctant to lend to SMEs and they suffer a credit gap. However, several public support programs have been launched to increase the credit availability for small firms. Therefore, whether the access to institutional credit significantly influences firm growth is an empirical question which we investigate in Chapter 5.

Theories of discrimination

Economics as a discipline started considering the issue of discrimination since the seminal publication of Gary Becker's *The Economics of Discrimination* in 1957. In the nearly six decades since the seminal work, the discipline has theoretically and empirically studied discrimination and its economic effects. However, such is the universal nature of the phenomena that Arrow wondered can "a phenomenon whose manifestations are everywhere in the social world really be understood, even in only one aspect, by the tools of a single discipline"? (Arrow, 1998). In the initial phase, the discipline of economics of discrimination mostly tried to answer the question: under what conditions can there exist differential wages for similar economic agents at market equilibrium (Stiglitz, 1973)? Theoretical literature propounds three major models on discrimination: taste-based discrimination (Becker, 1957), statistical discrimination (Phelps, 1972) and implicit discrimination (Bertrand et al., 2005). Early studies were confined to the experience in the labour market and the researchers' primary concern was the wage differentials among similarly qualified workers with different group memberships (race or gender). In the following subsections, we discuss in detail the theories of discrimination.

Taste-based discrimination

Becker's (1957) taste-based discrimination and its extensions dominated the early literature on the subject, particularly the application of the theory to understand the racial discrimination in the labour market. Under conditions of full information, a discriminating employer, *ceteris paribus*, will hire a white candidate over a black candidate. Following Altonji and Blank (1999), let "a" denote majority group membership and "b" denote minority group membership. Employers will maximise the following utility function:

$$U = pF(N_a + N_b) - w_a N_a - w_b N_b - dN_b \tag{2.1}$$

where p is the price level, F is the production function, N_x is the number of workers of group $x = \{a, b\}$ and w_x is the wage paid to members of each group. In equation 2.1, d is the taste-parameter of the firm. Prejudiced employers ($d > 0$) will consider the wage of b group workers as $w_b + d$. Therefore, they will hire b group members if $w_a - w_b \geq d$. The inclusion of the coefficient of discrimination (or "psychic costs") ensures that wage differences occur even at market equilibrium.

This distaste for members of group b creates incentives for segregation. A Pareto improvement can be attained if minority workers decide to work in their own businesses, thereby ensuring that no business owner has to bear the cost of their prejudice. In a competitive market, discriminating employers get competed out since workers should earn their marginal product.

Let $G(d)$ denote the Cobb-Douglass Function (CDF) of the prejudice parameter d in the employers. The optimal number of workers hired at each firm is determined by the solutions to the following equations:

$$pF'(N_a) = w_a$$

$$pF'(N_b) = w_b + d$$

Treating p as fixed and aggregating across firms in the economy leads to the market demand functions $N_a^d(w_a, w_b, G(d))$, $N_b^d(w_a, w_b, G(d))$ for each worker type. Wages are determined by the following where $N^s()$ are the supply functions.

$$N_a^d(w_a, w_b, G(d)) = N_a^s(w_a)$$
$$N_b^d(w_a, w_b, G(d)) = N_b^s(w_b)$$

The main conclusions from the previous discussion are as follows. Wage differential $w_b < w_a$ will arise if and only if the fraction of discriminating employers is sufficiently larger than the demand for B workers when $w_b = w_a$ is less than supply. Alternatively, *discrimination on the average does not imply discrimination at the margin.* If there are enough non-discriminating employers, then discrimination will be competed away. Another implication is that minority workers do not work for discriminating employers.

In a competitive, Constant Returns to Scale (CRS) model, discrimination will be competed away. At equilibrium, discriminating employers must fund the cost of their distaste out of their own pockets. The testable implication of this model is the wage differential, and preferential hiring. Interestingly, taste-based discrimination need not be perpetuated only by the employer. Group *a* workers, if prejudiced against *b* workers, may demand a premium from the employer to work alongside them. In another case, if the work involves interaction with customers prejudiced against *b* workers, their labour market returns will be affected.

It is important to note a crucial difference between "taste-based" discrimination and statistical discrimination discussed in the next subsection. In the former case, discrimination arises from an agent's distaste for people from a particular group. On the other hand, statistical discrimination occurs when rational agents use certain characteristics like race, gender and ethnicity to arrive at estimates of productivity or criminal tendencies. Becker (1957) acknowledges that in equilibrium, firms practising taste-based discrimination will be out-competed by other firms. Probably, due to this reason, subsequent research focused mostly on statistical discrimination.

Statistical discrimination

Just over a decade after Becker's taste-based discrimination, Phelps (1972) and Arrow (1972) introduced Statistical Discrimination into the literature. Statistical discrimination occurs when there is incomplete information regarding a prospective employee. In such cases, the employer may use group stereotypes (Fang, 2001) to evaluate the expected productivity as a solution to the signal extraction problem. While the candidate may have an observable performance score of *y*, what the employer is interested to know is the unobservable q, which indicates the candidate's skills and ability. When information on q is not available, employers substitute q with group mean $\hat{q}$.

Statistical discrimination models differ widely from Becker's taste-based models. The latter merely includes a "distaste" variable in the utility maximisation problem of the employer, which can be competed away at equilibrium. On the other hand, the statistical discrimination models cannot be competed away at equilibrium as it only replaces the unobservable q with group mean $\hat{q}$. It is arguably fairer and more efficient than taste-based discrimination. It is often difficult to test for statistical discrimination since it is impossible to observe how employers form expectations. We will explore a model of statistical discrimination below.

Model: difference in means

Assume that when workers apply for jobs, the employer sees race of the applicant $x = \{a, b\}$ and some error-ridden signal $\tilde{\eta}$ of productivity. Assume also that employers have learned the following from their experience:

$$\eta_x \sim N\left(\tilde{\eta}_x, \sigma_\eta^2\right) \text{ with } \tilde{\eta}_a > \tilde{\eta}_b \text{, and } \sigma_\eta^2 \text{ identical for } a \text{ and } b.$$

This indicates that b group members are less productive on average, but the dispersion (or variance) of productivity is the same for both groups. The productivity signal error may be represented as follows:

$$\eta_i = \eta_x + \varepsilon_i$$

$$\tilde{\eta}_i = \eta_i + i_i$$

$$i \sim N\left(0, \sigma_i^2\right) \text{ with } \sigma_i^2 > 0$$

Hence:

$$\tilde{\eta}_i = \tilde{\eta}_x + \varepsilon_i + i_i$$

$$E(\tilde{\eta}_i | \eta_i) = \eta_i$$

To compute the expectation of η given $\tilde{\eta}$ and x, the following regression equation has to be estimated:

$$E(\eta | \tilde{\eta}, x) = \tilde{\eta}_x (1 - \gamma) + \tilde{\eta}\gamma = \tilde{\eta}_x + (\tilde{\eta} - \tilde{\eta}_x)\gamma$$

$$\gamma = \frac{\sigma_i^2}{\sigma_\eta^2 + \sigma_i^2}$$

This implies that for a given $\tilde{\eta}$ the expected productivity of the *b* group of applicants is below *a* applicants – even though $\tilde{\eta}$ is an unbiased signal for both workers.

Coate and Loury (1993) and Moro and Norman (2004) have later advanced the Arrow-Phelps model of statistical discrimination. Fang and Moro (2011) provide a comprehensive review of the statistical discrimination models. These models assume that firm owners have less information about the workers' productivity. Due to the asymmetric information, the employers may rely on other characteristics like race, gender and ethnicity and the minorities may be assigned to low-skilled jobs. Moro and Norman (2003, 2004) formulated a general equilibrium model in which production technology consisted of two complementary inputs. Employers maximise profit by setting wages based on their information about the average productivity of a group. In this model, only relative group size is important. They show that the affirmative action can hurt the beneficiaries.

Implicit discrimination

While taste-based and statistical discriminations are *conscious* choices by the agent, Bertrand et al. (2005) based on extensive inputs from psychology put forward the concept of "implicit discrimination", which stands for discrimination that is unintentional and "outside of the discriminators' awareness". The authors cite several Implicit Association Tests (IATs) to empirically verify that agents may engage in discrimination without a conscious decision to discriminate for or against others.

IATs takes several forms, the most popular is "word associations". Respondents are shown pairs of compatible words (African-American and "bad", White and "good") and incompatible words (African-American and "good", White and "bad"). Quick responses were obtained for "compatible pairing", indicating a strong implicit discrimination against African Americans. The authors also caution that implicit attitudes may be "manipulated" by exposure to positive signals before the IATs. For instance, photographs of revered African Americans reduce the implicit discrimination against blacks. Increasing the time required to complete tasks also results in the reduction of discrimination.

Empirical testing and evidence

The empirical testing of discrimination is fraught with methodological challenges. Correctly identifying the extent and scope of discrimination (be it in the labour market or in the credit market) is hampered by omitted variables, specification bias, self-selection and sample selection and endogeneity (Blanchard et al., 2008). Better datasets with high quality data have at least partially addressed some of the concerns.

When an individual or a group of individuals are treated differentially "based on their actual or perceived membership in a certain group or social category" such acts may be labelled as discrimination. It is a pervasive world phenomena which takes varied forms and magnitudes and "restricts members of one group from opportunities or privileges that are available to another group, leading to the exclusion of the individual or entities". (Giddens et al., 2009).

Discrimination varies in form and magnitude – it can be based on, but not limited to, race, ethnicity, caste, language, nationality, disability, age, gender or sexual orientation. Although liberal democracies around the world over the past century have outlawed many forms of discrimination by the state, individuals or groups still practice it widely. The continued existence of this practice has social, political, legal and economic ramifications which has to be studied carefully to device suitable policy responses.

Credit market discrimination

After the initial emphasis on labour market discrimination, studies started exploring other markets, especially the credit market, to find evidence of discrimination. The discrimination could be based on race, gender, ethnicity or geography. More often than not, credit market discrimination is in the form of statistical discrimination.

The earliest and most influential study on mortgage lending discrimination is by Munnell et al. (1996) for Boston. The Home Mortgage Disclosure Act (HMDA) was passed to monitor the access to credit by minority households. With HMDA data, the authors estimate that minorities are twice as likely to be denied mortgage as whites. While this result does not decompose the effect of "discrimination" separately, with additional variables, the authors are able to show that race continued to play a significant role in the decision to grant a mortgage (Munnel et al., 1996).

Small business financing

The primary challenge in entrepreneurship is the financing of a new venture (Ebben and Johnson, 2006). "Entrepreneurs often draw on personal resources first, followed by financing from family and friends, and then debt and equity capital" (Berger and Udell, 1998).

Perhaps a unique problem faced by small firms in securing credit is "informational opacity" (Berger and Udell, 1998). Small firms rarely feature in the public gaze. Unlike large firms with tradable securities, small firms are mostly proprietorships or partnerships with low visibility. Some of them may not even have audited financial statements. This opacity hampers its ability to present a credible case to attract financing.

There are four other important factors that affect credit availability to small firms: age of the firm, size, past performance and the time and personal capital invested by the owner. When the lender cannot adequately compute the ability of repayment, it responds by ascribing group mean to the applicant. This may result in the rejection of the application or approval at terms markedly unfavorable to the borrower. Discrimination in the small business credit market creates a "vicious cycle" of low credit availability (Eddleston et al., 2016). Undercapitalisation affects the growth of the firm, which in turn affects its credit rating, thereby reducing its chances of a successful future loan application.

Small business credit-market discrimination

Racial discrimination

In one of the earliest empirical studies on the small business credit market, Blanchflower et al. (2003) find that black-owned firms are markedly more likely to be denied credit and are charged higher interest rates than comparable firms. The authors use the National Surveys of Small Business Finances (NSSBF) for the years 1993 and 1998. Availability of finance, and favorable interest rates, are self-reported by blacks as their major concern. Interestingly, they are less likely to apply for a loan due to the fear of rejection and the reported prejudice. Econometric evidence proves the presence of discrimination, even while controlling for credit worthiness, education of owner, firm and industry characteristics and characteristics of the financial firms. Asians and Hispanics too face higher loan denial rates, according to the study.

Later studies, notably by Blanchard et al. (2008) and Asiedu et al. (2012), confirm discrimination against black-owned businesses in the small business credit market. The former tests for different types of discrimination – taste-based and statistical – by including variables relevant to each and studying their interaction with group membership. The authors use the widely used NSSBF for the years 1993 and 1998 to arrive at their results. Results show that lenders spend extra time and effort to evaluate applications from minority borrowers, indicating the existence of statistical discrimination (Blanchard et al., 2008). Following a similar methodology, Asiedu et al. (2012) find black-owned firms face higher denial rates than all other ethnic groups, and the denial increased from 1998 to 2003. They also find that minority-owned firms (non-white) paid higher interest rates on loans than white-owned firms.

Fisman et al. (2017) provide evidence that the social proximity between lenders and borrowers improves loan outcomes. The study is focused on understanding and evaluating the individuals' treatment in-group and out-group preferential on the basis of the religion and caste of bank officers and borrowers from a bank in India. Data are obtained from the individual loan portfolio and personnel records of a large state-owned bank in India. The authors found that in-group loans are larger, less collateralised and less likely to default ex-post. Lower defaults persist after the in-group officer is replaced by an out-group one. The authors suggest that the information benefits of social proximity outweigh the effects of taste-based discrimination.

Bostic and Lampani (1999) examine racial differences in the small business access to credit associated with the local geography. The study considers two types of local geographic characteristics: (a) economic variables such as crime rates, costs of operation and profitability of the small business may influence firm risk and (b) other variables like racial composition of the local area may influence lender decisions. The authors used secondary data collected from the 1993 NSSBF. They found that there are no statistically significant differences in approval rates between white-owned firms and firms owned by Asians, Hispanics or women. The only racial disparity that is statistically significant is the difference in approval rates between white-owned and black-owned firms. Importantly, the study suggests that the economic and demographic characteristics of a firm's local geography should be considered for a more accurate quantification of these racial disparities.

Pan (2014) investigates racial and gender discrimination in the US small business credit market. The study analyses the causes of discrimination and also focuses on new credit line approval, credit line renewal provided by financial institutions and trade credit provided by suppliers. The study used data from the Survey of Small Business Finances (SSBF) for 2003. The author found that in new credit line approval, black-owned businesses face unfair outcomes and in credit line renewal, women-owned firms are slightly favored by lenders. In trade credit approval, no minority-owned firms appear to be discriminated against. They also show evidence that discrimination against minority groups is most likely to be based on statistical reasons instead of prejudice.

Coleman (2002) analyses the differences in the characteristics and borrowing experience of small firms by race and ethnicity. The study used data from the Survey of Small Business Finances for 1998. The findings of the study reveal that the minority firm owners were just as likely to apply for loans; however, the likelihood of approval were significantly less. Further, black small business owners were less likely to even bother applying for a loan since they assumed they would be denied.

Gender discrimination

While the literature on racial discrimination is unequivocal in confirming the presence of discrimination (taste-based, statistical or both), the evidence on gender discrimination is mixed at best. Several studies limit their analysis to sole proprietorship so that ownership can be clearly categorised as male or female. A few other studies look at other forms of ownership and categorise firms as female owned if the share of ownership is more than 50 percent.

Muravyev et al. (2009) analyse international data (the cross-country Business Environment and Enterprise Performance Survey) of sole proprietorships to conclude that female-managed firms are less likely to obtain a loan, and when approved are charged higher interest rates. Based on evidence from Italy, Alesina et al. (2013) find that although women are no more risky than men, they pay higher interest rates.

A significant addition to the literature was made by Eddleston et al. (2016) by augmenting the existing arguments with signalling theory and gender congruity theory. They argue that "capital providers reward business characteristics of male and female entrepreneurs differently to the disadvantage of women". For firms with comparable age, size and past performance, male-owned firms received higher loan amounts.

Madill et al. (2006) study on small businesses in Canada utilised Surveys of Financing of Small- and Medium-Sized Enterprises administered across Canada in the years 2001 and 2002. Using logistic regression, they show that the gender of SME ownership does not affect the loan turndown rates. However, the study does show a significant gender difference in the length of the lender-borrower relationship, with male-owned firms maintaining significantly longer relationship with lenders. This could potentially lead to more benefits to male-owned firms vis-à-vis female-owned firms (Madill et al., 2006).

Two studies from the UK gave contrasting evidence. Kwong et al. (2012) studied data from the Global Entrepreneurship Monitor (GEM) between the years 2005 and 2007. In a two-stage study, they conclude that a greater proportion of women are constrained by financial barriers than their male counterparts. The authors advocate for policy initiatives to enable easier access to finance by women. However, Irwin and Scott (2010) in their study of 400 SMEs found that women found it relatively easier to raise finance than men. Another study by Aristei and Gallo (2016) for 28 transitional European countries find that female-owned firms are likely to be more credit constrained than male-owned firms. This study also finds that female-owned firms are more likely to face rejection of loans.

The story from developing or underdeveloped regions is also not different. In two studies from the African continent, authors find significant evidence for discrimination in the credit market against women-owned businesses (Mohamed and Temu, 2009). Using the World Bank Enterprise Survey (WBES), Asiedu et al. (2013) show that even after controlling for observed and unobserved country characteristics and potential bias from omitted variables, there exists a statistically significant gap between male-owned and female-owned firms in their ability to access credit.

Using a mixed method technique, Derera et al. (2014) study the case of women entrepreneurs in South Africa. Out of 50 women entrepreneurs, 46 were either in the retail or services sector – a trend seen in South Africa as a whole where women rarely move out of the "traditional" female-dominated sectors. Most women approach the venture as an extension of their hobbies. Nearly 80 percent of the entrepreneurs surveyed reported that their source of seed capital came from personal savings or loans from friends and family. Only 1/5th of them approached banks for a short-term overdraft facility to kick-start their venture. A female expert interviewed by the author claimed that "people still undermine women in small businesses . . . [and that] banks do not take women seriously". Many of them started their business with insufficient capital. As a method of coping, many ask their husbands or male partners to apply for a loan and lend it to them. In their study on India, Coad and Tamvada (2012) find that enterprises managed by women have lower expected growth rates, and that size and age have a negative impact on firm growth.

Based on a new dataset from three Caribbean countries, Presbitero et al. (2014) show that "women-led businesses are more likely to be financially constrained than other comparable firms". Unlike most studies in this area, the authors do not restrict themselves to a sole proprietorship. Three distinct dummy variables are used to capture the gender dimension, looking at both the ownership and managerial levels of the firm. The study introduced two important variables – one to capture self-discrimination (i.e. when the owners decide not to apply for a loan in the expectation of an adverse result) and the other to capture the loan denial decision of the bank. The study uses firm-specific, industry-specific, and owner-specific control variables. Roughly 8 percent of the sample firms have majority female ownership. Using probit regression, the authors estimate that, although there is no evidence to support self-discrimination by female owners or managers, lending discrimination exists in the case of firms with majority owners and managers. One important feature of this study is the use of separate dummies to capture the presence of women at ownership and managerial levels respectively. The authors argue that the divergent results in literature could be due to the fact that the two factors are not separately estimated for.

In contrast, in a study based on three surveys in the US, Treichel and Scott (2006) find no evidence to suggest that gender plays a significant role in the acceptance rate of loan applications after controlling for firm level characteristics. They find that women enterprises are less likely to apply for a loan at the outset, due to the fear of being discriminated against. However, they did find evidence for discrimination in the loan size.

Perhaps two very interesting studies from SSA were carried out by Hansen and Rand (2014). In their first study, authors report that small firms owned by females are less credit constrained than male firms. Using the standard Oaxaca-Blinder decomposition, it is shown that the gap is purely due to gender effect – a result of "favoritism" to female-owned micro and small firms. In their second study, they used three different measures of credit constraints – perception, formal data and direct information yield three different results. They use the World Bank Investment Climate Survey for 16 SSA countries, with an exclusive focus on non-government manufacturing units. Female-owned firms are shown to be credit constrained by the first measure, while the difference dissipates when using formal data on access to financial services. Interestingly, it is the male-owned firms who appear to be credit constrained under the third model which takes into account firm level data.

Mijid and Bernasek (2013), interestingly, find evidence for self-rationing by women in the credit market in their study of small businesses in the US. This study also finds higher loan denial rates and lower loan application rates among female-owned firms. Mixed results are also reported by Bellucci et al. (2010), who find no discrimination in loan approval but reports discrimination in collateral requirements and loan size.

Caste discrimination

Social groupings in India in the form of caste affiliation are strongly entrenched in hierarchies and cultures. Emergence of caste is typically associated with occupation, which led to the stereotyping of certain "*dirty*" jobs to individuals affiliated to particular castes. Even though caste affiliation may not determine occupations anymore, a pervasive feature of the Indian society still at large is the prevalence of caste as a means of gaining access to power as well as tangible and intangible capital. The SCs (or Dalits) account for approximately 16 percent of India's population. Nearly 66 percent of them are landless with a lack of accumulated wealth or income generating employment. When it comes to the ownership of private capital, there exists a widespread disparity among the upper castes and the marginalised communities (Thorat and Sadana, 2009). This concern is evident from the fact that there is a decline in the proportion of units owned by SCs and STs. Deshpande and Sharma (2013) report a decline in the share of SC (ST)-owned enterprises from 7.7 (3.5) percent in 2001–2002 to 6.7 (2.9) percent in 2006–2007. Since the onset of liberalisation policies in India, the state has tried to influence the economic outcomes of the socially disadvantaged sections (SCs and STs) through affirmative action programmes in several spheres. This includes quotas for jobs reserved for SC and ST communities in the public sector. In a similar vein, in order to annihilate the skewness in the distribution of private capital, the state has made various attempts to help the socially disadvantaged sections to gain access to financial resources and promote entrepreneurship. In spite of the honest attempts made by the policy makers, SC/ST entrepreneurs face severe hurdles in the credit market and discrimination in the labour market due to absence of networks and their lower position in the social hierarchy (Jodhka, 2010). In the context of India, several studies have raised concerns about labour market discrimination against SCs and STs who earn significantly lower wages and often engaged in economic activities which are "polluting and impure" (Banerjee and Knight, 1985; Madheswaran and Attewell, 2007; Das and Dutta, 2007; Deshpande and Sharma, 2016). It is possible that this discrimination may be prevalent in the credit markets as well. Using a nationally representative survey, Chaudhuri and Cherical (2012) report difficulty by ST households in obtaining credit from the Credit Cooperative Society (CCS), the Self-Help Group (SHG) and SHG-Banks. In a similar vein, Burgess et al. (2005) show that rural SC/ST households are much less likely to obtain loans from formal financial institutions.

In the Indian context, very little is known about the social group affiliation of small business owners and access to formal finance. Further, lack of comprehensive data in India has affected studies on loan acceptance rate, interest charged, etc. as observed in international studies. Kumar et al. (2017) report that farmers belonging to SCs are less likely to have access to institutional credit than those belonging to STs and OBCs. More recently, Fisman et al. (2017) found cultural similarity influencing loan outcomes based on a unique dataset comprised of loan officers and borrowers who are clients of a large public sector bank in India. But the study is limited to borrowers that received a loan from a single bank.

However, three important studies have looked at the sector to present important evidence on the impact of caste in entrepreneurship. In a significant study of Dalits in business, Jodhka (2010) surveyed 118 SC entrepreneurs in Panipat and Saharanpur. They had little or no social capital to rely on with illiterate parents. However, the entrepreneurs were educated – everyone had completed schooling. Motivated by the desire to have a livelihood not dependent on traditional caste jobs or as slaves to upper castes, they started out with capital from friends or family (Jodhka, 2010). Coad and Tamvada (2012) in their study identify the lack of access to credit as a primary reason for the "sickness" of firms (Coad and Tamvada, 2012). In another influential study, Deshpande and Sharma (2013) find clear and persistent caste disparities in virtually all enterprise characteristics. The share of SC/ST ownership has declined over the period between the Third and Fourth Registered MSME Census. SC/ST firms tend to be smaller, rural rather than urban, more owner-operated (single employee) units and grow slower than higher caste-owned firms. The majority of the workforce is employed by non-SC/ST firms, with evidence of homophily among OBC and upper caste firms. It is interesting to note that almost all of the leather units are owned by SCs, traditionally a "dirty" job. Nearly 20 percent of all firms owned by SCs are in the leather industry (Deshpande and Sharma, 2013).

Small business performance

Literature on small business performance seems to indicate the fact that female-owned businesses underperform vis-à-vis their male counterparts, although available empirical literature seems to be divided on the issue. In their study, Rietz and Henrekson (2000) examine the "female underperformance hypothesis" with a sample of 4200 Swedish entrepreneurs (with 405 female entrepreneurs). While at an aggregate level the authors do find evidence for underperformance, when the authors decompose performance variables, and employ multivariate regression with several control variables, the difference disappears in all but one indicator: sales. Profitability is found to be unaffected by the gender of the entrepreneur, as are production and employment indicators.

While the Swedish case seems to indicate the negation of the female underperformance hypothesis, evidence from the US suggest otherwise. Robb and Fairlie (2009) using confidential micro-data investigate the performance of female-owned businesses find that female-owned firms underperform significantly and have lower survival rates, profits, employment and sales. In a study of the US, Cheng (2015) using Kauffman Firm Survey Data studies 4928 firms from their start-up phase onwards to estimate the effect of different financial sources on its survival. Using the Cox proportional hazards method, with four types of control variables (individual, establishment, regional and financing), the author estimates six model specifications. The study concludes that only government financing is a statistically significant variable in increasing the probability of the firm surviving. Overall, it is found that "creditable, college educated, experienced, and older entrepreneurs across racial and ethnic background" tend to survive the start-up phase.

Evidence from developing countries is also mixed at best. In a cross-region study (Latin America (LA), SSA and Eastern Europe and Central Asia (ECA)), Bardasi et al. (2011) use WBES Data to estimate the impact of gender of the principal owner on the growth and productivity of the firm. According to the study, female-owned firms perform significantly worse only in Latin American countries, while the gap is not statistically significant in the other two regions.

When credit constrained firms are given a sudden capital infusion (in cash or kind), theory predicts that these firms should grow rapidly, taking advantage of the unexpected availability of funds. Two similar studies were carried out in Ghana and Sri Lanka as randomised experiments (Fafchamps et al., 2014; De Mel et al., 2012). Firms were randomly allotted to three groups: one control group, and two groups of which one received $150 in cash and the other received inventory items of the same value. In-kind intervention resulted in large increases in business profit for both female-owned and male-owned firms, with a larger effect on the former. However, in-cash intervention did not result in a significant increase in profits for female-owned firms. Male-owned firms did manage to increase their profits, though not to the levels of in-kind intervention.

Concluding remarks

This chapter reviews key studies to offer an understanding of access to finance and firm growth nexus. We also provide a summary of the previous literature on credit market access and the ownership characteristics in terms of gender, race, ethnicity and caste. In the case of the gender gap in credit access, studies have found conflicting results. Explanations provided by the previous studies for differences between male- and female-owned firms with respect to formal credit is due to discrimination, gender differences in abilities and preferences. However, studies on credit access differences based on race and ethnicity provide a clear picture of discrimination.

Note

1 Gibrat's (1931) law posits that firm growth rates are independent of the initial firm size.

3

MICRO, SMALL AND MEDIUM ENTERPRISES (MSMEs) ACCESS TO FINANCE AND POLICY INITIATIVES

Introduction

Small firms play a crucial role in developing economies in the form of employment generation, poverty alleviation and industrial development. Some studies regarded small firms as the vehicle to achieve growth and equity. Recognising their considerable importance to the economy, policy makers in developing countries try various instruments to enhance their growth. These instruments include subsidies, tax incentives, product market reservation and credit to boost the productivity and incomes of the small firms (Katrak, 1999). The key objective of these policy measures is to enhance the performance of the small firms.

The Indian scenario is no different if one traces the historical evolution of this sector during the last six decades. In a labour surplus economy like India, there is an increasing realisation among the policy makers that the only feasible way to generate employment for the vast labour pool is the development of the MSME sector (Mohan, 2002). Since these firms are a dominant feature in the labour-intensive sectors and mostly located in rural areas, the development of this sector can lead to a geographic dispersion of industrial activities. It is also widely accepted that a necessary condition for the birth of large firms is through the transformation of the small firms. With this objective, industrial policy in India, since independence, has laid an emphasis on the promotion of the small-scale sector (BalaSubrahmanya, 1995). The first five-year plan focused on creating boards to encourage the MSME sector, namely: (a) Khadi and Village Industries Board; (b) Handloom Board; (c) Handicrafts Board; (d) Coir Board; (e) Sericulture Board; and (f) Small-Scale Industries Board (SSIB). The major thrust of this strategy was to promote traditional segments of the sector. However, other measures like technology, marketing, financial support and reservation of certain sectors exclusively for the small firms was considered as the means to achieve modernisation of the MSME sector (BalaSubrahmanya, 1995).

Initially, measures like infrastructure development, regional development centres and technical and financial assistance were formulated to enhance the growth of small enterprises (Little et al., 1987). Subsequently, with the growing concern that the growth and performance of the small firms were severely hampered by the competition from large firms, efforts were made to protect this sector by enacting a product market reservation policy. This was first rolled out in 1967 with the reservation of 47 items exclusively under the domain of small businesses. Subsequently, the list of reserved products expanded considerably, and by 1989 the list included 836 products. The objective of all these policy measures apparently had varying impacts on social welfare (Shah et al., 2007; Raj and Sen, 2016). Policies targeted at technological enhancement may help in the overall efficiency of the firms. On the other hand, scholars argue that policies like exclusive reservations of products for small firms may not have the desired outcome since it protects this sector from competition and makes the firms remain small (Katrak, 1999).

The lack of availability of timely and adequate finance is most often highlighted as one of the major bottlenecks to the growth of Indian SMEs. Realising the importance of addressing this issue, the GOI has introduced a number of measures to extend financial services to small enterprises. In this chapter, we make an attempt to trace the evolution of these policy initiatives and examine how successful they are in terms of coverage and magnitude with greater focus on the period post-financial liberalisation. There has been an increasing realisation that certain segments of society like the historically disadvantaged groups like SC/ST and women entrepreneurs face severe obstacles in obtaining external finance. Therefore, another objective of this chapter is to trace the trends and recent bout of policy initiatives to provide credit to weaker sections of society including SC/ST and women entrepreneurs.

This chapter is organised as follows. The next section outlines the evolution of the MSME sector credit policies and the role of banking and financial sector during the pre- and post-liberalisation period. The third section presents an overview of the MSME-centric credit policies while the fourth section highlights the recent policy initiatives.

Financial sector

In India, the banking sector plays a vital role in meeting the finance requirements of the small-scale industries. The banking sector provides services to the disadvantaged section including small firms through the branch licensing policy and Priority Sector Lending (PSL) programme (Nikaido et al., 2015). The supply of credit to the small industries was mainly met through the extensive branch networks.

It is interesting to note that for nearly two decades after independence, the financial sector in India operated in a liberalised mode with relatively fewer controls (Cole, 2009). During this period, much of the credit flow was towards the non-food credit sector while the agricultural sector received less than three percent of the credit (Sen and Vaidya, 1997). In order to divert the flow of credit to the priority sector,[1] nationalisation of banks was implemented in two phases. The first phase was rolled out in July 1969 where 14 private banks were nationalised followed by 6 banks in 1980. One of the major objectives of this measure was to help small firms obtain institutional credit without much difficulty. Further, the government established Regional Rural Banks in 1975 to improve the institutional credit delivery to small and marginal farmers, agricultural labourers and rural artisans.

In the post-bank nationalisation phase, nothing much happened in terms of new policy initiatives to improve the credit availability to firms. Reforms during the mid-eighties mainly focused on lowering direct tax rates, expanding the role of the private sector and liberalising trade (Ahluwalia, 2002). However, it was during the early phase of the 1990s that India witnessed radical changes in the form of economic reforms which led to an array of policy measures being introduced in the industrial, trade and banking sectors. Based on the recommendations of the Narasimhan committee, the then government decided to lower the Statutory Liquidity Ratio (SLR) and the Cash Reserve Ratio (CRR). An important policy reform was the deregulation of the administered interest rates by the commercial banks. The banks were allowed to fix their own lending rates. Another noteworthy reform in the banking sector was the entry of foreign banks and allowing public sector banks to raise capital from the public (up to 49 percent). The objective of these measures was to increase the supply of credit and remove the financing constraints from the firms. However, empirical studies provide mixed evidence regarding the impact of financial liberalisation on the financial constraints of firms. Bhaduri (2005) find that large firms had easier access to capital than small firms during the post-reform period. The study attributes the difficulty of small firms in obtaining formal credit to growing information asymmetry. On the other hand, Ghosh (2006) shows that financial liberlisation significantly improved the credit access of Indian firms. Interestingly, the effect was more manifested in the case of small firms.

Branch expansion programs

Given the vast geography of India, to bring about financial inclusion, it is necessary to ensure that banks are not concentrated in select regions. To achieve this objective, Section 23 of the Banking Regulation Act 1949 stipulated that commercial banks will have to obtain a licence in order to open a branch. To achieve equitable distribution of bank branches and reduce state disparities, the Reserve Bank of India (RBI) formulated a licensing norm which required banks to open three branches in an unbanked area if they wished to open a new branch in an already banked area (Burgess and Pande, 2005).[2] The success of the policy is evident from the fact that between 1977 and 1990, 80 percent of all new branches opened were in unbanked centres (Burgess and Pande, 2005).

However, this policy ceased to be in effect after 1990. Since then, the criteria for branch expansion is based on the "need, business potential, and financial viability of the location" (GOI, 1991). At present, RBI follows a flexible policy with respect to branch expansion and closure. Prior approval of the RBI is not required to open branches in rural, semi-urban, and urban areas in the north-eastern states. Similarly, banks are also free to open new branches in towns with populations of up to 50,000. However, if a particular bank is the sole bank in a rural area then it does not enjoy the discretion to close the branch at its will. Further, domestic banks are entitled to close any branch in metropolitan, urban and semi-urban areas without prior approval. The branch expansion policy of the RBI led to expansion of bank branches in rural, urban and semi-urban areas post-nationalisation of banks (Table 3.1). However, the post-liberalisation era (1994–2009) witnessed a slowdown in the growth of rural bank branches whereas there was a large-scale expansion of branches in the metropolitan, semi-urban and urban centres. However, we witness a revival of rural banking with the number of rural branches significantly increased during the recent period (2013–2017).

The government appointed various committees to provide suggestions to improve the access to credit for small firms. The RBI instituted the P. R. Nayak committee in 1991 to examine the issues faced by small firms in obtaining institutional finance. The committee recommended the opening of one specialised bank branch in each district. Banks were allowed to convert branches with more than 60 percent of advances to small businesses into specialised small industry branches to fulfil the credit needs of the sector.[3] The Kapur Committee (1992) (a high level committee on credit to SSIs) also recommended opening up more specialised SSI branches. A working group on flow of credit to the SSI sector (Ganguly Committee 2004) emphasised the need to establish specialised small scale industries branches in industrial clusters. The committee also recommended the need to adopt new instruments by banks in order to enhance the flow of credit to rural artisans, rural industries and rural entrepreneurs.[4]

Another RBI-appointed committee, headed by F. K. F. Nariman recommended the formulation of a lead bank scheme in 1969. The scheme envisages the assignment of lead roles to banks within a particular district. The responsibility of heading deposit mobilisation and credit allocation in a particular district was entrusted with a bank having a relatively large network of branches in the rural areas and adequate financial and manpower resources in that district. The lead bank is assigned the task of formulating District Credit Plans (DCPs) and Annual Action Plans (AAPs) in order to achieve the social objective of credit allocation to the priority sectors. RBI requires bank branches to maintain a credit-deposit ratio of 60 percent in order to avoid rural areas becoming the supplier of urban credit. In 2007, a high level committee reviewing the lead bank scheme under Usha Thorat recommended the provision for banking facilities at least once a week at every village with a population of over 2,000 (RBI, 2009).

Table 3.1 Evolution of Commercial Banking

	1969 June	*1974 March*	*1979 March*	*1984 March*	*1989 March*	*1994 March*	*1999 March*	*2004 March*	*2009 March*	*2013 March*	*2017 March*
1. No. of commercial banks	89	83	136	247	278	276	303	291	170	157	154
Scheduled Commercial Banks (SCBs)	73	74	131	243	274	272	302	286	166	153	150
of which, Regional Rural Banks (RRBs)	–	–	56	162	196	196	196	196	86	64	56
Non-SCBs	16	9	5	4	4	4	1	5	4	4	4
2. No. of bank offices in India[1)]	8262	16936	30202	45332	57699	61803	64939	66970	79056	104647	13770
Rural	1833	6166	13337	25380	33014	35329	32857	32080	31489	38451	48232
Semi-urban	3342	5116	7889	9326	11,166	11,890	14168	15018	18764	27822	37880
Urban	1584	3091	5037	6116	7524	8745	9898	10990	15325	20127	24877
Metropolitan	1503	2563	3939	4510	5995	5839	8016	8882	13478	18247	26781
3. Population per office (in thousands)[2)]	64	35	22	16	14	15	15	16	14	12	NA
4. Per capita deposits of SCBs (Rs)	88	182	434	878	1821	3,596	7286	14089	34372	NA	NA
5. Per capita credit of SCBs (Rs)	68	133	290	593	1097	1854	3763	8273	24945	NA	NA

Source: RBI, Banking Statistics, Quarterly Statistics on Deposits and Credit of SCBs and Nikaido et al. (2012). NA denotes not available.

PSL

Soon after the nationalisation of banks was rolled out, sectoral allocation of credit was fixed by the RBI. Along these lines, in 1972 the RBI came up with a list of "priority" sectors which included agriculture and allied activities and small-scale and cottage industries. The banks are free to set interest rates under the PSL programme based on the risk assessment of the borrower. The monitoring power of the PSL programme is vested with the RBI which monitors the PSL performance of the banks on a quarterly basis. A target of 33 percent lending to the priority sector was set in 1975 which was subsequently raised to 40 percent (to be achieved by 1985). RBI also laid down the sub-targets for banks to provide 16 percent of lending to agriculture and 10 percent to the "weaker sections" (Table 3.2). In spite of the noteworthy reforms introduced in the banking sector, "priority sector" lending continues to be untouched.

Although a targeted lending programme like PSL is necessary to provide preferential status to small businesses, some studies have been apprehensive about the benefits trickling down to the priority sector (Kale, 2016; Bhue et al., 2019). Existing evidence points to medium-sized firms appropriating most of

Table 3.2 Targets and Sub-Targets for Lending to Micro and Small Enterprises Sector by Domestic Banks and Foreign Banks Under Priority Sector Lending (PSL)

Sectors	*Domestic Banks and Foreign Banks With More Than 20 Branches*	*Foreign Banks With Less Than 20 Branches*
Agriculture	18 percent	NA
Micro enterprises	7.5 percent of Net Bank Credit (NBC) or Credit Equivalent Amount of Off-Balance Sheet Exposure	NA
Export credit	2 percent of NBC or Credit Equivalent Amount of Off-Balance Sheet Exposure	32 percent of NBC or Credit Equivalent Amount of Off-Balance Sheet Exposure
Micro credit	NA	NA
Education loans	NA	NA
Housing loans	NA	NA
Social infrastructure	NA	NA
Renewable energy	NA	NA
Weaker sections	10 percent of NBC or Credit Equivalent Amount of Off-Balance Sheet Exposure	NA
Total priority sector	40 percent	40 percent (to be achieved in a phased manner by 2020)

Source: http://iibf.org.in/documents/priority-sector-lending.pdf. NA: Not Applicable.

the funds from the PSL regime (Rao, 2014). A committee appointed under the Chairmanship of M. V. Nair to review the PSL regime recommended the need to focus on the micro businesses and suggested the need to discourage lending to medium-sized firms. A flip side of the PSL regime is the absence of motivation for the micro units to grow since moving to a large scale denies them such types of institutional credit. Probably to overcome this shortcoming, more recently, RBI mandated a sub-target of 7.5 percent of adjusted Net Bank Credit (NBC) or credit equivalent for microenterprises under PSL (RBI, 2015).[5] If we look at the share of MSME sector credit to gross bank credit during 2008–2017, we notice only a marginal increase but in absolute terms the amount allocated to the MSME sector increased considerably from Rs 252071 crore to Rs 901972 crore during the same period under the PSL advances (Table 3.3).

It is evident from Table 3.4 that the credit from commercial banks to the small enterprises increased from Rs 46045 Crore to Rs 104703 Crore during 2000–2007. However, when we look at the share of the credit to the

Table 3.3 Deployment of Gross Bank Credit

Year	*Priority Sector Advances: Micro & Small Enterprises*			*Gross Bank Credit: Non-Food Credit (Rs Crore)*	*Share of Micro, Small and Medium Enterprise (MSME) Credit to Gross Bank Credit (in percent)*
	Micro & Small Enterprises (Rs Crore)	*Manufacturing (Rs Crore)*	*Services (Rs Crore)*		
2008	252071	132698 (52.64)	119373 (47.36)	2204801	11.43
2009	309195	168997 (54.66)	140198 (45.34)	2601825	11.88
2010	373530	206401 (55.26)	167130 (44.74)	3039615	12.29
2011	442848	210206 (47.47)	232642 (52.53)	3667354	12.08
2012	498625	236657 (47.46)	261969 (52.54)	4289745	11.62
2013	562296	284348 (50.57)	277947 (49.43)	4869563	11.55
2014	707813	348194 (49.19)	359618 (50.81)	5529601	12.80
2015	800343	380028 (47.48)	420314 (52.52)	6002952	13.33
2016	847587	371467 (43.83)	476120 (56.17)	6546903	12.95
2017	901972	369731 (40.99)	532241 (59.01)	7094490	12.71

Source: www.epwrfits.in/.

Table 3.4 Credit Flow to the Micro, Small and Medium Enterprise (MSME) Sectors

	2000	*2001*	*2002*	*2003*	*2004*	*2005*	*2006*	*2007*
Net Bank Credit (NBC)	316427	341291	396954	477899	558849	718722	1017614	1317705
Credit to Medium and Small Enterprises (MSEs)	46045	48400	49743	52988	58278	67634	82492	104703
MSEs credit as percentage of NBC	14.6	14.2	12.5	11.1	10.4	9.4	8.1	8.0
Credit to micro enterprises	24742	26019	27030	26937	30826	34315	33314	44311
Micro enterprises credit as percentage of NBC	7.8	7.6	6.8	5.6	5.5	4.8	3.3	3.4

Source: https://dcmsme.gov.in/Final_Report.pdf.

medium and small enterprise sector, the NBC recorded a decline from 14.6 percent to 8 percent during the same period (Table 3.4). In the case of micro enterprises, the decline in share of credit is even sharper (from 7.8 percent to 3.4 percent during 2000–2007). This finding is not entirely surprising, since some of the studies show that bank loans are increasingly getting concentrated in large-sized loans. The small-sized loans (Rs 25000 and less) in total bank credit declined from about 6 percent in 2002 and to less than 1 percent in 2014 while a share of large loans (Rs 10 crore and above) went up from 21 percent in 1995 to about 55 percent in 2014 (Das, 2015).

Policy initiatives to improve institutional credit to small firms

The Ministry of MSMEs in the GOI handles all matters pertaining to MSMEs. A primary function of the Ministry is to design and implement policies and promotion programmes for the growth of the MSME sector through its administrative arms. In this regard, the Office of the Development Commissioner (Development Commissioner MSME – DCMSME) attached with the Ministry of MSME is the apex body which advise, coordinate and formulate policies and programmes for the MSME sector. Within the DCMSME, the Small Industries Development Organisation (SIDO) is another principal organisation which is given the power to formulate policies for the development of MSMEs in India. The Small Industries Development Bank of India (SIDBI) was established to take care of the exclusive credit needs of the SSIs. The government also used various policy tools to enhance the growth of the small-scale sector including financial, fiscal, general incentives, special incentives in backward areas and the reservation of items for SSIs (BalaSubrahmanya (1995). This section analyses the other policy directives undertaken to help address the financing of micro and small enterprises in India.

Credit-Linked Capital Subsidy for Technology Upgradation (CLCS-TU)

The key objective of this scheme is to provide capital subsidy up to ₹ 15.00 lakhs to micro and small enterprises including tiny, khadi, village and coir industrial units to facilitate technology upgradation. Currently, the scheme aids subsidy to 51 sub-sectors/products.

The Credit-Linked Capital Subsidy Scheme (CLCSS)

CLCSS was launched on 1st October, 2000 to provide capital subsidy on institutional credit availed by the micro and small enterprises for the modernisation of the plant and machinery and techniques. Initially, this scheme intended to provide a loan ceiling of ₹ 40 lakhs and was subsequently raised ₹ 1.00 crore from 2005. This scheme is being implemented with the help of Commercial

Table 3.5 Performance of Credit-Linked Capital Subsidy Scheme (CLCSS) (2001–2002 to 2018–2019)

Year	*Number of Micro and Small Firms*	*Total Subsidy (Rs crore)*
2001–2002 to 2011–2012	16295	854.05
2012–2013	5713	343.79
2013–2014	6279	421.49
2014–2015	7246	448.85
2015–2016	5047	322.43
2016–2017	4011	256.53
2017–2018	4081	260.54
2018–2019	14155	980.44

Source: http://my.msme.gov.in/MyMsme/Reg/COM_ClcssAppForm.aspx.

Banks, SIDBI and the National Bank for Agriculture and Rural Development (NABARD). The scheme is intended to provide subsidy to 51 sub-sectors/products including khadi and village industries. The beneficiaries of this scheme include sole proprietorships, partnerships, cooperative societies and private and public limited companies in the SSI sector. An interesting feature of this scheme is the priority given to the women-led enterprises. In order to claim subsidy under aegis of this programme, the micro and small enterprises are required to apply online through Primary Lending Institutions (PLIs), from where they availed a term loan for the upgradation of technology. From Table 3.5, we observe that during the period 2001–2002 to 2011–2012, the amount of subsidy disbursed under this scheme was to the tune of 854.05 crores. By the year 2018–19, subsidy worth Rs 980.44 crore has been provided to 14155 units. In order to bring about inclusion of SC/ST and women entrepreneurs, a Special Credit-Linked Capital Subsidy Scheme (SCLCSS) has been introduced under National SC/ST Hub. The key feature of this scheme is 25 percent capital subsidy (ceiling of Rs 1 crore) on investment in plant and machinery, equipment and technology upgradation for SC/ST and women enterprises.

Credit guarantee fund scheme for micro and small enterprises

One of the major hurdles for the micro enterprises and first-generation entrepreneurs is the non-availability of finance. This issue is further exacerbated by the lack of collateral with these enterprises to offer to the financial institutions in order to obtain credit. In order to overcome this difficulty, the government introduced credit guarantees for MSMEs through the Credit Guarantee Fund Trust for Micro and Small Enterprises (CGTMSE), a joint initiative by the GOI and SIDBI. This scheme was formerly known as the "Credit Guarantee Fund Trust for Small Industries" (CGTSI).

The prime objective of the CGTMSE is to support the MSE sector and encourage entrepreneurship and innovation by providing easy access to finance. Further, the scheme is expected to encourage lending institutions to adopt innovative lending strategies to the MSE sector by using de-risking measures, thereby making easy and timely flow of funds to the sector. The borrower availing the guarantee facility should provide both term loan and working capital facilities (composite loan) from a single source. The Credit Guarantee Scheme (CGS) is a means to reassure the lending institutions that, in the case of default by a micro and small unit, which availed collateral free credit facilities, the trust will provide compensation in the form of repayment up to a maximum of 85 percent of the credit availed.

This scheme launched in the year 2000 ensured collateral-free loans through banks and financial institutions. The corpus for the fund is Rs 2500 crore and the sharing ratio between the GOI and SIDBI is 4:1. Under this scheme, new or existing micro enterprises are eligible for loans and working capital up to Rs 1 crore without any collateral or third party guarantee. The cover under the scheme is for the terms of the credit facility while in the case of working capital, the guarantee cover is for five years. In the case of enterprises becoming sick, the assistance rendered by the lender is also covered under the ambit of this scheme.

A bank or lending institution should become a member with CGTMSE (called a "Member Lending Institution" or "MLI") in order to benefit from the scheme. Over the years, the CGS has been expanding its coverage and as of 31st March 2016 it had 119 MLIs. The growth in the number of MLIs over the years is presented in Figure 3.1.

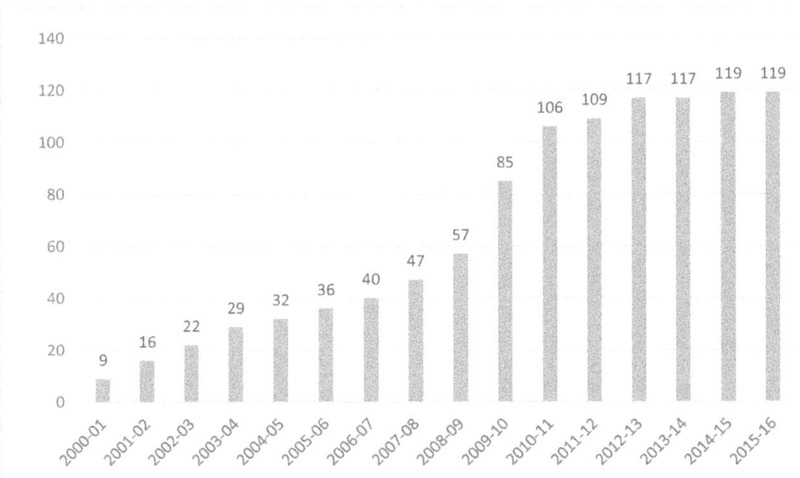

Figure 3.1 Number of Member Lending Institutions (MLIs)

Source: Based on http://dcmsme.gov.in/schemes/sccrguarn.htm.

The scheme provides a guarantee up to 85 percent of the sanctioned credit (Table 3.6). A guarantee cover of 85 percent is provided in the case of micro enterprises with loans up to Rs 5 lakh. However, the guarantee cover reduces to 80 percent for medium and small enterprises owned by females and further to 75 percent for loans amounting to Rs 50 lakh. The trust charges an annual guarantee fee of 1 percent per annum of the sanctioned credit facility, while in the case of women-led micro enterprises the annual fee is only 0.85 percent (for loans above 5 lakhs and up to 1 crore). It is clearly evident from Figure 3.2 that the number of proposals for credit guarantee cover increased from 951 in the year 2000–2001 to 513978 in

Table 3.6 Credit Guarantee

Category	*Maximum Guarantee Cover*		
	Up to Rs 5 lakh	*Above Rs 5 lakh Up to Rs 50 lakh*	*Above Rs 50 lakh Up to Rs 200 lakh*
Micro enterprises	85 percent of the amount	75 percent of the amount	75 percent of the amount
Women entrepreneurs	80percent of the amount in default subject to a maximum of 40 lakh		
Other borrowers	75 percent of the amount		
Activity	From 10 lakh up to 100 lakh		
MSE retail trade	50 percent of the amount in default		

Source: www.cgtmse.in/About_us.aspx.

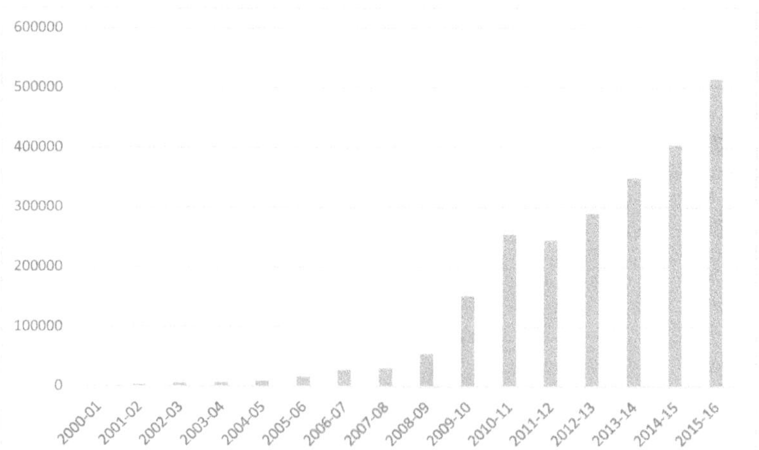

Figure 3.2 Number of Credit Guarantees Approved

*Source:*http://dcmsme.gov.in/schemes/sccrguarn.htm.

Table 3.7 Year-Wise Amount of Guarantee Cover Approved

Year	*Amount Approved (Rs crore)*
2000–2001	6.06
2001–2002	29.52
2002–2003	58.67
2003–2004	117.6
2004–2005	267.46
2005–2006	461.91
2006–2007	704.53
2007–2008	1055.84
2008–2009	2199.4
2009–2010	6875.11
2010–2011	12589.22
2011–2012	13783.98
2012–2013	16062.48
2013–2014	18188.12
2014–2015	21274.82
2015–2016	19949.38

Source: http://dcmsme.gov.in/schemes/sccrguarn.htm.

the year 2015–2016. Alongside this, the coverage of the CGTMSE in terms of approved amount is also increasing (Table 3.7).

Credit Guarantee Fund for Micro Units (CGFMU) came into effect in 2015. This fund was set up to guarantee payment against default in micro loans (collateral free loans up to 10 lakhs) by banks, non-banking companies and other financial intermediaries. According to this scheme, the first 5 percent of the default amount will be given by the lending institution while the amount in default above 5 percent will be settled by the CGFMU.

Trade-Related Entrepreneurship Assistance and Development (TREAD) scheme

Given the fact that women entrepreneurs encounter difficulties in obtaining formal credit due to limited access to resources, during the ninth five-year plan the government decided to launch the Trade-Related Entrepreneurship Assistance and Development (TREAD) scheme. The key focus of the scheme is to provide credit to the most disadvantaged section like illiterate and semi-literate women in rural and urban areas. Loan assistance to women applicants is routed through Non-Governmental Organisations (NGOs) which are assisting women in training and empowerment activities. Since 2005, Micro Finance Institutions (MFIs) are also allowed to raise loans on behalf of women beneficiaries under the TREAD scheme. This scheme also provides assistance to NGOs which are providing training to women entrepreneurs. Women beneficiaries are given a grant of up to 30 percent of the loan/credit with a maximum of up to Rs 30 lakhs. In the case of organisations providing training to women entrepreneurs, a grant of up to Rs 1 lakh is given per programme with the condition that such organisations should contribute a minimum of 25 percent of the government grant.

Rashtriya Mahila Kosh (RMK)

This initiative began with the setting up of National credit fund for women in the year 1993. The main objective of this funding organisation under the Ministry of Women and Child Development is to provide credit exclusively for poor women. The Rashtriya Mahila Kosh (RMK) provides loans, both working capital and term loans, to women self-help groups and women entrepreneurs. It also provides micro credit to women in the informal sector and microenterprises. The RMK also undertake capacity building initiatives by imparting training in financial management, project management, enterprise development, skill upgradation and exposure visits to women entrepreneurs. In order to improve their livelihood, women entrepreneurs are provided marketing assistance and the scheme aims at the holistic development of women entrepreneurs. It began with an initial corpus of Rs 31 crore which has been further raised to Rs 284 crore.

Recent developments

Micro Units Development and Refinance Agency (MUDRA) bank initiative

Among the recent initiatives, Pradahan Mantri Mudra Yojana (PMMY), a refinancing scheme was launched in 2015 to meet the credit needs of micro and small enterprises. Under this scheme, Micro Units Development and Refinance Agency (MUDRA) bank was launched with the funding of Rs 200 billion for lending and Rs 30 billion for provision of credit guarantees. The loans are classified under three categories: (a) Sishu (up to Rs 50000); (b) Kishor (between Rs 50000 and Rs 500000); and (c) Tarun (between Rs 500000 and Rs 1000000). These loans are given by commercial banks, Regional Rural banks (RRBs), small finance banks, MFIs and Non-Banking Financial Companies (NBFCs). Under this initiative, banks, non-bank finance companies and MFIs can obtain refinance facility for loans disbursed under this scheme. It is expected that under all categories of loans preference is given to microenterprises and 60 percent of the funds are to be allocated under the first category of loan (Sishu). The MUDRA

Table 3.8 Share of Loan Accounts and Amount Sanctioned by Categories of Borrowers

Category	*2017–2018*		*Cumulative for Three Years**	
	Number of Accounts	*Amount Disbursed (Rs crore)*	*Number of Accounts*	*Amount Disbursed (Rs crore)*
Up to Rs 50000	42669795 (88.7)	104228.05 (42.3)	111568654 (90.9)	250147.6 (45.1)
Between Rs 50000 and 5 lakh	4653874 (9.7)	83197.09 (33.8)	9386837 (7.6)	175333.5 (31.6)
Between Rs 50000 and 10 lakh	806924 (1.7)	59012.25 (23.9)	1757073 (1.4)	129223.1 (23.3)
Total	**48130593**	**246437.39**	**122712564**	**55470430**
Women	33558238 (69.7)	100170.55 (40.6)	90333397 (73.6)	241610.80 (43.6)
Scheduled Caste/Scheduled Tribe/Other Backward Class (SC/ST/OBC)	26224114 (54.5)	83686.97 (34.0)	67125807 (54.7)	199163.10 (35.9)

Source: www.mudra.org.in/.

Note: Figures in parenthesis indicate their share in the total. * Refers to 2015–2016 to 2017–2018.

bank initiative is launched with the objective of increasing the fund availability and reduced interest cost of credit to the borrowers. There is cap on the interest rate chargeable by various types of lenders to the MUDRA segment. Under the interest rate ceilings, regional rural banks and cooperatives can only charge up to 3.50 percent over and above the MUDRA refinance rate from the final borrower while for NBFCs an interest limit of 6 percent over and above the MUDRA refinance rate is stipulated by RBI. Based on the latest data available, the share of loan accounts of the underprivileged sections of society – SC, ST, OBC and women are significant. The share of women borrowers in the total loan accounts currently stands at 47 percent while that of SC/ST/OBC borrowers stands at 36 percent of the total loan accounts (Table 3.8). Even though there is no publicly available disaggregated level data for the affirmative action category borrowers to analyse the trend since the initiation of the scheme, the annual report of the 2017–2018 MUDRA mentions the share of SC, ST and OBC categories as 18 percent, 5 percent and 32 percent, respectively, in terms of number of loan accounts sanctioned.[6] In terms of the total amount sanctioned, the share of women borrowers is 43 percent for the three years (2015–2016 to 2017–2018), while SC/ST/OBCs borrowers account for 35 percent during 2015–2016 to 2017–2018.

Stand-up India

To improve the credit availability and establishment of small businesses by women and SC/ST entrepreneurs, the government under the leadership of SIDBI started the Stand-up India initiative in 2016 for setting up greenfield enterprises in the manufacturing, retail and services sectors. Under this scheme, the banks are supposed to provide loans ranging from Rs 10 lakh to Rs 1 crore for the first-time women and SC/ST entrepreneurs. The loan can cover 75 percent of the project cost and the borrower is expected to contribute a minimum 10 percent of the cost. The coverage of loan includes both term loan and working capital. The loan is expected to be paid back in 7 years. The interest rate charged under this scheme is a maximum of 3 percent above base rate plus tenor premium.

Start-up India

To improve the start-up ecosystem in India, the government launched the Start-up India initiative in 2016. Start-ups are those enterprises incorporated for less than seven years with a turnover not exceeding Rs 25 crores. These enterprises are working towards development, production or distribution of new products, processes or services.[7] This initiative is expected to empower the start-up ecosystem through simplification and handholding, funding and incentives, incubation and industry-academic partnership. The initiative is through the inception of Rs 25 billion initial corpus and the expectation is to reach Rs 100 billion by 2020. These funds will be channelled through venture capital funds registered with the Securities and Exchange Board of India (Shankar, 2019). Several state governments have come up with policies to promote start-ups. Some states like Andhra Pradesh, Bihar and Odisha have special policies to encourage women start-ups.

"59-minute-one-crore-MSME-loan" initiative

This is a recent initiative which considerably simplifies and eases the process of obtaining institutional credit by MSMEs. An online platform (psbloansin59minute.com) serves as the medium for applying for a loan (term loan and working capital loan). There are more than 25 banks and NBFCs registered with this platform. The scheme is designed in such a way that the borrower is expected to receive loan approval in 59 minutes. Disbursement of the loan amount will be within seven to eight days. Business loans ranging from Rs 1 lakh to Rs 5 crore are provided with or without collateral. Interest rates payable start at 8.5 percent and the borrower is given the freedom to choose the lending institution.

Credit rating and performance scheme

In order to further improve credit access to the MSME sector, the government recently initiated the Credit Rating and Performance Scheme. It is expected that firms with a credit rating will find it easier and cheaper to obtain formal credit. According to this scheme, a fee will be charged by the rating agencies and the fee is fixed according to the sales turnover of the enterprises. However, units are eligible for a share of reimbursement of the rating fee from the Ministry of MSME. Eligibility is prescribed under three slabs based on the turnover: up to Rs 50 lakh – 75 percent of the fee or Rs 25000; between Rs 50 and 200 lakh – 75 percent of the fee or Rs 30000; and more than Rs 200 lakh – 75 percent of the fee or Rs 40000. In the case of SC/ST enterprises, for the initial rating 90 percent subsidy is provided by the rating agency. In the case of the renewal of ratings, SC/ST enterprises with a rating of up to five is eligible for a subsidy of 50 percent. During 2016–2017, 395 SC/ST enterprises received ratings under this scheme (Ministry of MSME, 2018).[8]

Conclusion

The overall discussion in this chapter clearly suggests that there have been considerable changes in the policies and programmes introduced to address the credit needs of small firms in the Indian manufacturing sector. For the remainder of the book, we will investigate the implications of these policies on the growth and performance of MSMEs as well as their role in addressing discrimination in the small-business credit market. In Chapter 4, we will present some stylised facts about the firms in the MSME sector. Chapter 5 will investigate the relationship between access to credit and firm growth. In Chapters 6 and 7 of the book we will explore the crucial relationship between ownership characteristics and credit access, and whether and how the nexus between the two influences the performance of small firms. In particular, we examine the role of gender on credit access in Chapter 6 and caste affiliation of the firm owner on credit access in Chapter 7.

Notes

1 This includes agriculture and related activities, small scale sector, retail, transport operators, professionals and craftsmen.
2 In 1977, RBI revised this to four branches from the previous three branch criteria (Shah et al., 2007; Burgess and Pande, 2005).
3 http://laghu-udyog.gov.in/publications/comitterep/nayak.html.
4 www.rbi.org.in/Scripts/PublicationReportDetails.aspx?ID=394.
5 www.rbi.org.in/Scripts/NotificationUser.aspx?Id=9688&Mode=0.
6 Mudra, Annual Report 2017–18. www.mudra.org.in.
7 Source: Startup India website (www.startupindia.gov.in/).
8 https://msme.gov.in/relatedlinks/annual-report-ministry-micro-small-and-medium-enterprises.

4

MICRO, SMALL AND MEDIUM ENTERPRISES (MSMEs) IN INDIA

Their characteristics and evolution over time

Introduction

There exists substantial literature on the evolution, performance and characteristics of firms in developed countries (McGahan, 1999; Bamiatzi and Hall, 2009). In recent years, there has been a burgeoning amount of literature that has delved into the characteristics and behaviour of firms in the Indian manufacturing sector (Topalova and Khandelwal, 2011; Nagaraj, 2012). However, most of these studies have primarily focused on large firms in India. On the other hand, there is a dearth of studies that probed the evolution and performance of small firms in the sector. This is indeed surprising, given the fact that large firms constitute a very small share in the Indian manufacturing sector. Like large firms, small firms too combine labour and capital to produce output, and some firms do it better than others. This depends on the inherent abilities of managers and owners, and specific characteristics of firms such as firm size and age. In comparison with large firms that mostly operate in monopolistic or oligopolistic market structures (that have implications for their behaviour and performance), small firms operate in market structures which are close to perfect competition or are characterised by monopolistic competition (Raj and Sen, 2016).

In this chapter, we make an attempt to present some stylised facts about the firms in the MSME sector, using the unit level data drawn from the MSME survey for the year 2000–2001 and 2006–2007. We start by examining the evolution of firm size, growth and productivity at the aggregate level. We also capture this evolution at the aggregate level by firm type (micro, small and medium), registration status (formal and informal) and location (rural and urban). We then examine the differences in firm size, output growth and firm productivity across states and industries. We also look at firm size, growth and productivity by different sets of firms characteristics (ownership, age and gender and social group of the owner) to see if there are observable differences in firm size, growth and productivity across firms of different characteristics.

One of the main concerns about small firms is that they pay lower wages to workers than large firms do. We look at differences in wages paid to workers by specific characteristics of firms such as type of enterprise, registration status, location, ownership and gender and social group of the owner. Finally, we also examine one specific issue which is the main focus of this book – access to credit. We explore the relationship between finance, firm size and productivity. To be specific, we see the firms' access to credit and examine whether the firms rely mostly on institutional or non-institutional sources of finance. We also see whether access to credit differs across firms of different characteristics and whether there exists substantial differences in size, growth and productivity for firms with access to credit vis-à-vis firms which have reported as having no access to credit.

Size and productivity of MSMEs: evolution over time

In this section, we first examine the evolution of firm size and productivity at the aggregate level and then by state and industry.

Aggregate trends

Figure 4.1 presents trends in average size of a firm over the period 2001–2006. We use average number of workers to represent firm size. We find a consistent increase in the size of an average firm in the MSME sector over time. The average size has increased from 5.46 workers in 2001 to over 5.9 workers in 2006. This firm size expansion is evident in both registered and unregistered sectors (Figure 4.2). The size of an average firm, however, differ significantly between registered and unregistered MSME sectors. Our rural-urban comparison of firm size mirrors the pattern that we observed at the aggregate level (Figure 4.3). We observe a rise in average firm size between 2001 and 2006 for firms in rural as well as urban areas. But these changes are more striking for firms in urban areas than in rural areas. In other words, urban firms observed a faster increase in firm size as compared to rural firms. Firms in urban areas are expected to be larger than those in rural areas and our findings do not contradict this expectation. Figure 4.3 shows that urban firms, on average, employed 6.74 workers and are 41.6 percent larger than their counterparts in rural areas. We also find that the difference in firm size between rural and urban firms increased from 0.35 in 2001 to 0.61 in 2006. As expected, the firms in the medium enterprise category are larger in size followed by small and micro firms (Figure 4.4). On average, medium firms employed 77.58 workers, small firms employed 16.41 workers and micro firms employed 3.65 workers. Thus, in terms of size, the medium firms are 4.7 times larger than small firms, which are 4.5 times the size of micro firms. This size difference between enterprise types can be observed in both registered and

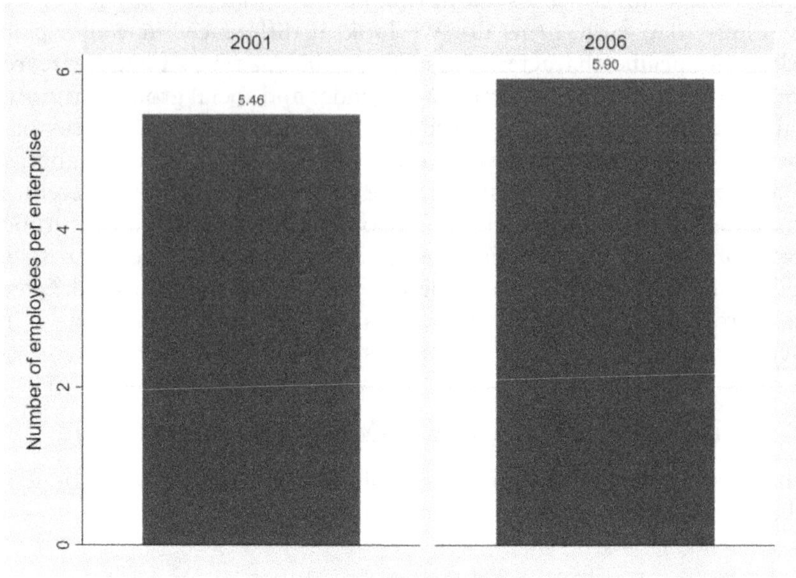

Figure 4.1 Changes in Firm Size, 2001–2006
Source: Authors' estimates.

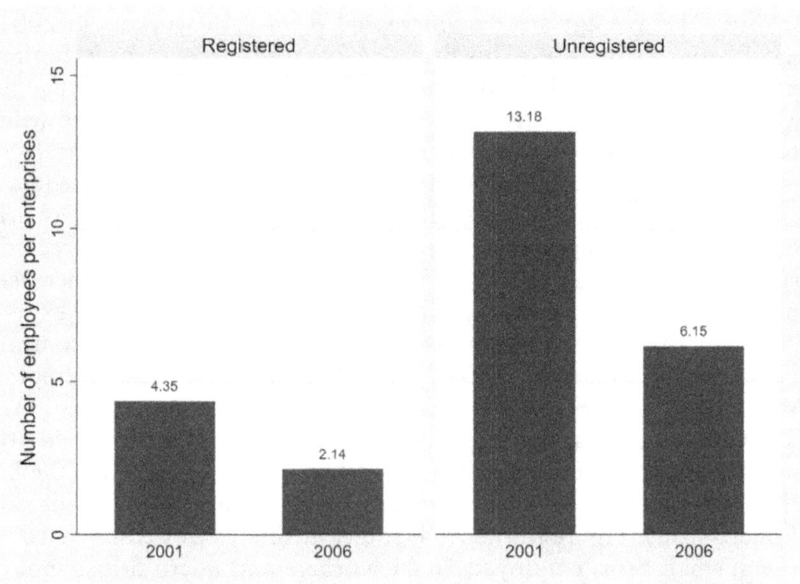

Figure 4.2 Firm Size by Registration Status
Source: Authors' estimates.

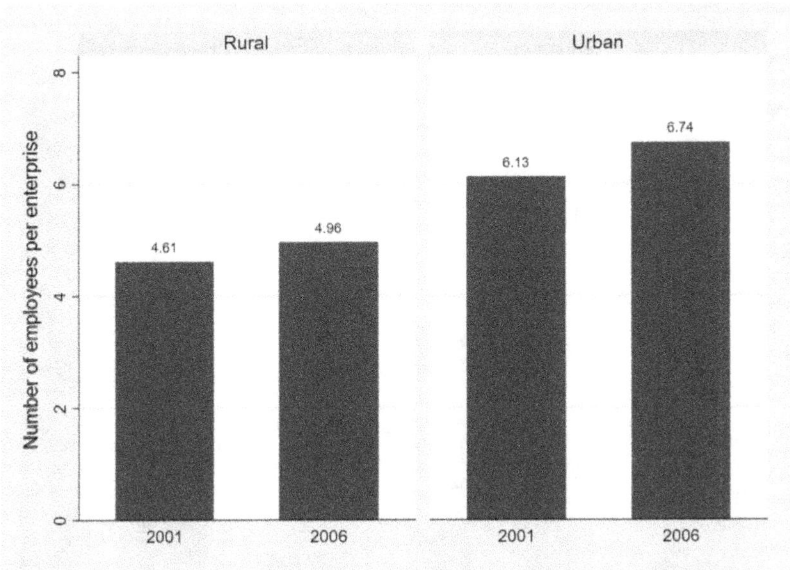

Figure 4.3 Firm Size by Location
Source: Authors' estimates.

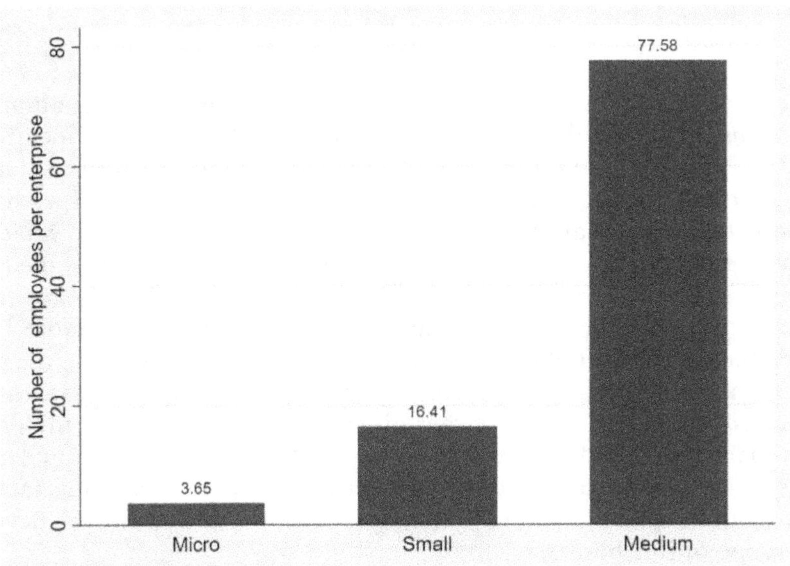

Figure 4.4 Firm Size by Enterprise Type
Source: Authors' estimates.

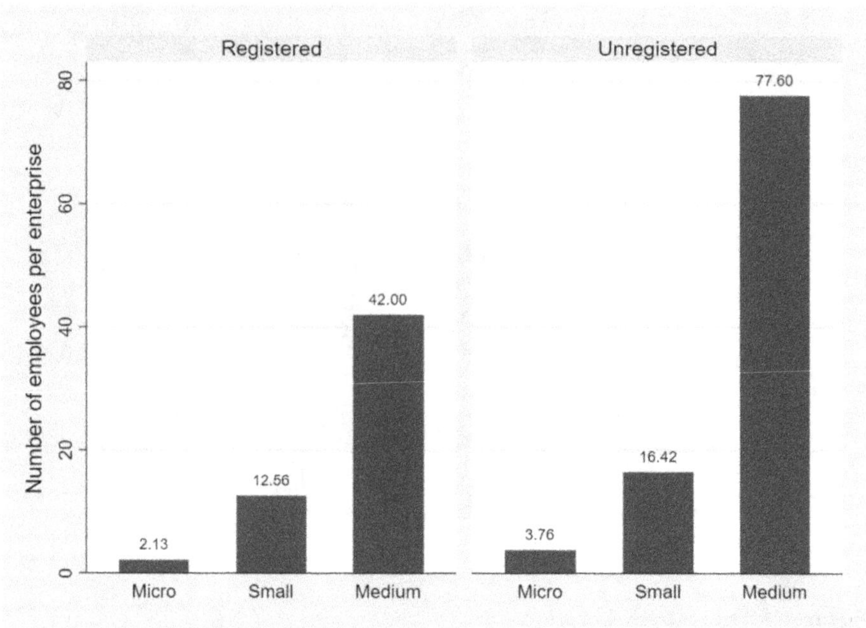

Figure 4.5 Firm Size by Enterprise Type and Registration Status
Source: Authors' estimates.

unregistered sectors (Figure 4.5). A similar pattern is also observed for firms in the rural and urban areas (Figure 4.6). In both locations, medium firms are found to be larger than small and micro firms. However, perhaps the most striking finding from our analysis emerges when we do the rural-urban comparison by enterprise type. Unlike what we observed earlier, our findings point to a relatively larger size of medium firms in the rural areas vis-à-vis those in urban areas. As is apparent from Figure 4.6, an average medium firm in rural areas is more than twice the size of a similar firm in urban areas. This seems to be the case for firms in the "small" enterprise type too. One would have rather expected urban firms to be larger given that the markets for the products made by these firms would be larger due to the higher population density in these areas. Further research is needed to locate the factors that would explain this unexpected outcome, which is, however, beyond the scope of this book.

When we look at the labour productivity levels, the pattern is more or less in accordance with what we observed for firm size. We use the ratio of total sales to total employment to proxy labour productivity. Available

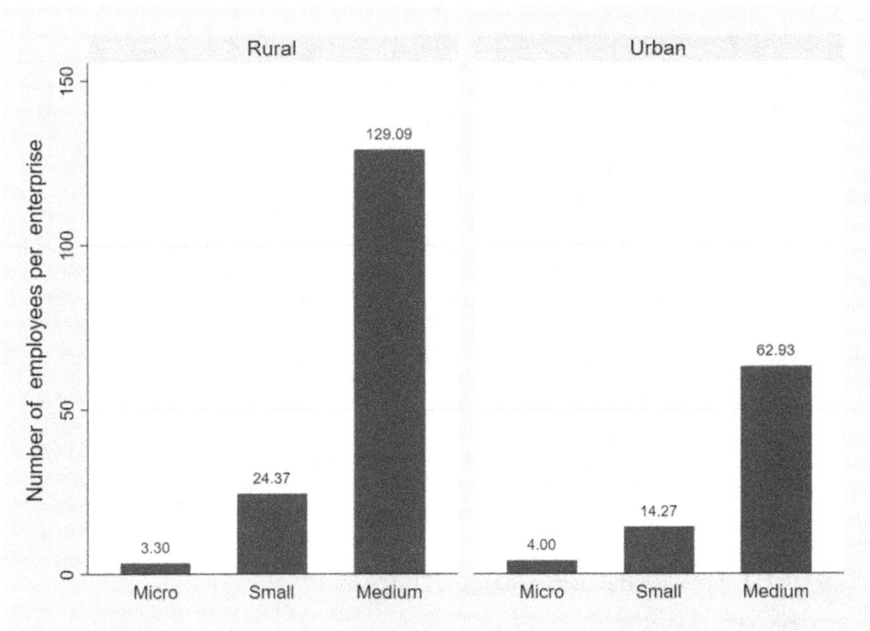

Figure 4.6 Firm Size by Enterprise Type and Location

Source: Authors' estimates.

evidence shows that the sector has experienced a significant rise in labour productivity between 2001 and 2006 (Figure 4.7). Our computations reveal that the output per labour has increased at a rate of 5.9 percent per annum during this period. This acceleration in productivity can be observed in both registered and unregistered sectors (Figure 4.8). Predictably, the average productivity levels are higher among firms in the registered sector. While productivity grew at a rate of 1.5 percent per annum in the registered sector, it reported a decline of 0.35 percent in the unregistered sector. Similar productivity improvements are noticed in rural and urban firms too. Urban firms are, on average, more productive than rural firms, and also reported a faster increase of labour productivity over time (Figure 4.9). As expected, the average productivity levels are found to be highest among the medium firms, followed by small firms and micro firms (Figure 4.10). We find that medium firms are 1.12 times more productive than small firms, which are 1.07 times more productive than micro firms. This difference in productivity levels between enterprise types is clearly evident for registered and unregistered firms (Figure 4.11) as well as for rural and urban firms (Figure 4.12).

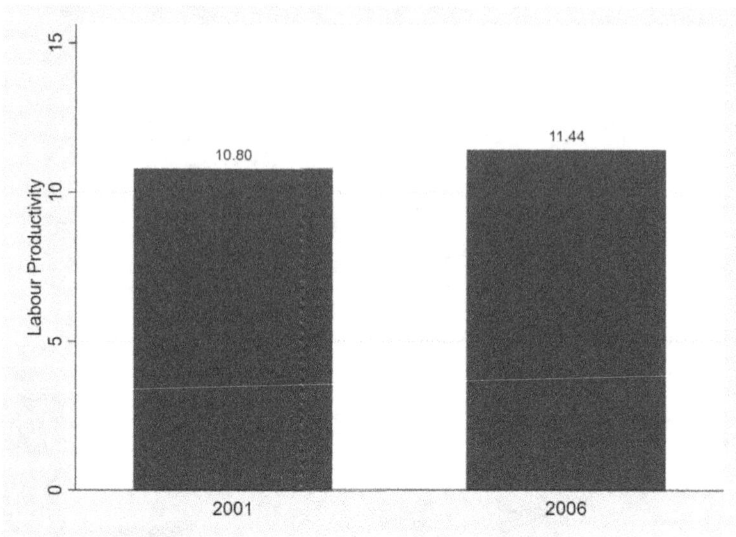

Figure 4.7 Labour Productivity Changes, 2001–2006

Source: Authors' estimates.

Labour Productivity is expressed in log form.

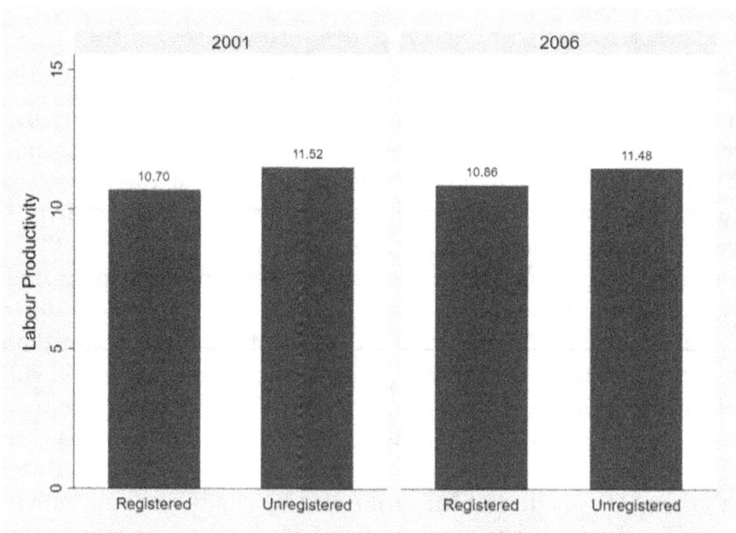

Figure 4.8 Labour Productivity by Registration Status

Source: Authors' estimates.

Labour Productivity is expressed in log form.

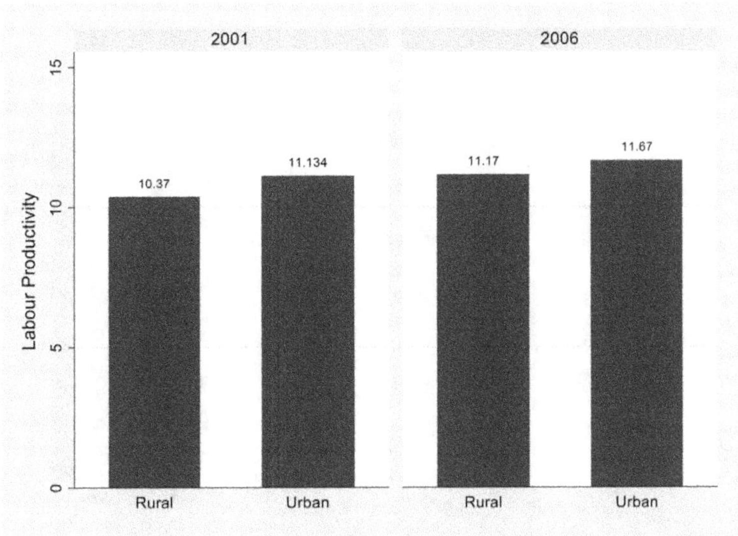

Figure 4.9 Labour Productivity by Location

Source: Authors' estimates.

Labour Productivity is expressed in log form.

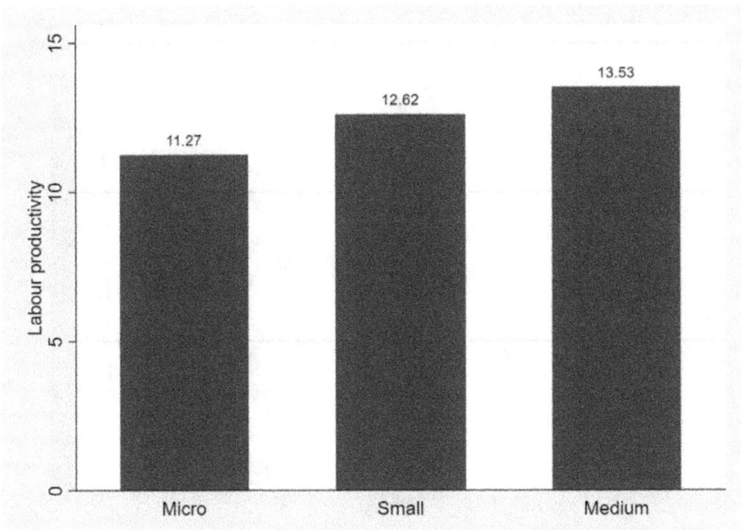

Figure 4.10 Labour Productivity by Enterprise Type

Source: Authors' estimates.

Labour Productivity is expressed in log form.

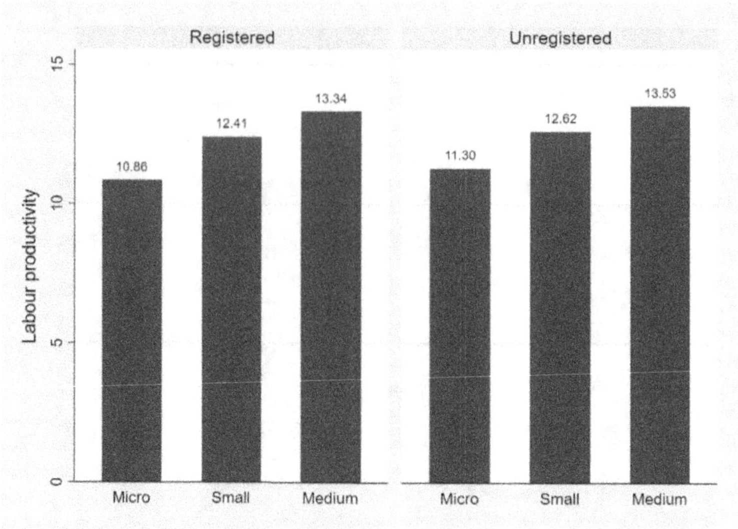

Figure 4.11 Labour Productivity by Enterprise Type and Registration Status

Source: Authors' estimates.

Labour Productivity is expressed in log form.

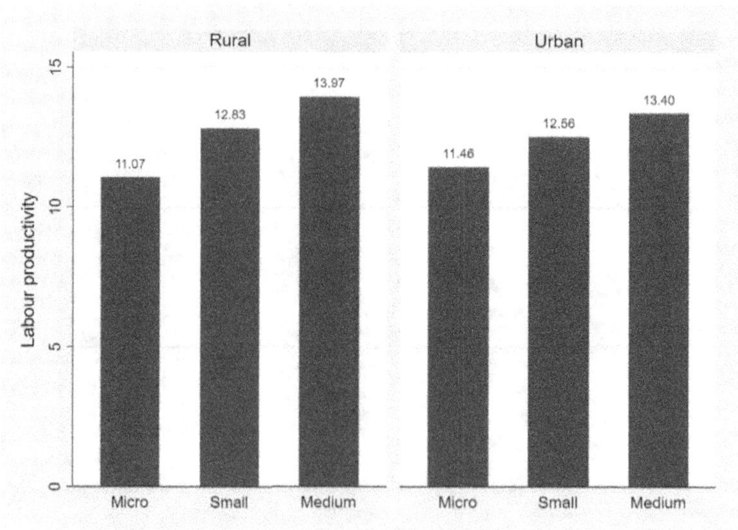

Figure 4.12 Labour Productivity by Enterprise Type and Location

Source: Authors' estimates.

Labour Productivity is expressed in log form.

We next examine histograms of frequency of firms and firm growth and productivity across different size classes for the years 2001 and 2006. We identified six size categories based on the number of workers employed by the firms. They include firms with 1–2 workers, those with 3–5 workers, those with 6–9 workers, those with 10–15 workers, firms with 16–19 workers and those firms that employ 20 or more workers. Over the period from 2001 to 2006, we noticed a steady increase in number of firms in smaller size classes (firms employing 1–2 workers and 3–5 workers) and larger size classes (10–15, 16–19 and 20 or more size categories) (Figure 4.13). In contrast, the number of firms in the intermediate size classes employing 6–9 workers witnessed a decline. It is also evident from Figure 4.13 that the histogram is skewed to the right indicating that the majority of the firms are concentrated in the smaller size categories (1–2 and 3–5 workers). What is even more interesting is the fact that there has been hardly any transformation in firm size distribution in the five year period between 2001 and 2006. This finding possibly lends support to the argument that very few small firms make transition to larger firms. Evidence also points to a substantial economic distance between small and large firms in the MSME sector. As evident from Figures 4.14 and 4.15, large firms report substantially higher

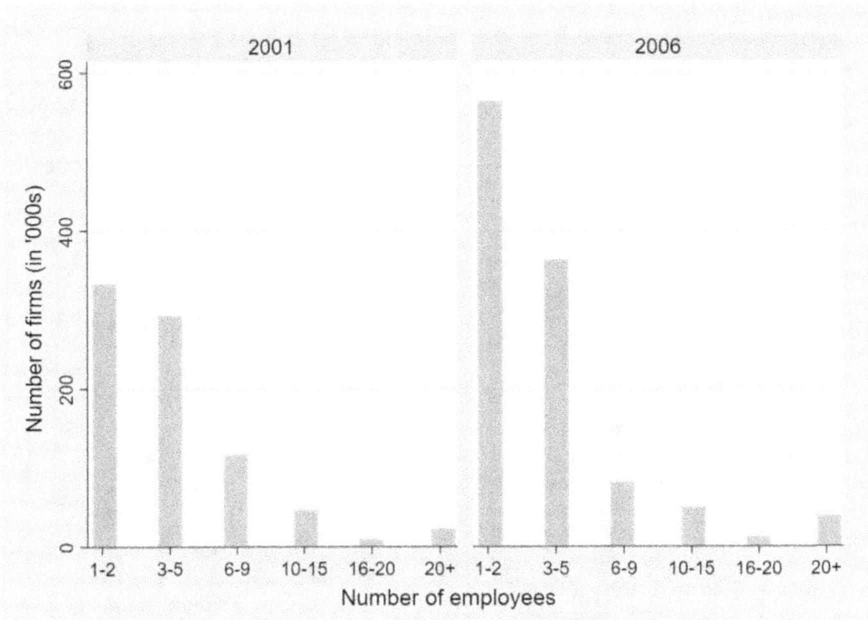

Figure 4.13 Firm Distribution Across Different Size Classes
Source: Authors' estimates.

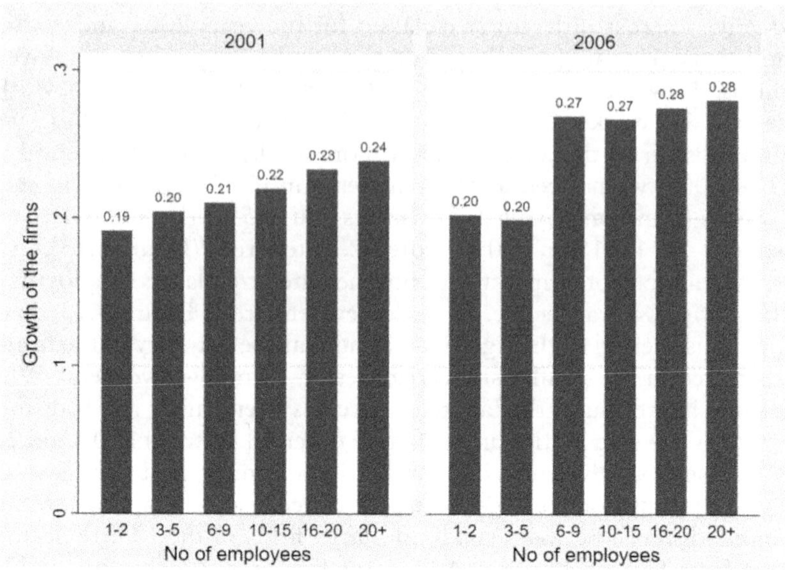

Figure 4.14 Output Growth Across Different Size Classes

Source: Authors' estimates.

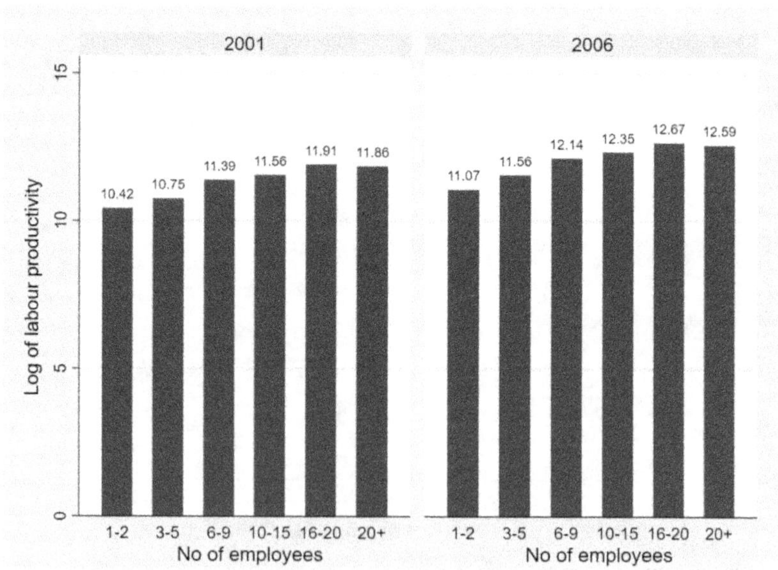

Figure 4.15 Labour Productivity Across Different Size Classes

Source: Authors' estimates.

output growth and productivity as compared to the small firms. Moreover, the economic distance between the two categories widened during 2001–2006. On the whole, the discussion of firm size distribution suggests the clustering of firms in smaller size categories pointing to the lack of vertical progression of firms in the MSME sector. Our evidence based on growth and productivity distribution also shows why such limited firm transition is a drag on the overall growth and productivity of the sector.

State and industry differences

The changes in the distribution of firm size, output growth and productivity at the industry and state levels are captured in this section. We capture the changes for the period 2001–2006. We find that the average firm size increased in the majority of the industries (Figure 4.16). We observe that 15 out of 22 industries recorded an increase in firm size over the five year period. Among the industries, tobacco goods experienced the fastest increase in firm size followed by basic metals, petroleum products and transport equipment. Firms, on average, are larger in size in the tobacco industry and, according to our estimates, an average firm in the tobacco industry

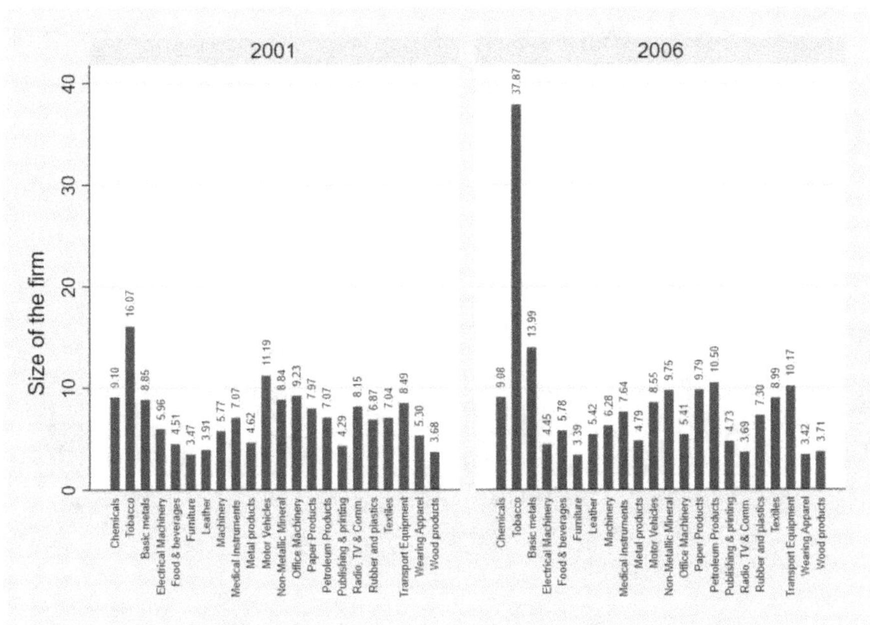

Figure 4.16 Firm Size by Industry

Source: Authors' estimates.

has more than doubled its size, from 16 workers in 2001 to 38 workers in 2006. Interestingly, even though basic metal industry is ranked second in terms of average size, a typical firm in this industry is only 1/3rd of the size of an average firm in the tobacco industry. On the other side, seven industries report size contraction: chemicals, electricals, furniture goods, motor vehicles, office machinery, radio, television (TV) and communication equipment and wearing apparel. The firms in the motor vehicle industry and office machinery industry experienced the largest contraction in firm size; in the motor vehicle industry, the average firm size declined from 11 workers in 2001 to 8 workers in 2006 while in office machinery industry the size declined from 9 workers in 2001 to 5 workers by 2006. In other industries, we witness only a marginal decline in size.

However, when we discern the trend at the state level we observe a similar picture of what we observed at the industry level. The average firm size experienced an increase in most of the states; about 3/4th of the states reported an increase in average firm size (Figure 4.17). While the size contraction is evident mainly in some of the major states, size expansion is mostly confined to the smaller states of India. Among the major states, the highest reduction in firm size is reported in Tamil Nadu, Uttar Pradesh,

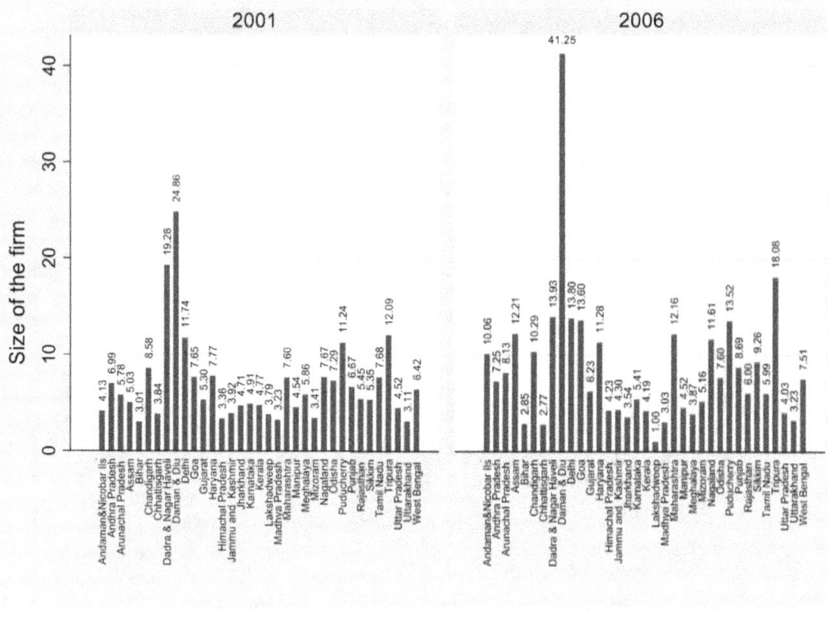

Figure 4.17 Firm Size by State

Source: Authors' estimates.

Bihar, Madhya Pradesh and Jharkhand. On the other hand, the states that experienced the largest increase in firm size include Maharashtra, Assam, Haryana, Delhi and Punjab.

Do substantial economic differences between firms exist across states and industries too? We investigate this question based on Figures 4.18, 4.19, 4.20 and 4.21, which report inter-state and inter-industry variations in output growth and labour productivity over the period 2001–2006. As expected, output growth shows substantial improvement in most of the industries and states over the period 2001–2006. The rate of growth of output improved in 13 out of 22 industries and in 23 out of 35 states. Our evidence also points to considerable regional-level and industry-level variations in output growth. At the industry level, output growth rates are found to be the lowest in the tobacco goods industry and the highest in industries producing basic metal and paper products (Figure 4.18). When we look at the changes between 2001 and 2006, significant gains in output growth are reported in basic metals, motor vehicles, publishing and printing industries. On the other hand, manufacture of tobacco products and office machinery goods witnessed considerable deceleration in the output growth rate during the same period. There are substantial regional-level variations in output growth too (Figure 4.19). The lowest output growth rate is reported

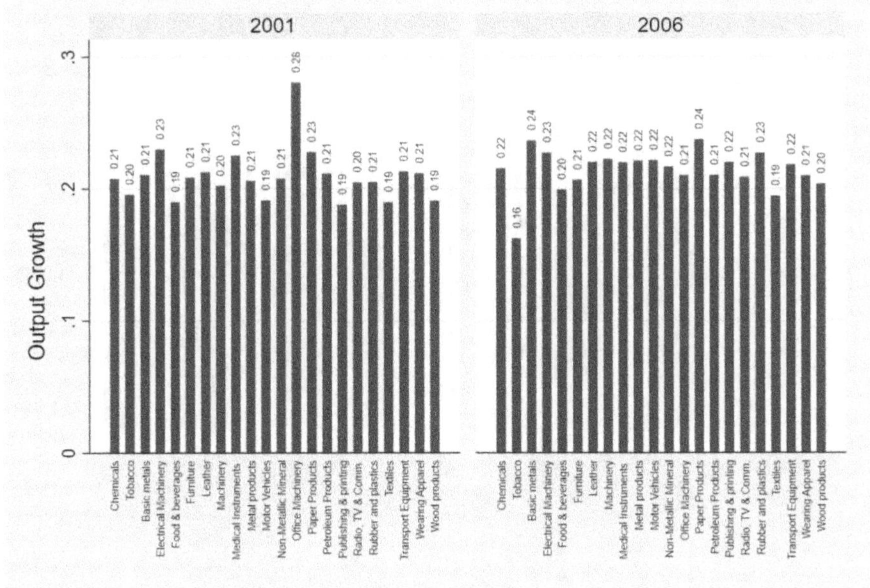

Figure 4.18 Output Growth by Industry

Source: Authors' estimates.

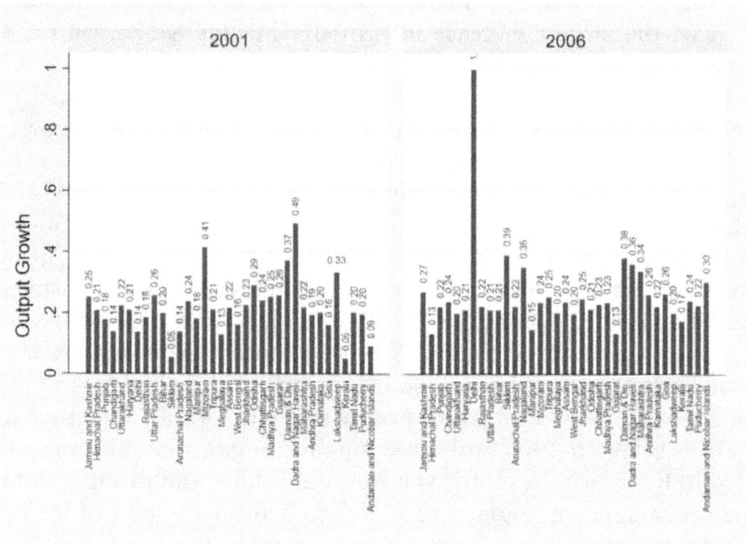

Figure 4.19 Output Growth by State

Source: Authors' estimates.

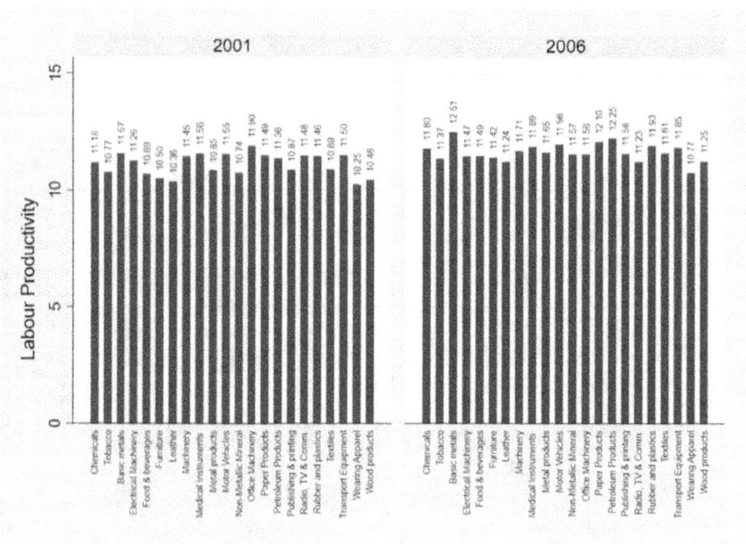

Figure 4.20 Labour Productivity by Industry

Source: Authors' estimates.

Labour Productivity is expressed in log form.

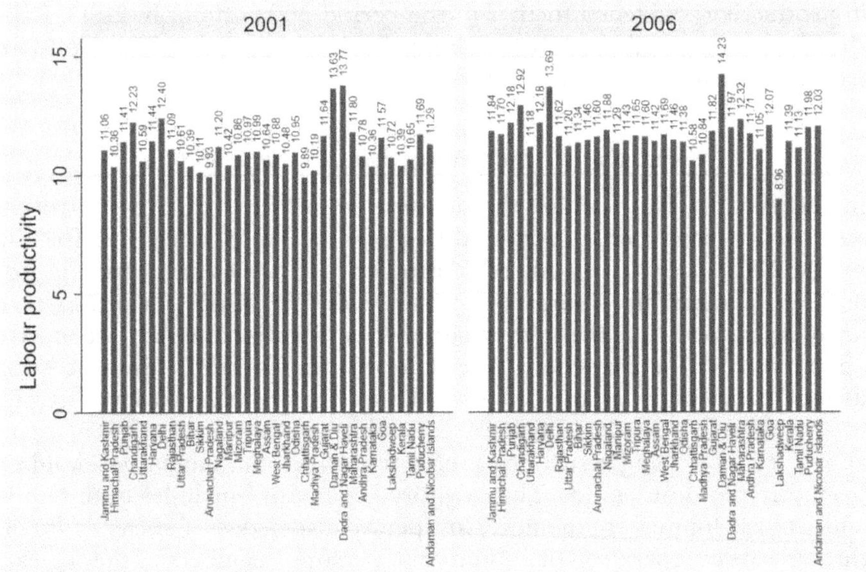

Figure 4.21 Labour Productivity by State

Source: Authors' estimates.

Labour Productivity is expressed in log form.

in the states of Himachal Pradesh and Gujarat and the highest growth rate is in Delhi. Over the period 2001–2006, substantial acceleration in output growth occurred in the states of Delhi, Kerala, Sikkim and Maharashtra. Meanwhile, output growth slowed down significantly in Gujarat and a few smaller states such as Mizoram, Dadra and Nagar Haveli and Himachal Pradesh.

Along the expected lines, except for a few, all industries and states witnessed a significant surge in productivity levels during 2001–2006. At the industry level, only two industry groups, office machinery and radio, TV and communication equipment witnessed an erosion in productivity levels (Figure 4.20). At the same time, considerable gains in productivity are observed in basic metals, non-metallic minerals, leather products, furniture and food and beverages. Among the industry groups, output per worker is found to be the lowest in wearing apparel and the highest in basic metals in 2006. More or less a similar trend is observed at the regional level too. Only in the case of the two union territory – Dadra and Nagar Haveli and Lakshadweep – did we see a drop in labour productivity between 2001 and 2006 (Figure 4.21). The largest gains in productivity are reported in Delhi and Kerala. Evidence also points to significant inter-regional variations in productivity levels; and this variation in productivity widened further in the period 2001–2006. In 2006, Lakshadweep registered the lowest labour productivity and Daman and Diu recorded the highest productivity level.

Size, growth and productivity by ownership

In this section, we examine the differences in firm size, output growth and labour productivity across different ownership categories for the period 2001–2006. Five ownership categories of firms are identified: proprietary, partnership, company, cooperatives and others. In proprietary firms, an individual is the sole owner of the enterprise and they are mostly operated from the household. The report of the Fourth All India Census defines partnership as the "relation between persons who have agreed to share the profits of a business carried on by all or any one of them acting for all". The partners may be drawn from the same household or from different households. The category "company" includes both public and private limited companies. Co-operative society is a society formed through the co-operation of a number of persons (members of the society) to benefit the members. If the enterprise does not fall under the previously mentioned four categories, then it is included under the category "others". For example, if the enterprise is owned by a trust, then it is treated as "others".

The main objective here is to examine whether the average firm size, output growth and labour productivity vary across these five ownership categories. We capture this in Table 4.1. In line with our expectations, it is found that the average firm size is high in the "company" category. This implies that public and private limited companies are, on average, larger in size as compared to their counterparts. This category of firms also witnessed a significant size expansion over the five-year period 2001–2006. On average, their size has increased from 22 workers in 2001 to 37 workers in 2006. On the other hand, the average firm size is relatively smaller for proprietary firms. According to our estimates, an average proprietary firm in 2006 is 9 times smaller than the size of an average firm in the "company" category. We also examine the size differences across ownership categories by registration status and location of firms. Trends similar to the ones observed at the aggregate level are noticed for registered and unregistered firms and rural and urban firms too; average size is higher for firms in the "company" category and lower for proprietary firms. We also find that large firms tend to be more productive and grow faster (second and third panel of Table 4.1). It is clearly evident from the table that public and private limited companies are the ones that grow faster and are more productive. On the other hand, proprietary firms reported slower growth and were found to be less productive. This relationship holds irrespective of the registration status and location of firms.

Table 4.1 Size, Growth and Productivity by Ownership

Category	*2001*					*2006*				
	Proprietary	*Partnership*	*Company*	*Cooperative*	*Others*	*Proprietary*	*Partnership*	*Company*	*Cooperative*	*Others*
	Firm Size					Firm Size				
Registration										
Unregistered	3.77	8.82	14.02	13.41	5.51	2.13	3.27	20.75	4.63	2.29
Registered	8.25	17.95	29.92	31.68	29.92	4.38	17.19	37.28	29.27	11.60
All Firms	4.19	11.55	21.89	16.91	9.69	4.23	16.97	37.27	29.02	11.03
Sector										
Rural	3.63	12.95	22.51	18.18	7.33	3.64	18.12	42.71	29.47	7.68
Urban	4.69	11.06	21.61	15.42	11.88	4.79	16.48	34.77	28.44	14.25
All Firms	4.19	11.55	21.89	16.91	9.69	4.23	16.97	37.27	29.02	11.03
	Labour Productivity (in log)					Labour Productivity (in log)				
Registration										
Unregistered	10.59	11.76	11.99	10.41	10.71	10.86	11.45	13.20	10.77	10.62
Registered	11.12	12.18	12.60	11.29	11.48	11.37	12.76	12.92	11.53	11.70
All Firms	10.64	11.88	12.29	10.57	10.84	11.33	12.73	12.92	11.52	11.63
Sector										
Rural	10.26	11.66	12.21	10.27	10.44	11.10	12.60	12.87	11.30	11.36
Urban	10.97	11.96	12.33	10.94	11.21	11.55	12.79	12.94	11.81	11.90
All Firms	10.64	11.88	12.29	10.57	10.84	11.33	12.73	12.92	11.52	11.63
	Output Growth					Output Growth				
Registration										
Unregistered	0.20	0.20	0.26	0.15	0.20	0.21	0.20	0.17	0.31	0.21
Registered	0.21	0.20	0.25	0.19	0.24	0.21	0.26	0.29	0.22	0.22
All Firms	0.20	0.20	0.25	0.16	0.21	0.21	0.26	0.29	0.22	0.22
Sector										
Rural	0.19	0.22	0.28	0.14	0.21	0.20	0.25	0.29	0.22	0.25
Urban	0.21	0.19	0.24	0.17	0.20	0.21	0.26	0.29	0.23	0.20
All Firms	0.20	0.20	0.25	0.16	0.21	0.21	0.26	0.29	0.22	0.22

Source: Authors' estimates.

Age, firm size and productivity

Do MSMEs increase in size and become more productive as they grow older? Available evidence in the context of other countries points to an inverse relationship between age and growth (Sleuwaegen and Goedhuys, 2002). Some scholars have observed the existence of an inverse U-shape relationship between age and productivity (Jensen et al., 2001; Van Biesebroeck, 2005; Fernandes, 2008). In contrast, Anyadike-Danes and Hart (2017) show that age matters critically for both survival and growth. When it comes to India, existing studies reported a negative association between age and firm growth (for example see, Deshpande and Sharma, 2013). However, according to Majumdar (1997), older firms are more productive and less profitable. In this section, we explore whether any relationship exists between age, size and productivity for MSME firms. The MSME survey dataset we utilise in this book provide information on the year of initial operation of the firms. Using this information, we arrive at the age of the firms, which is defined as the number of years since the commencement of the firm operation. We first report the average age for micro, small and medium size categories in Figure 4.22 and find that average age does not vary significantly across the three size categories. Though there exists a marginal age difference between

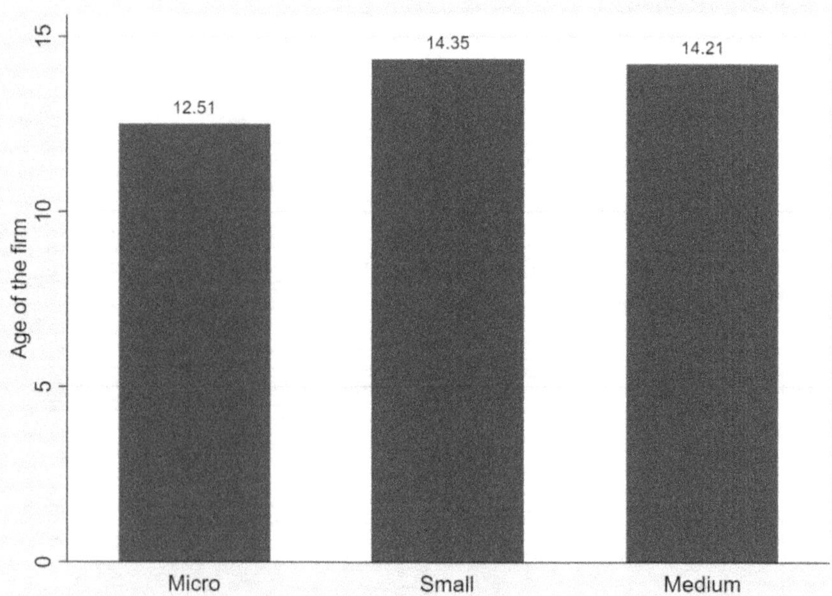

Figure 4.22 Firm Age by Enterprise Type

Source: Authors' estimates.

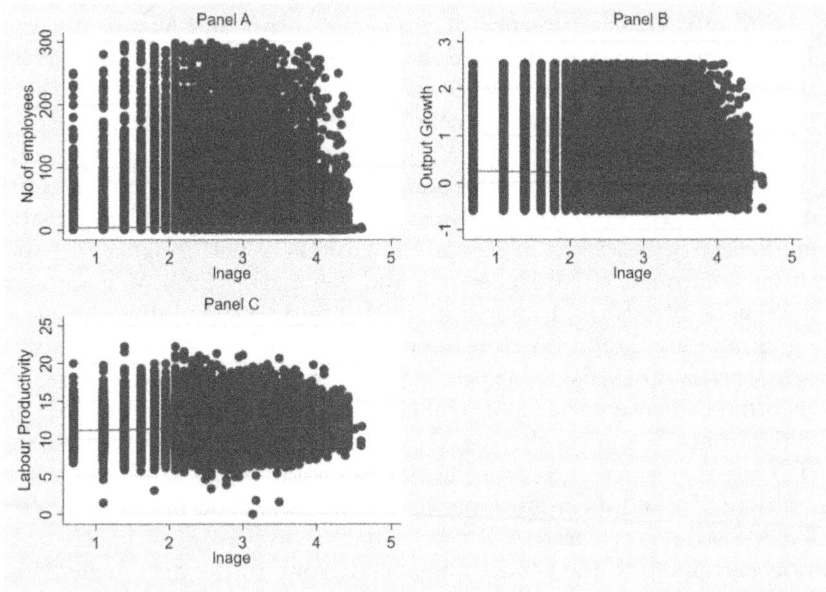

Figure 4.23 Relationship Between Age and Firm Size

Source: Authors' estimates.

micro and other firms, there is hardly any difference in average age of SMEs. Our findings thus fail to suggest any precise relationship between firm age and firm size. Given that the larger firms tend to survive longer, one would generally expect a positive relationship between the two and, hence, would see the average age increasing with firm size. In Figure 4.23, we explore this relationship further and found no evidence to support any precise relationship between firm age and employment. Our analysis fails to produce any conclusive evidence on the relationship between firm age and labour productivity and output growth. The other scatter plots in Figure 4.23 show absence of any such relationship between firm age and output growth and labour productivity.

Firm characteristics by gender and social group of the owner

Recent years witnessed a growing number of studies that attempted to locate the role of gender and social group of the owner on the size, growth and performance of firms. One common finding emerging from these studies relates to the underrepresentation of firms owned by women entrepreneurs and entrepreneurs belonging to SCs and STs (Deshpande and Sharma, 2013; Iyer et al., 2013). Further, these studies also observed that the firms run by women were smaller in size, less productive and grew slower as compared to enterprises owned by their male counterparts (Deshpande and Sharma, 2013; Iyer et al., 2013). The presence of women and SCs and STs are relatively higher in occupations which record the highest rates of poverty (such as agricultural labour in rural areas and casual workers in urban areas), and there is mixed evidence on the degree of occupational mobility of these groups, especially in the post-reform period. While some studies argue that the performance of female-owned firms compares well with that of male-owned firms (Bardasi et al., 2011), others show evidence of significant gender gaps both at market entry as well as in several dimensions of performance of female-led firms (Marques, 2015; Hellerstein and Neumark, 1999). When it comes to caste-wise differences, Kapur et al. (2010) find clear mobility of SCs from being agricultural labourers to being owners of Own Account Manufacturing Enterprises (OAMEs) using primary data from Uttar Pradesh. Gang et al. (2017) find evidence of occupational convergence among SCs towards non-SC/STs but not STs in rural areas. On the other hand, Thorat and Neuman (2012) find that social and economic discrimination significantly restricts the mobility of SCs and their entry into "non-traditional" occupations.

The MSME survey datasets that we utilise in this book also collected information pertaining to the gender and social group of the firm owner, which enables us to examine the differences in size, growth and productivity by the gender of the owner and social group affiliation. For social group, we identified three categories of firms: (a) Firms owned by those belonging to SCs or STs (SC/ST); (b) Those owned by OBCs; and (c) Those owned by the general category (GEN). We first look at the composition of firms in the MSME sector by gender and social group and how the composition has changed over time (Table 4.2). As anticipated, male-owned firms dominate the MSME sector. Our estimates suggest that about 87 percent of firms in the sector are male-owned firms. We also find that female-run firms witness an increase in their share over the period 2001–2006 (an increase from 9 percent in 2001 to 14 percent in 2006). When we look at the ownership by social group, the firms owned by the GEN category occupied the largest share, closely followed by the OBCs. They together constitute 90 percent of the firms in the MSME sector while the SCs- and STs-owned firms are only 10 percent. We find that OBC-owned firms improved their share between 2001 and 2006 but firms owned by the GEN category and the SCs and STs reported a decline in their share. The male dominance in ownership of firms is evident in both registered and unregistered firms, though the share witnessed a marginal decline over time in both types of firms. The preponderance of male ownership is visible among rural and urban firms too and more so for urban firms where the share exceeded the all-India average. We also observe this pattern across different ownership categories. As expected, male dominance is more apparent in the "company" category and less evident among firms in the cooperative society category. In tune with the aggregate trend, the share of male-owned firms has declined in all ownership categories.

Table 4.2 Composition of Micro, Small and Medium Enterprise (MSME) Firms by Gender and Social Group

Characteristics	*2001*					*2006*				
	Gender		*Caste*			*Gender*		*Caste*		
	Male	*Female*	*Scheduled Caste/ Scheduled Tribe (SC/ST)*	*Other Backward Class (OBC)*	*General (GEN)*	*Male*	*Female*	*SC/ST*	*OBC*	*GEN*
All Firms	91.45	8.55	10.84	36.02	53.14	86.51	13.49	10.45	40.70	48.85
Registration Status										
Unregistered	91.41	8.59	10.59	35.75	53.66	86.7	13.3	9.87	40.22	49.91
Registered	91.67	8.33	14.82	40.27	44.91	86.49	13.51	19.48	48.13	32.39
Enterprise Type										
Micro	–	–	–	–	–	85.20	14.80	11.46	44.50	44.04
Small	–	–	–	–	–	95.60	4.40	3.35	14.42	82.24
Medium	–	–	–	–	–	96.92	3.08	2.99	9.26	87.74
Location										
Rural	90.25	9.75	15.16	42.6	42.24	84.28	15.72	14.50	46.59	38.92
Urban	92.4	7.6	7.43	30.81	61.77	88.47	11.53	6.89	35.51	57.59
Ownership										
Proprietary	91.32	8.68	11.6	38.37	50.03	86.09	13.91	10.89	42.47	46.64
Partnership	92.55	7.45	5.41	21.8	72.79	91.26	8.74	4.48	23.78	71.74
Company	94.27	5.73	4.38	13.59	82.03	93.95	6.05	5.20	14.23	80.57
Cooperative	73.17	26.83	14.02	31.34	54.64	75.94	24.06	14.83	33.52	51.66
Others	91.16	8.84	10.34	24.81	64.84	85.84	14.16	8.50	29.58	61.93

Source: Authors' estimates.

We now examine whether there exist considerable differences in size, growth and productivity across male- and female-owned firms and firms owned by different social groups. The results are more or less in line with our expectations. Male-owned firms are larger in size as compared to female-owned firms (Table 4.3). In 2006, an average male-run firm employed 6 workers while a female-run firm employed only 4 workers. Evidence also confirms that, over the period 2001–2006, male-owned firms witnessed an expansion in their average firm size while female-owned firms experienced size contraction. When we examine firm size by social group, we observe that firms owned by the GEN category, on average, employ more workers, followed by firms owned by OBCs and SC/STs. The average firm run by the GEN category is double the size of an average OBC-run firm and SC/ST-run firm. Barring a few exceptions, such gender-wise and social group-wise differences in firm size are clearly evident across registered and unregistered firms, rural and urban firms and firms belonging to various ownership categories too (Table 4.3). Strikingly, female-run firms are found to be larger than male-run firms in "partnership" and "company" categories. We notice more or less a similar pattern for labour productivity too. Male-owned firms are more productive than female-owned firms (Table 4.4). Similarly, firms owned by the GEN social group category reported the highest productivity levels, followed by firms owned by the OBCs, the SCs and the STs. This variation in firm productivity between male- and female-owned firms and between firms owned by various social groups is also visible across various categories of firms namely, registered firms, unregistered firms, rural firms, urban firms and firms belonging to different ownership categories. As regards output growth, our results do not show any substantial difference between male- and female-owned firms (Table 4.5). Neither was there any significant gap in output growth among firms owned by various social groups. However, we do find gender-wise and caste-wise differences in net worth and profitability of the firms. We capture this in Table 4.6, which reports net worth and profitability of an average firm by gender and social group of the firm owner. It is clearly apparent from the table that male-run firms outperformed female-run firms in both the indicators – net worth and profitability. In other words, the net worth and profitability of firms are substantially higher for male-run firms as compared to female-run firms. With regard to social group, our findings are on expected lines as we find that the firms owned by the GEN category outperformed all other categories in total net worth and profitability. This pattern is evident even when we look at the levels separately for registered and unregistered firms, rural and urban firms and firms belonging to different ownership categories. Overall, our findings point to clear differences in firm size, net worth, productivity and profitability, with the SCs and STs being the most disadvantaged, followed by the OBCs, and with the firms owned by the GEN category group (forward castes, along with the non-Hindus who are also non-SC/ST and OBC) being the largest in terms of size and net worth and the most productive and profitable.

Table 4.3 Firm Size by Gender and Social Group of the Owner

Firm Characteristics	*2001*					*2006*				
	Gender		*Social Group*			*Gender*		*Social Group*		
	Male	*Female*	*Scheduled Caste/ Scheduled Tribe (SC/ST)*	*Other Backward Class (OBC)*	*General (GEN)*	*Male*	*Female*	*SC/ST*	*OBC*	*GEN*
All Firms	5.22	5.48	3.19	4.34	6.67	6.18	4.14	3.92	3.97	7.93
Registration Status										
Unregistered	4.213	4.365	2.852	3.804	5.086	2.217	1.653	1.939	2.060	2.388
Registered	12.521	13.238	6.862	9.908	15.132	6.438	4.300	4.178	4.125	8.170
Location										
Rural	4.248	4.650	2.536	3.730	6.244	5.248	3.396	3.158	3.579	7.283
Urban	6.223	6.123	4.263	5.027	6.905	6.962	5.036	5.350	4.437	8.329
Ownership										
Proprietary	4.068	4.210	2.875	3.725	4.867	4.426	3.090	3.258	3.393	5.244
Partnership	13.112	11.425	7.424	10.957	12.035	16.814	18.624	15.341	13.922	18.087
Company	21.087	21.944	10.044	17.107	23.321	36.849	43.916	25.270	30.543	39.241
Cooperative	12.632	18.482	8.168	21.938	16.274	33.353	15.365	30.986	22.311	32.817
Others	7.427	9.916	3.977	8.235	11.167	11.968	5.353	4.771	3.942	15.283

Source: Authors' estimates.

Table 4.4 Firm Productivity by Gender and Social Group of the Owner

Firm Characteristics	*2001*					*2006*				
	Gender		*Social Group*			*Gender*		*Social Group*		
	Male	*Female*	*Scheduled Caste/Scheduled Tribe (SC/ST)*	*Other Backward Class (OBC)*	*General (GEN)*	*Male*	*Female*	*SC/ST*	*OBC*	*GEN*
All Firms	10.422	10.83	10.15	10.43	11.18	11.51	10.96	10.95	11.17	11.77
Registration Status										
Unregistered	10.301	10.733	10.108	10.386	11.054	10.922	10.485	10.613	10.869	11.005
Registered	11.295	11.540	10.636	10.885	11.861	11.555	10.994	11.000	11.193	11.805
Location										
Rural	9.981	10.420	9.861	10.180	10.761	11.248	10.800	10.770	11.050	11.482
Urban	10.871	11.156	10.627	10.705	11.409	11.742	11.160	11.301	11.308	11.946
Ownership										
Proprietary	10.285	10.674	10.090	10.363	10.980	11.404	10.899	10.914	11.133	11.615
Partnership	11.737	11.894	11.241	11.427	12.067	12.760	12.478	12.066	12.249	12.938
Company	12.127	12.301	11.242	11.390	12.497	12.942	12.583	12.184	12.168	13.101
Cooperative	9.604	10.937	9.802	10.239	10.974	11.751	10.800	11.422	10.912	11.947
Others	10.080	10.916	10.168	10.309	11.154	11.742	11.006	11.104	11.227	11.907

Source: Authors' estimates.

Labour Productivity is expressed in log form.

Table 4.5 Output Growth by Gender and Social Group of the Owner

Firm Characteristics	*2001*					*2006*				
	Gender		*Social Group*			*Gender*		*Social Group*		
	Male	*Female*	*Scheduled Caste/Scheduled Tribe (SC/ST)*	*Other Backward Class (OBC)*	*General (GEN)*	*Male*	*Female*	*SC/ST*	*OBC*	*GEN*
All Firms	0.18	0.20	0.21	0.18	0.21	0.21	0.22	0.21	0.20	0.21
Registration Status										
Unregistered	0.17	0.20	0.21	0.18	0.21	0.20	0.22	0.18	0.18	0.17
Registered	0.18	0.20	0.19	0.19	0.22	0.21	0.22	0.18	0.17	0.17
Location										
Rural	0.16	0.20	0.21	0.17	0.21	0.20	0.21	0.20	0.20	0.21
Urban	0.19	0.20	0.22	0.18	0.21	0.21	0.23	0.23	0.21	0.21
Ownership										
Proprietary	0.17	0.20	0.21	0.18	0.21	0.20	0.22	0.21	0.20	0.20
Partnership	0.20	0.20	0.21	0.18	0.20	0.25	0.27	0.26	0.23	0.26
Company	0.26	0.25	0.23	0.25	0.25	0.29	0.29	0.25	0.26	0.29
Cooperative	0.13	0.16	0.17	0.12	0.17	0.21	0.25	0.21	0.22	0.22
Others	0.17	0.21	0.22	0.20	0.20	0.21	0.22	0.27	0.22	0.21
Enterprise Type										
Micro	–	–	–	–	–	0.21	0.22	0.21	0.20	0.21
Small	–	–	–	–	–	0.21	0.26	0.21	0.22	0.20
Medium	–	–	–	–	–	0.23	0.29	0.22	0.23	0.23

Source: Authors' estimates.

Table 4.6 Net Worth and Profitability by Gender and Social Group of the Owner (Rupees Thousand Crore) for 2006

Firm Characteristics	*Categories*	*Gender*		*Social Group*		
		Male	*Female*	*Scheduled Caste/ Scheduled Tribe (SC/ST)*	*Other Backward Class (OBC)*	*General (GEN)*
Net Worth						
	All Firms	2296.77	1223.90	1132.63	847.06	3458.47
Registration	Unregistered	133.24	66.21	88.58	111.25	164.81
	Registered	2435.56	1296.61	1263.08	902.84	3594.03
Location	Rural	1665.60	626.93	701.22	650.32	2821.65
	Urban	2825.31	1939.94	1929.56	1073.75	3836.86
Ownership	Proprietary	1047.19	491.51	650.39	537.70	1438.73
	Partnership	7768.11	8421.57	4970.55	4768.34	9018.63
	Company	27778.04	38232.63	26217.84	18797.54	30254.65
	Cooperative	18778.90	1688.19	5470.29	5869.31	23017.67
	Others	4123.67	887.65	631.56	847.23	5427.43
Profitability						
	All Firms	1103.09	568.80	568.85	378.04	1631.49
Registration	Unregistered	40.72	6.40	−7.62	39.04	55.86
	Registered	1161.25	597.77	629.57	400.08	1688.64
Location	Rural	722.70	382.06	428.98	267.95	1198.88
	Urban	1403.10	787.20	805.18	499.74	1880.13
Ownership	Proprietary	416.96	254.32	298.48	254.43	534.90
	Partnership	4204.65	4034.00	6145.34	2454.69	4651.26
	Company	14039.77	12593.58	7514.32	5661.34	15825.12
	Cooperative	6350.86	804.21	7134.79	1573.68	6653.98
	Others	2443.54	1628.85	308.98	293.82	3458.77

Source: Authors' estimates.

We also analyse various important firm characteristics, which we use later in the empirical analysis, by gender and social group of the owner. We consider four important firm characteristics: (a) Whether the firm is located in a cluster; (b) Whether the firm maintains an account; (c) Whether the firm possesses quality certificates (from Quality Management System-International Standardisation Organisation (QMS-ISO) or Environmental Management System-International Standardisation Organisation (EMS-ISO)) such as QMS-ISO:9000-1 and EMS-ISO:14001-2; and (d) Whether the firm is an exporting firm. We analyse how these characteristics vary across male- and female-owned firms and firms owned by different social groups. Table 4.7

Table 4.7 Firm Characteristics by Gender and Social Group of the Owner

Firm Characteristics	*Categories*	*Gender*				*Social Group*					
		Male		*Female*		*Scheduled Caste/ Scheduled Tribe (SC/ST)*		*Other Backward Class (OBC)*		*Others*	
		Numbers	Percent	Numbers	Percent	Numbers	Percent	Numbers	Percent	Numbers	Percent
Located in a Cluster?	Yes	70201	89.48	8253	10.52	6436	8.21	22599	28.81	49398	62.98
	No	893317	86.28	142052	13.72	109925	10.62	430427	41.6	494393	47.78
Maintains an Account?	Yes	308318	90.83	31128	9.17	97543	5.54	367923	25.07	308291	69.38
	No	655200	84.61	119177	15.39	18818	12.61	85103	47.55	235500	39.84
Quality Certificate?	Yes	36171	87.03	5390	12.97	112053	10.37	440004	31.34	519567	58.3
	No	927347	86.49	144915	13.51	4308	10.46	13022	41.06	24224	48.48
Exporting?	Yes	32784	92.2	2772	7.8	113902	6.92	447203	16.39	516537	76.69
	No	930734	86.32	147533	13.68	2459	10.57	5823	41.5	27254	47.93

Source: Authors' estimates.

reports these results. According to our estimates, less number of firms are reported to be located in a cluster; only 7 percent of the firms replied that they are part of a cluster. Out of these cluster firms, the majority are owned by men. About 90 percent of the cluster firms are male-owned firms. Account maintenance is another aspect that we examined. While 30 percent of the firms in the MSME sector reported to be maintaining an account, this practice is most prevalent among male-run firms. Only one in ten firms that maintained an account is found to be owned by a female entrepreneur. With regard to the possession of quality certificates, only 3.7 percent of the firms are reported to be in the possession of such certificates. And even among those who possessed quality certificates, about 80 percent are owned by male entrepreneurs. The story is no different when we look at the share of firms that are involved in exporting and the share of female-owned firms involved in it. Out of the 3.2 percent of firms that export, a significant majority of them are owned by male entrepreneurs. As stated before, we also analyse these characteristics by social group of the firm owner. The findings in general support our conjectures. They suggest that the firms owned by the GEN category occupied a larger share (3/5th or more) among cluster firms, firms that maintained account, firms with quality certificates and exporting firms. OBC-run firms accounted for the second largest share, with 28 percent, 25 percent, 31 percent and 16 percent among cluster firms, firms that maintained account, firms with quality certificates and exporting firms, respectively. The firms maintained by the SCs and STs occupied a lower share in all four firm types.

Wages, firm size and productivity

Do the wages paid to the workers vary by enterprise type? Do wages differ by firm location and gender and social group of the owner and are the most productive firms paying the highest wages? In this section, we present some stylised facts about wages in the MSME sector and examine whether wages per worker differ by firm type, registration status, firm location and gender and social group of the owner. We use wages and salaries payable in cash or in kind as the measure of wages in this book and we do not consider the value of social security contributions paid by the employer. We find clear evidence that the medium-sized firms pay higher wages, followed by the small firms and then the micro firms (Figure 4.24).

Our computations show that the medium-sized firms pay wages 1.38 times higher than those paid by the small firms, and twice more than the wages paid by micro firms. It is very much possible that large firms demand a higher quality of labour defined by observable characteristics such as education, job tenure, and a higher fraction of full-time workers, hence they end up paying higher wages. A part of the reason could also lie in higher productivity and stability of the workforce in large firms. The findings thus

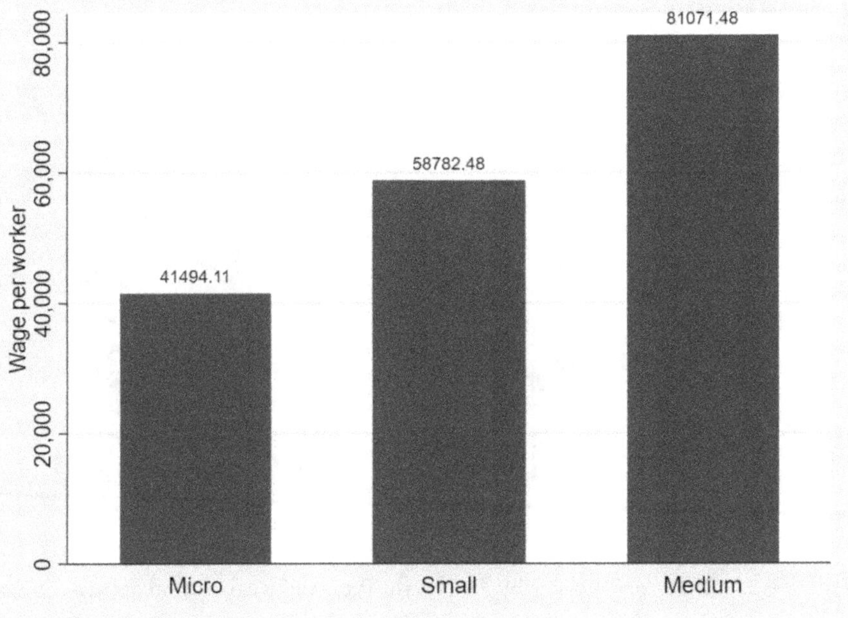

Figure 4.24 Wages per Worker by Enterprise Type

Source: Authors' estimates.

possibly point to the importance of ensuring vertical progression of firms in the MSME sector, from smaller size to medium size and then to larger size, so as to improve the living conditions of workers employed in these firms. This difference in wages per worker is clearly visible even when we do this analysis by registration status (Figure 4.25), location (Figure 4.26), gender (Figure 4.27) and social group of the firm owner (Figure 4.28).

As expected, the wages paid by firms in the registered sector are much higher than the wages paid by unregistered firms (Table 4.8). Our estimates suggest that an average worker in a registered firm received 1.8 times the wages of an average worker in an unregistered firm. Between rural and urban firms, the average wages are higher in firms that are located in urban areas. When we consider the gender of the firm owner, we find that firms owned by male entrepreneurs pay the highest wages. Our estimates also show that firms owned by the GEN social group pay the highest wages compared to firms owned by SC/STs and OBCs. Finally, the scatter plots presented in Figure 4.29 show the absence of strong evidence supporting the positive relationship between wages paid to workers and firm productivity, and wages paid to workers and firm size.

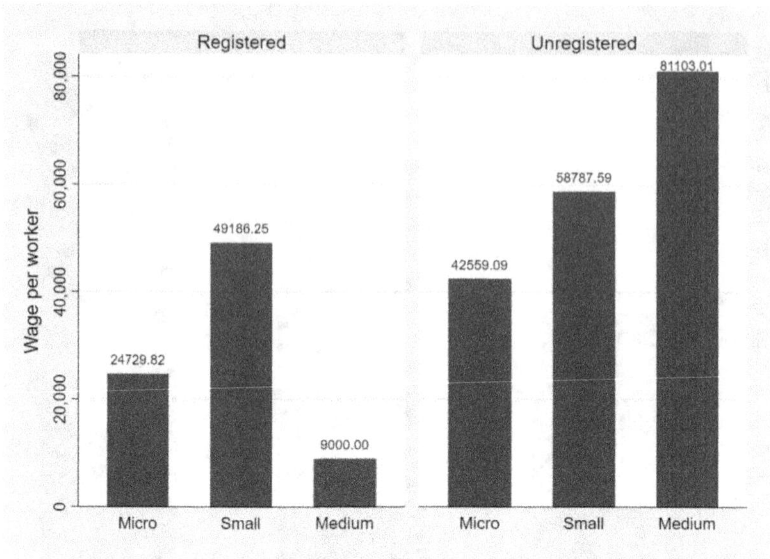

Figure 4.25 Wages per Worker by Enterprise Type and Registration Status
Source: Authors' estimates.

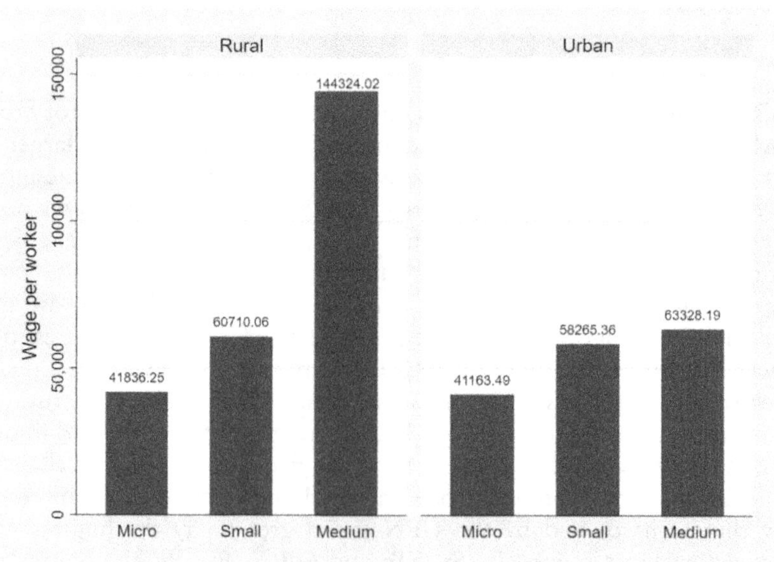

Figure 4.26 Wages per Worker by Enterprise Type and Location
Source: Authors' estimates.

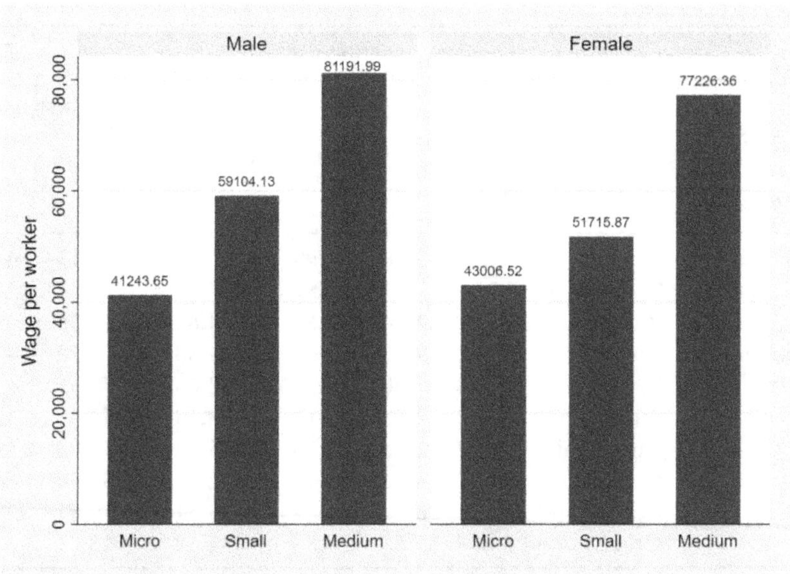

Figure 4.27 Wages per Worker by Gender of the Owner

Source: Authors' estimates.

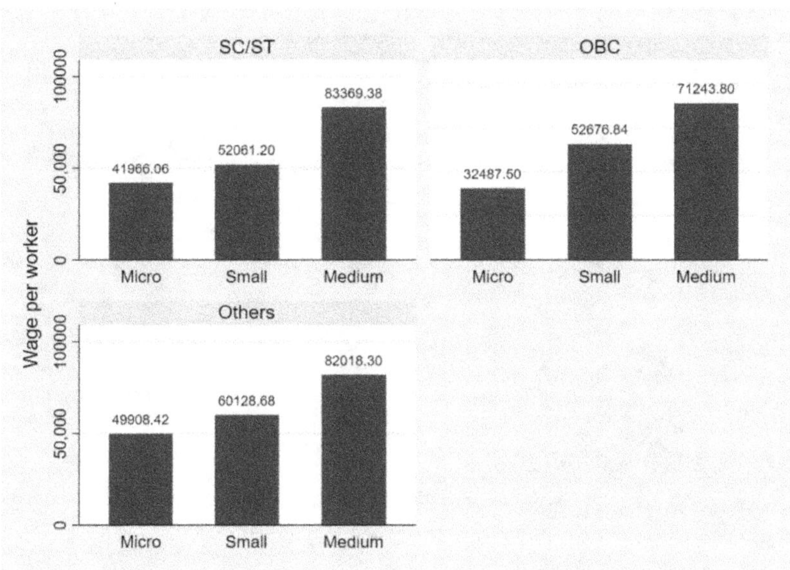

Figure 4.28 Wages per Worker by Social Group of the Owner

Source: Authors' estimates.

Table 4.8 Wages per Worker and Firm Characteristics

Firm Characteristics	*Categories*	*Gender*		*Social Group*			*Total*
		Male	*Female*	*Scheduled Caste/ Scheduled Tribe (SC/ST)*	*Other Backward Class (OBC)*	*General (GEN)*	
All Firms		44.67	43.50	42.99	33.71	53.19	44.51
Registration	Unregistered	25.76	17.61	45.81	19.38	21.27	24.76
	Registered	45.70	44.84	42.69	34.64	54.36	45.59
Location	Rural	44.62	39.73	33.07	34.63	57.72	43.87
	Urban	44.70	47.90	59.78	32.68	50.59	45.04
Ownership	Proprietary	43.53	43.58	43.11	33.18	52.40	43.53
	Partnership	51.97	41.26	35.56	45.13	53.95	51.03
	Company	67.08	56.76	55.19	52.53	69.64	66.46
	Cooperative	42.58	26.03	41.85	35.51	39.91	38.76
	Others	39.83	35.68	29.88	32.58	43.31	39.29

Source: Authors' estimates.

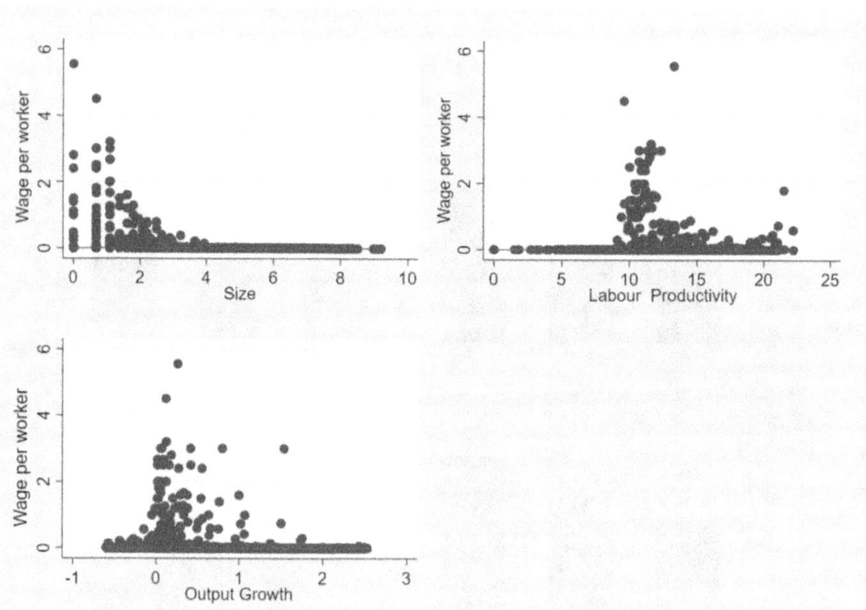

Figure 4.29 Wages per Worker, Labour Productivity and Firm Size

Source: Authors' estimates.

Note: Wage per worker is in 10*[8].

Finance, firm size and productivity

We now make an attempt to present some descriptive evidence on the relationship between finance, firm size and productivity. Before we trace this relationship, we first examine the share of firms who had access to finance from external sources. As is evident from Figure 4.30, only a quarter of firms in the sector reported to have obtained finance from external sources. Further, there is a significant change in the share of firms with loans between 2001 and 2006. The share of firms who obtained financial support through outside sources is found to be substantially lower among the micro firms as compared to small and medium firms; while about 10 percent of micro firms claimed to have had access to credit, the share was 17 percent and 21 percent, respectively, for small and medium firms (Figure 4.31). We also find that the share of firms with credit access is higher among rural firms as compared to the ones located in urban areas (Figure 4.32). While 23 percent of firms in rural areas had access to loans in 2006, the share was just 9 percent for firms in urban areas. Do the firms source their loans from institutional or non-institutional sources? The graphical illustration in Figure 4.33 clearly shows that firms that sourced loans from institutional sources constituted

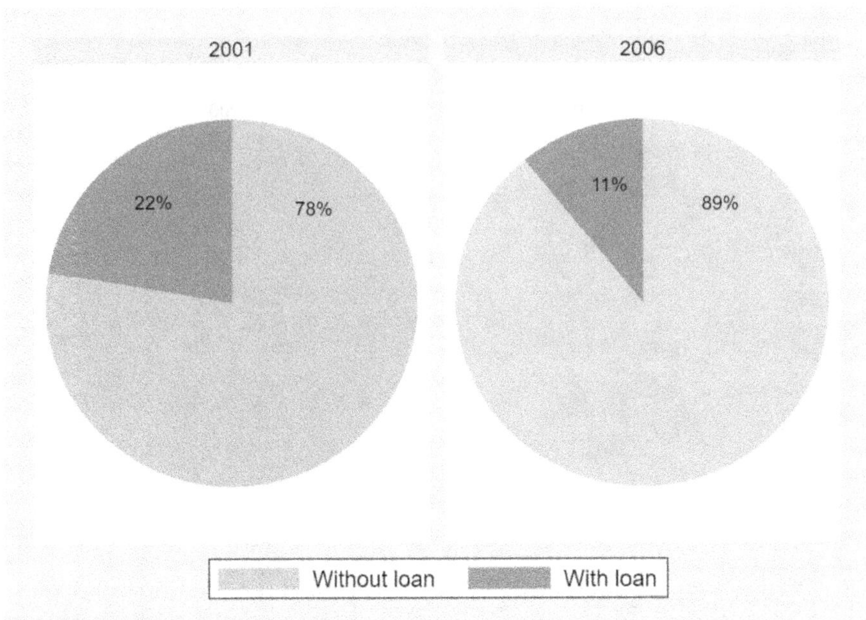

Figure 4.30 Status of Loan, 2001–2006

Source: Authors' estimates.

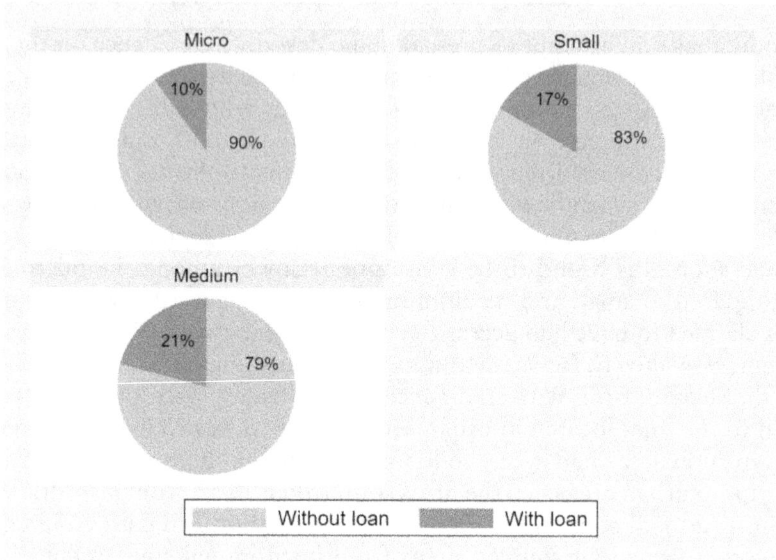

Figure 4.31 Status of Loan by Firm Size, 2006
Source: Authors' estimates.

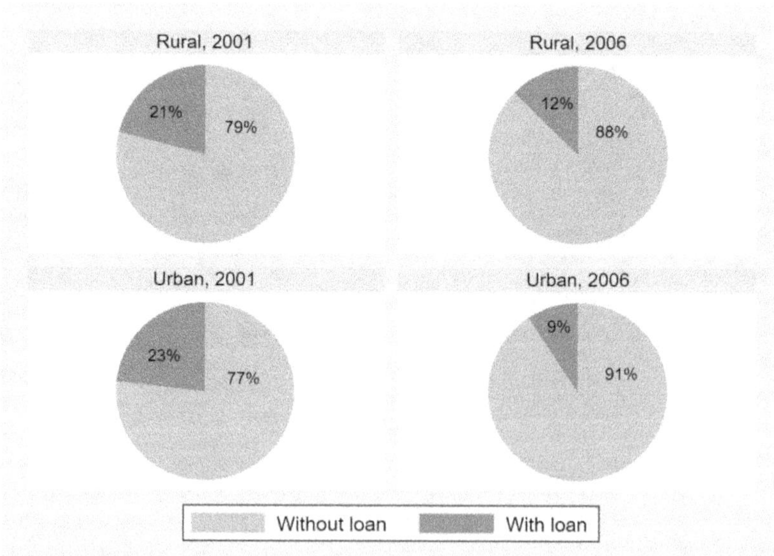

Figure 4.32 Status of Loan by Location
Source: Authors' estimates.

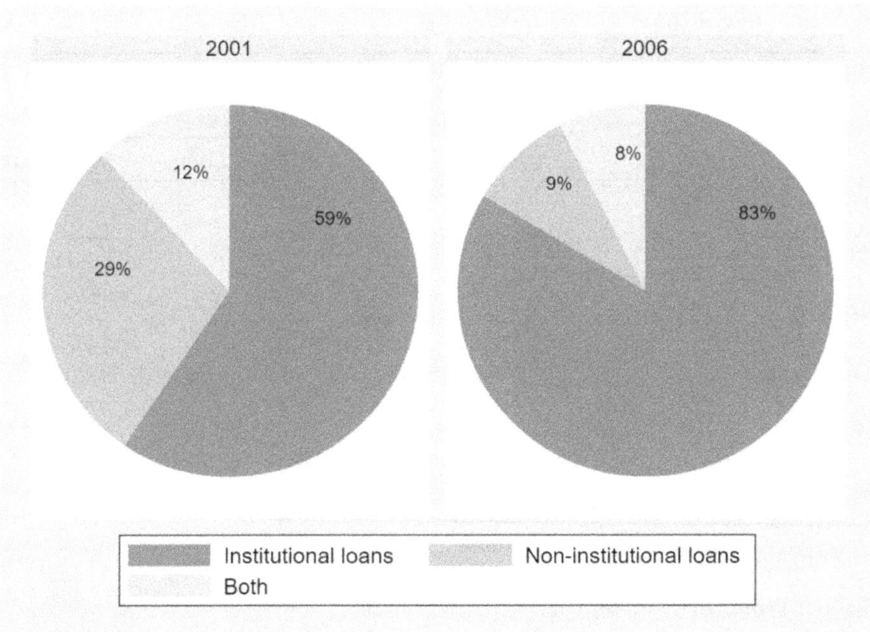

Figure 4.33 Loan by Source, 2001–2006

Source: Authors' estimates.

the majority. About 83 percent of the firms that had loans in 2006 sourced it from institutional sources while non-institutional sources accounted for a meagre 9 percent.

Does access to external finance influence firm size? Available descriptive evidence suggests that credit access and firm size are positively related. This is clearly evident in Table 4.9 where it can be seen that average firm size is higher for firms with credit access as compared to firms that are credit constrained. According to our estimates, firms with loans are more than double the size of firms which did not have loans. This seems to be the case for registered and unregistered firms as well as rural and urban firms. A similar pattern can be also discerned among firms of various sizes and those belonging to various ownership categories. Does credit access enhance productivity? We capture this in Table 4.9 and find that the firms with loans reported higher productivity levels vis-à-vis firms that did not have loans. Such gains in productivity via credit access are also observed for registered firms, unregistered firms, rural firms, urban firms, firms of all sizes and firms belonging to various ownership categories. Another related finding that we observe

Table 4.9 Finance, Firm Size and Productivity by Registration Status, Location and Ownership

Firm Characteristics	*Categories*	*2006*	
		Loan Status	
		Without Loan	*With Loan*
Firm Size			
All firms		5.14	12.14
Registration Status	Unregistered	2.11	3.41
	Registered	5.36	12.28
Sector	Rural	4.23	9.96
	Urban	5.92	14.76
Ownership	Proprietary	3.94	7.07
	Partnership	15.12	21.80
	Company	32.39	51.53
	Cooperative	22.52	49.08
	Others	10.40	17.11
Enterprise Type	Micro	3.42	5.65
	Small	13.69	30.01
	Medium	68.40	112.29
Labour Productivity (in log)			
All firms		11.37	12.02
Registration Status	Unregistered	10.85	11.27
	Registered	11.41	12.03
Sector	Rural	11.10	11.72
	Urban	11.60	12.38
Ownership	Proprietary	11.29	11.73
	Partnership	12.56	13.18
	Company	12.65	13.72
	Cooperative	11.52	11.51
	Others	11.60	11.98
Enterprise Type	Micro	11.22	11.67
	Small	12.46	13.40
	Medium	13.34	14.24
Output Growth			
All firms		0.20	0.23
Registration Status	Unregistered	0.21	0.20
	Registered	0.21	0.24
Sector	Rural	0.20	0.22
	Urban	0.21	0.26
Ownership	Proprietary	0.21	0.23
	Partnership	0.25	0.27
	Company	0.27	0.34
	Cooperative	0.23	0.19
	Others	0.22	0.24
Enterprise Type	Micro	0.21	0.22
	Small	0.20	0.30
	Medium	0.19	0.38

Source: Authors' estimates.

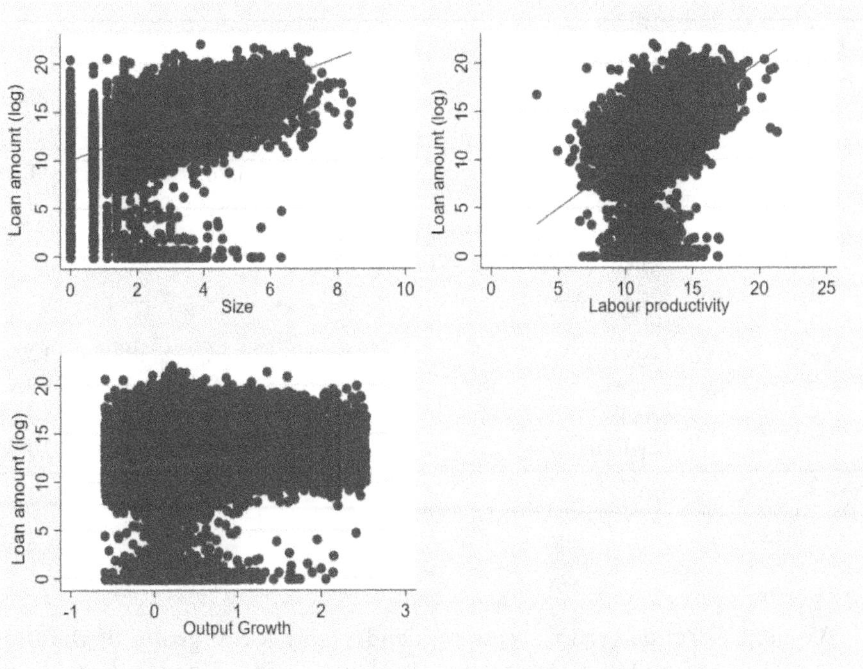

Figure 4.34 Finance, Firm Size, Productivity and Growth

Source: Authors' estimates.

from Table 4.9 is the role that credit access plays in firm growth. We find that firms with credit access displayed a faster growth of output as compared to those without any credit access. Based upon the descriptive evidence presented previously, we may conclude that credit access plays a critical role in the size, growth and productivity of firms in the MSME sector. We explore these relationships further in Figure 4.34 in three scatter plots, where we capture the relationship between loans and employment, loans and productivity and loans and output growth. The three plots unambiguously suggest a positive relationship between outstanding loans and firm size, growth and productivity. In other words, firms that are larger, more productive and grew faster are those that had access to external finance. The visual examination suggests that credit access is very much important for improving the size, productivity and growth of firms in the MSME sector. The descriptive analysis is suggestive and, therefore, demands a much deeper analysis of the potential interactions between loans and firm performance, which we perform in the next chapter.

Table 4.10 Finance by Gender and Social Group of the Owner

Characteristics	*Categories*	*2001*		*2006*	
		Without Loan	*With Loan*	*Without Loan*	*With Loan*
Gender	Male	73.24	26.76	88.91	11.09
	Female	78.17	21.83	90.65	9.35
Social Group	Scheduled Caste/ Scheduled Tribe (SC/ST)	82.95	17.05	90.59	9.41
	Other Backward Class (OBC)	79.60	20.40	90.21	9.79
	Others	75.44	24.56	87.94	12.06
Enterprise Type	Micro	–	–	90.03	9.97
	Small	–	–	83.32	16.68
	Medium	–	–	79.09	20.91

Source: Authors' estimates.

We next examine credit access by gender and social group of the firm owner. Using available descriptive evidence, our objective here is to derive some insights on whether gender-wise and caste-wise discrimination exists in the credit market and how they influence the performance of the firms. If the figures presented in Table 4.10 are an indication, then the evidence points to the existence of gender- and caste-wise discrimination in the credit market. Within the firms, those who have had access to loans, only 9.35 percent, have reported to be owned by female entrepreneurs. Across social groups too, we find that the firms owned by the GEN category had a greater share in firms who had obtained loans while the share of SC/ST-owned firms stood at 9.41 percent. We also observe that around 20 percent of medium-sized firms have received credit, followed by 16 percent for small firms and only 9 percent in the case of micro firms. The estimates presented in Table 4.11 clearly points to the benefits that credit access accrues to firms and firm owners. The substantial difference in size, productivity levels and growth rates between firms with loans and those without loans points to the critical role played by credit access in improving the performance of firms in the MSME sector. The overall lower performance of the female-led firms can thus be possibly linked to their relatively lesser access to credit from external sources. We shall see in the next chapter whether this observed relationship survives the scrutiny of an econometric exercise.

Table 4.11 Finance, Firm Size and Productivity by Gender and Caste of the Owner

Firm Characteristics	*Categories*	*Male*		*Female*		*Scheduled Caste/ Scheduled Tribe (SC/ST)*		*Other Backward Class (OBC)*		*Others*	
		Without Loan	*With Loan*	*Without Loan*	*With Loan*	*With Loan*	*Without Loan*	*With Loan*	*Without Loan*	*With Loan*	*Without Loan*
Firm Size											
Registration Status	Unregistered	2.18	3.41	1.62	3.38	1.91	2.99	2.04	2.98	2.33	4.06
	Registered	5.62	12.69	3.76	9.24	3.53	9.82	3.66	8.12	7.13	15.48
Sector	Rural	4.48	10.38	2.98	7.06	2.77	6.76	3.18	6.86	6.16	13.29
	Urban	6.12	15.05	4.38	12.27	4.38	15.56	3.94	9.77	7.34	17.32
Ownership	Proprietary	4.12	7.21	2.80	6.13	2.86	7.28	3.13	5.99	4.94	7.93
	Partnership	14.96	21.59	16.72	24.21	13.54	20.87	12.30	18.75	16.21	22.73
	Company	31.72	51.81	42.74	47.27	21.57	41.91	24.54	52.68	34.65	51.80
	Cooperative	25.51	55.83	13.76	21.72	19.11	74.26	18.34	36.03	26.43	50.36
	Others	11.27	19.01	4.98	8.21	3.70	16.87	3.56	7.24	14.56	22.64
Labour Productivity (in log)											
Registration Status	Unregistered	10.91	11.33	10.48	10.62	10.60	10.92	10.86	11.18	10.99	11.53
	Registered	11.49	12.08	10.92	11.65	10.97	11.26	11.15	11.61	11.71	12.45
Sector	Rural	11.17	11.78	10.74	11.35	10.74	11.00	11.00	11.42	11.36	12.14
	Urban	11.67	12.41	11.08	12.06	11.26	11.77	11.26	11.86	11.86	12.71
Ownership	Proprietary	11.36	11.77	10.85	11.47	10.89	11.13	11.10	11.48	11.57	12.06
	Partnership	12.59	13.20	12.29	13.02	11.92	12.50	12.07	12.77	12.78	13.34
	Company	12.67	13.74	12.30	13.40	11.98	13.10	11.89	13.20	12.84	13.82
	Cooperative	11.77	11.71	10.81	10.74	11.56	10.92	10.88	11.03	11.96	11.92
	Others	11.70	12.17	11.00	11.07	11.09	11.20	11.21	11.42	11.86	12.39

(*Continued*)

Table 4.11 (Continued)

Firm Characteristics	*Categories*	*Male*		*Female*		*Scheduled Caste/ Scheduled Tribe (SC/ST)*		*Other Backward Class (OBC)*		*Others*	
		Without Loan	*With Loan*	*Without Loan*	*With Loan*	*With Loan*	*Without Loan*	*With Loan*	*Without Loan*	*With Loan*	*Without Loan*
Output Growth											
Registration Status	Unregistered	0.21	0.19	0.23	0.25	0.21	0.21	0.21	0.20	0.21	0.19
	Registered	0.21	0.24	0.22	0.24	0.22	0.21	0.21	0.21	0.21	0.26
Sector	Rural	0.20	0.22	0.21	0.22	0.21	0.20	0.20	0.20	0.21	0.24
	Urban	0.21	0.26	0.24	0.28	0.23	0.21	0.22	0.23	0.21	0.29
Ownership	Proprietary	0.20	0.22	0.22	0.24	0.21	0.20	0.21	0.21	0.20	0.25
	Partnership	0.25	0.27	0.27	0.27	0.27	0.25	0.23	0.23	0.26	0.28
	Company	0.27	0.34	0.29	0.32	0.24	0.31	0.27	0.27	0.28	0.35
	Cooperative	0.22	0.19	0.27	0.21	0.20	0.26	0.23	0.18	0.24	0.18
	Others	0.22	0.24	0.23	0.23	0.27	0.34	0.22	0.20	0.21	0.25

Source: Authors' estimates.

Conclusion

In this chapter, we made an attempt to explore some stylised facts about firms in the MSME sector using unit record data from the MSME surveys for two years, 2001 and 2006. We started off by examining the evolution of firm size and productivity at the aggregate level and also across regions and product groups. We then proceed to examine observable differences in firm size and productivity across firms of different characteristics. In the penultimate section, we tried to identify the vital factors in explaining variations in wages paid to workers in the sector. Finally, we strive to unravel the linkage between access to finance, firm size and performance.

We observe an expansion of the firm size from 2001 to 2006. Among them, the rate of increase is higher in urban areas than in rural areas. We find a positive relation of size of the firm with labour productivity and output growth. Further, we notice a considerable variation in output growth and labour productivity among different industries and regions. It is also observed that output growth and labour productivity are higher among partnership and company firms than proprietary firms.

Our analysis also reveals that the MSME sector is dominated by male-owned firms irrespective of the registration status. However, the share of female-owned firms recorded a marginal increase during the 2001–2006 period. Looking at the social background of the owner, we find the SC/ST-owned firms are only 10 percent of the total MSMEs in India. In the case of the OBC, their share increased from 2001–2006 whereas the share of other groups declined. The size of the SC/ST and OBC category firms are much smaller compared to the GEN category firms and they are mostly confined to the rural areas. In addition, we also observe that most of SC/ST and OBC firms are in the cooperative and proprietary owned categories. Regarding the firm performance, both female-owned and SC/ST firms exhibit lower productivity than their counterparts.

Our analysis on the access to external finance indicates that only 11 percent of the firms report credit access. Among them, along the expected lines, the share of medium-sized firms having external finance are relatively higher (21 percent), followed by small (17 percent) and micro (9 percent) firms. In addition, we also observe that MSMEs are more reliant on the institutional sources of funds. It is also evident that registered firms receive more funds from financial institutions. Both cooperative and company firms obtained higher credit, followed by partnership, while proprietary firms received miniscule shares. While examining the productivity-finance nexus, we unambiguously observe that firms with external funds are more productive and growth-oriented. The major chunk of the external credit flows to male-owned firms (89 percent), while female-owned firms receive around 10 percent. An identical trend is visible in the case of the SC/ST-owned firms (9.41 percent).

5

ACCESS TO CREDIT AND SMALL FIRM GROWTH

Introduction

The growth constraints on firms in developing countries are well documented by a recent but growing body of studies. Among the set of growth-inhibiting factors, World Bank firm level surveys carried out across regions unambiguously identify finance as the *numero uno* factor. It has been argued that credit constraints hamper firms' ability to fund investments, which hinders its growth (Rahaman, 2011). Unlike large firms, the impediments to credit access are severe for small firms which are touted as the engines of economic growth in developing countries. Therefore, it becomes imperative to analyse the importance of access to finance in fostering firm growth. Further, the need to analyse the role of financial factors behind small firms' growth is crucial in the case of developing economies since they play a key role in employment generation, exports and value added.

There is extensive literature on the importance of the finance constraint on firm growth. Most of these studies do not address the issue of the finance-firm growth nexus directly. Mostly, these studies test the investment cash flow sensitivity which may not be relevant for small firms. Even though this literature is filled with abundant evidence of the importance of finance on firm growth, these studies are mostly confined to the experience of developed markets. In the case of the Indian context, studies exploring the relationship between access to finance and firm growth are few. Therefore, in this chapter, we set forth to examine this relationship and investigate the relationship between access to finance and firm growth.

Further, some of the studies which directly test this relationship often do not distinguish between the importance of sources of finance and firm growth. Very recently, a new strand of literature has emerged which analyses the role of relative importance of sources of finance – formal versus informal. The use of informal sources or non-bank credit is attributed to convenience. Among the set of studies, one strand emphasises the role of informal sources of finance in enhancing firm growth while another body of literature posits that bank finance fosters firm growth. It is important to make this distinction since small firms which are constrained for institutional sources of credit substitute it with non-institutional sources like friends, relatives and money lenders. Therefore, in this chapter, we attempt to analyse the importance of financing sources (formal and informal) for MSMEs in India, using the data obtained from the Fourth Census of the MSMEs carried out in 2007. In doing so, this book complements recent studies that focus on the growth obstacles of Small and Medium Enterprises (SMEs), mostly in the context of emerging and developing economies.

Methodology

To examine the association between access to finance and firm growth, we estimate the following baseline firm growth regression model based on OLS estimation:

$$Growth_{jis} = \beta_0 + \beta_1 FIN_{jis} + \sum_{k>1} \gamma_k X_{jis} + \delta_j + \theta_s + \varepsilon_{jis} \tag{5.1}$$

The dependent variable, *Growth*, represents output growth. The main explanatory variable of interest is Finance (*FIN*), a measure of access to formal finance for MSMEs. The coefficient of *FIN* (β_1) would, therefore, capture the effect of access to formal finance on firm growth. We expect the estimate of β_1 to be positive and significant, as we hypothesise that there is a positive association between the use of formal finance and firm growth. In other words, a positive and significant coefficient of β_1 indicates that access to formal finance enhances the growth of output in MSMEs. We also estimate alternative specifications where we replace formal finance with informal sources of finance, which include financing sources such as friends, relatives and money lenders. We also include a bunch of owner-specific and firm-specific control variables that are likely to influence the growth of firms in the MSME sector. These control variables are firm size, firm age, location of the firm, ownership of the firm, the use of external technical knowledge, whether the firm is part of a cluster and a dummy variable for gender of the owner, and they are represented by vector X_j in equation (5.1).[1] δ_i are industry-specific fixed effects and θ_s are state-specific dummies. Since some industries are more reliant on external finance than others (Rajan and Zingales, 1998), we include industry-fixed effects as controls to capture industry-specific external finance requirements which may exert an independent influence on firm growth over and above that exerted by the finance constraint that the firm faces. Inclusion of industry dummies also helps us to account for the unobserved heterogeneity at the industrial level. State dummies, on the other hand, control for the advantages and disadvantages of being located in a particular state (region) and their influence on firm growth.

Endogeneity issues

While estimating equation 5.1, even though we get a positive coefficient for the access to finance variable, the result may be due to the simultaneity (Ayyagari et al., 2008, 2010). It is possible that the firms with certain characteristics are the ones seeking formal finance from banks. That makes the loan variable endogenous since the firms self-select to apply for formal finance. This leads to the problem of self-selection bias which needs to be corrected using appropriate econometric techniques. In the presence of the selection bias, OLS estimation is found to be biased and inconsistent. To address this potential endogeneity, the Heckman (1979) two-stage approach, a popular modelling choice adopted in the empirical literature to overcome the selection bias, is employed. The Heckman (1979) procedure involves two stages. The first step involves estimating a probit model to locate the determinants of the probability that a MSME will receive a loan. In the second stage, a pooled OLS regression function is estimated, where an Inverse Mills ratio (IMR) obtained in the first stage along with loan and other control variables enter as explanatory variables. However, there is some scepticism about the appropriateness of including Mills ratio to alleviate the exclusion restriction criteria (Wolfolds and Siegel, 2019). To alleviate such concerns and estimate the selection model (first step), we need to identify a variable that is correlated with access to bank finance but uncorrelated with firm growth. Following Ayyagari et al. (2010), we employ collateral as an exclusion restriction which influences firms' access to bank loans. As shown by prior studies (Johnson et al., 1999), collateral does not influence firm growth. We define the selection model as follows:

$$Loan_{jis} = \beta_0 + \beta_1 Collateral_{jis} + \sum_{k>1} \gamma_k X_{jis} + \delta_i + \theta_s + \varepsilon_{jis} \quad (5.2)$$

where the selection equation describes the probability of receiving a bank loan (*Loan* = 1) influenced by a host of explanatory variables (collateral, age, size, ownership, location, woman-owned and a set of industry and regional dummies).

The second stage involves estimating the following OLS model:

$$\text{Growth}_{jis} = \beta_0 + \beta_1 Loan_{jis} + \sum_{k>1} \gamma_k X_{jis} + \lambda_j + \delta_i + \theta_s + \varepsilon_{jis} \quad (5.3)$$

In order to address the selection issue, we include the IMR (λ) generated for each firm observation from the first step equation as an additional variable to estimate the regression equation (5.3).

Quantile regression

In order to capture the differential effects of various sources of finances on firms with varying growth rates, we estimate the previous model using quantile regressions pioneered by Koenker and Basset (1978). Quantile regression is increasingly used in the literature to identify the determinants of firm growth (Coad and Rao, 2008). The quantile regression approach is particularly suited to study firm growth since the distribution is often characterised by heavy tails. Another advantage is the robustness associated with quantile regression in the presence of outliers. Quantile regression facilitates the estimation of the effect of availability of finance on firm growth at various quantiles of the conditional distribution of the dependent variable, and not only the conditional mean in the case of the OLS method. To be precise, the parameters of equation 5.1 are estimated at various quantiles of the conditional distribution of firm growth (*Growth*).

Variable description and summary statistics

Variable description

Dependent variable

Previous research has identified firm performance using a variety of measures (profits, sales, employment, output, etc.). These measures are used extensively by earlier studies. Our main variable of firm performance is the output growth which is computed as the logarithmic differences in firm output over the period 2005–2007. Following the previous studies, we define growth of the firm ($Goutput_{it}$) as follows:

$$Goutput_{it} = \ln(output_{it}) - \ln(output_{it-2})$$

where $Goutput_{it}$ denotes firm growth measured by the gross output between periods t and t–2. In the dataset employed for the analysis, there may be concern about the reliability of the data due to short term shocks. Therefore, to overcome such inconsistencies, we smooth our growth rate variable by measuring growth over a two-year period (2004–2005 to 2006–2007) instead of measuring the growth over one-year period. We believe that the data smoothening over two years will considerably reduce the year-on-year fluctuations.

Explanatory variables

Access to finance is considered a key facilitator of firm growth (Beck and Demirguc-Kunt, 2006, 2008). As the main variable of interest, we have a dummy variable representing access to finance (*loan*) which takes the value of 1 if the firm reported a bank loan. It takes the value of 0 if the firm reported no loan from formal financial sources. The role of informal finance complementing formal financial sources is increasingly recognised since they meet the requirements of small entrepreneurs. Therefore, we also consider alternative sources of finance for firms from informal sources, friends and relatives. The *informal loan* dummy takes the value of 1 if the firm reports a loan from informal sources, friends and relatives and 0 otherwise.

In order to evaluate the effectiveness of access to finance on firm growth, we need to control for certain factors which are correlated with access to finance and firm growth. Control variables included can be categorised as enterprise and entrepreneur characteristics. Firm characteristics include size, age, sector, ownership structure and location. Firm size is considered a fundamental determinant of firm growth. Therefore, logarithm of gross output is included to proxy firm *size*. Age (*lnage*) of the firm is reported as the number of years since the year of initial production. Age variable indicates how the firm grows over a period of time. Jovanovic (1982) posits that younger firms are likely to grow faster. The variable on ownership structure indicates whether the owner is a sole proprietor. Location is considered an influential factor in determining firm growth. Firms located in urban areas benefit from the availability of skilled workers, better infrastructure and financial resources (Rosenthal and Strange, 2004). Therefore, firms located in urban areas are likely to achieve faster growth than those located in rural areas. To capture the locational advantages, we assign a dummy variable with a value of 1 for those firms located in urban areas and 0 for other firms. Owner characteristics include the gender of the owner (*woman*). We assign a dummy with a value of 1 if the enterprise is owned and operated by a female. Firm growth is expected to vary across industries. To control for industry heterogeneity, we include a host of industry dummies at the two digit NIC level. The variables used in our empirical analysis are presented and defined in Table 5.1.

Summary statistics

Table 5.2 presents the summary statistics of the variables (both dependent and independent variables) included in the empirical analysis. Average annual output growth of MSMEs between 2004–2005 and 2006–2007 is 8 percent, with a Standard Deviation (SD) of 10 percent and ranging from –45 to 63 percent. Of the total number of firms, only 11 percent have relied on external finance and a meagre 1 percent report using non-institutional sources of finance. In our dataset, the average age of firms is 13 years. Single ownership is the most dominant form of firm ownership structure. More than 90 percent of the firms are run by sole proprietors while firms operating on a partnership basis and public and private limited companies constitute the residual. Urban firms constituted 53 percent of the total firms in our dataset. About 12 percent of the firms report to have obtained technical know-how from outside sources and a meagre 7 percent formed part of a cluster. Not so surprisingly, only one out of ten firms in our sample are owned and operated by women entrepreneurs.

Table 5.1 Variable Description

Variables	*Definition*
Goutput	Growth of output between 2004–2005 and 2006–2007
Loan	Binary variable; 1= Firm has access to external finance, 0 = Firm does not have access to external finance
Non-institutional loan	Binary variable; 1= Firm has access to finance from non-institutional sources, 0 = Firm does not have access to finance from non-institutional sources
Size of the firm	Log of firm output
Age of the firm	Log of age of the firm (number of years since it began operations)
Rural area	Binary variable; 1 = Rural firm, 0 = Urban firm
Firm is part of a cluster	Binary variable; 1 = Firms that are part of a cluster, 0 = Firms that are not part of a cluster
Technical know-how	Binary variable; 1 = Firm obtained technical know-how from any source, 0 = Firm did not obtain any technical know-how from any source
Proprietary ownership	Binary Variable; 1 = Firm is a proprietary organisation, 0 = Firm is a non-proprietary organisation
Women-owned firm	Binary variable; 1 = Female-run firm, 0 = Male-run firm
Collateral	Ratio of fixed assets to total assets
Bank density	Number of bank branches per 10000 population in the district

Source: Authors' construction.

Table 5.2 Summary Statistics (All Firms)

Variables	*N*	*Mean*	*Standard Deviation (SD)*	*Min*	*Max*
Goutput	1113823	0.172	0.197	–0.90	1.26
Loan	1113823	0.109	–	0	1
Non-institutional loan	1113823	0.010	–	0	1
Size of the firm	1113823	12.288	1.699	0	22.90
Age of the Firm	1113823	12.745	8.872	1	99.00
Log of age	1113823	2.417	0.661	0.69	4.61
Urban area	1113823	0.532	–	0	1
Firm is part of a cluster	1113823	0.070	–	0	1
Technological know-how	1113823	0.118	–	0	1
Proprietary ownership	1113823	0.914	–	0	1
Women-owned firm	1113823	0.098	–	0	1
Collateral	1113823	0.105	–	0	1
Bank density	1113823	0.865	0.905	0	103.84

Source: Authors' estimates.

Table 5.3 Descriptive Statistics by Access to Credit

Variables	*Firms With Loan*		*Firms Without Loan*	
	Mean	*Standard Deviation (SD)*	*Mean*	*SD*
Goutput	0.175	0.249	0.171	0.189
Size of the firm	13.025	1.861	12.019	1.426
Age of the firm	2.363	0.684	2.417	0.659
Urban area	0.441	0.497	0.531	0.499
Firm is part of a cluster	0.070	0.255	0.061	0.239
Technological know-how	0.161	0.368	0.108	0.311
Proprietary ownership	0.858	0.349	0.937	0.242
Women-owned firm	0.074	0.262	0.106	0.307

Source: Authors' estimates.

In Table 5.3, the summary statistics of these variables are compared for firms with a loan and without a loan. Evidence in Table 5.3 possibly points to the positive role of external finance on output growth. This is evident from the fact that annual output grew marginally faster for firms that received external finance vis-à-vis firms without access to any external finance. The table also reveals that firms with external finance are younger but larger, and are mostly located in rural areas. As compared to firms without a loan, firms with a loan constitute a larger share in industrial clusters, in firms with technological know-how obtained from outside sources and in non-proprietary ownership firms. As expected, when it comes to women-owned businesses, their share is relatively low in firms with credit access as compared to firms that did not receive any credit; only 7 percent of firms in the former category are female-run firms while they constitute 11 percent of firms in the latter category of firms.

The previous discussion based on descriptive statistics is suggestive of the fact that there exists a positive relationship between firms' access to finance and output growth. We shall next see whether this observed relationship survives the scrutiny of regression analysis. In what follows, we carry out a formal evaluation of the relationship between external finance and growth of output using multivariate regression analysis.

Finance and growth: regression results

Our baseline OLS estimates of the parameters in equation 5.1 are presented in Table 5.4.[2] Five different specifications are estimated. Two model specifications are estimated for the full sample. The basic specification estimating the effect of finance on growth is presented in column 1. We introduce all

Table 5.4 Access to Finance and Firm Growth
Dependent Variable: Growth of Output

Variables	*(1)*	*(2)*	*(3)*	*(4)*	*(5)*
	All Firms	*All Firms*	*Young Firms*	*Mature Firms*	*Oldest Firms*
Loan	0.008***	0.009**	0.0161**	0.001	0.004*
	(0.001)	(0.001)	(0.001)	(0.001)	(0.002)
Size		-0.009***	-0.012***	-0.007***	-0.005***
		(0.0002)	(0.0003)	(0.0002)	(0.0004)
Age		-0.019***	-0.033***	-0.009***	-0.015***
		(0.0003)	(0.001)	(0.001)	(0.002)
Urban		0.013***	0.012***	0.013***	0.016***
		(0.0004)	(0.0006)	(0.0006)	(0.001)
Cluster		-0.001	0.0001	-0.003***	-0.005***
		(0.001)	(0.001)	(0.001)	(0.002)
Know-how		0.014***	0.013***	0.015***	0.015***
		(0.001)	(0.001)	(0.001)	(0.002)
Proprietary		-0.034***	-0.040***	-0.030***	-0.023***
		(0.001)	(0.001)	(0.001)	(0.002)
Female		-0.002**	-0.005***	0.002	0.006
		(0.001)	(0.001)	(0.001)	(0.003)
Industry effects		Yes	Yes	Yes	Yes
State effects		Yes	Yes	Yes	Yes
Constant	0.171***	0.390***	0.462***	0.328***	0.307***
	(0.0001)	(0.003)	(0.005)	(0.005)	(0.010)
N	1113823	1113823	543372	570451	192428
R^2	0.000	0.056	0.044	0.068	0.090

Source: Authors' estimates.

Note: (a) Standard errors in parentheses; (b) * $p < 0.05$, ** $p < 0.01$, *** $p < 0.001$; and (c) Young firms = Age < 10 years, Mature firms = 10 =<Age< 20 years and Oldest firms = Age => 20 years.

of the control variables and industry and state dummies in column 2. In column 3, following Coad and Tamvada (2012), we restrict the sample to young firms, defined as firms in their first ten years of existence. We limit our sample to mature firms, defined as those in operation for more than ten years but less than 20 years, in column 4. In column 5, the analysis is further restricted to the oldest firms, defined as firms that have been in operation for at least 20 years.

Our results clearly suggest that credit access and output growth are positively related. The coefficient of the loan is positive and significant at the conventional levels in all specifications except in column 4. The coefficient value of the loan variable in the full sample with controls and industry and state effects (column 2) is 0.009 implying that a firm financing its capital from external sources experienced nearly 1 percent more growth over the two-year period than a firm that did not obtain any financial support from external sources. Further, as the statistically significant and positive coefficients of the loan variable in columns 3 and 5 suggest, the finance-firm growth nexus is more striking in the case of young firms as compared to the oldest firms in the sample, perhaps indicating that younger firms, which are in the expansion stage, are likely to have higher credit demand than older firms. There is some evidence in the existing literature that younger firms find it more difficult to secure external finance (Cowling et al., 2018; Regasa et al., 2019), and those which could overcome this barrier grew faster (Haltiwanger et al., 2013).

It can be seen that most of our control variables yield a significant impact on firm growth. In line with the evidence in the literature, there is faster output growth among smaller firms. The coefficient of the size variable is negative and significant in all specifications (Table 5.4). Our computation based on the estimate of size coefficient in column 2 suggests that the rate of growth experienced a decline of 1.52 percent for a one SD increase in firm size.[3] As anticipated, age (*lnage*) has a negative impact on output growth. The coefficient on age variable in the full sample (in column 2) yields a value of –0.019, implying that a 1 SD increase in firm age results in a decline of 1.26 percentage points in the growth rate. Our finding on age corroborates the findings of other studies which have indicated that firm age is an important determinant of firm growth, with younger firms growing faster than older firms (Haltiwanger et al., 2013). It also lends support to the liability of age argument suggesting that as the economic environment improves the sensitivity of firm age on output growth becomes stronger, hence older firms might suffer from a "liability of obsolescence" and also a "liability of senescence" (Barron et al., 1994). Further, the statistically significant and positive coefficient of *Urban* variable suggests that urban firms experience faster growth than rural firms – the difference is about 1.3 percentage points. Also, comparing the coefficients of "Urban" in columns 3 and 5, we find that older urban firms tend to grow faster than their younger counterparts, perhaps because the latter face obstacles initially while establishing themselves in urban markets.

In Table 5.4, we also observe statistically positive coefficients on the knowledge source variable across all specifications, suggesting that output grows faster for firms that derive knowledge from outside sources. Again, the growth benefits are marginally higher (0.2 percent) for the older firms vis-à-vis the younger firms, possibly indicating that the superior ability of the older firms to learn from outside knowledge sources enables them to achieve faster growth. Single ownership has a significant negative association with output growth. Firms with a single owner recorded output growth rate that is 3.4 percentage points less than firms established as partnerships or limited companies. Further, the proprietary firms face much lower expected growth rates among young firms than old firms.

Credit access and female-owned businesses

How important is the availability of credit for the growth of women-owned businesses? It is evident from Table 5.4 that the gender of the owner is an important determinant in firm growth. Results in Table 5.4 show that firms owned and managed by women grew at a slower rate than male-owned firms, a finding which is in consonance with the evidence available from other studies. The coefficient value of the variable *Female* in the full sample with controls and industry and state effects (column 2) is –0.002, suggesting that women-owned businesses experience significantly slower output growth to the tune of 0.2 percentage points. One possible explanation offered in the existing literature is that women-owned firms tend to locate in poorly performing sectors (Coad and Tamvada, 2012). Our dataset does not permit us to undertake an analytical exercise to explain if this indeed is the case. But we do make an attempt to locate the determinants of growth for female-owned firms in order to identify the factors that aid the growth of such firms or inhibit it. In other words, what we do here is to estimate the same specifications as in Table 5.4 for a subsample of firms that are owned and managed by women entrepreneurs.

The results presented in Table 5.5 suggest that credit availability has a larger impact on the growth of female-owned firms compared to the growth of an average firm in the MSME sector. The coefficient value 0.016 indicates that female-owned firms that have loans and credit lines grow 1.6 percentage points faster than female-owned firms without any external financial support. In the case of an average firm, this difference in growth rate was is 0.9 percentage points (see Table 5.4). The effect of size, age and type of ownership is bigger for female-run firms than for an average firm in the sector as seen from the coefficients in Tables 5.4 and 5.5. It shows that large, older firms and proprietary firms tend to grow slower if they are owned by female entrepreneurs. One finding that separates the female-owned firm from an average firm is the significant growth benefits the former derives from being part of a cluster. As the positive and significant coefficient of *Cluster* variable in column 2 of Table 5.5 shows, female-owned firms that are part of a cluster show much faster growth – to the tune of 1.8 percent. Also, the growth benefits are more evident in their first ten years of existence, as the significance of the coefficient disappears for older firms. In summary, women-owned firms with access to formal finance are more likely to achieve significant growth.

Table 5.5 Access to Finance and Firm Growth: Women-Owned Enterprises
Dependent Variable: Growth of Output

Variables	*All Firms*	*All Firms*	*Young Firms*	*Mature Firms*	*Oldest Firms*
Loan	−0.004	0.016***	0.028***	−0.014**	0.009
	(0.003)	(0.003)	(0.004)	(0.006)	(0.013)
Size		−0.024***	−0.027***	−0.018***	−0.019***
		(0.001)	(0.001)	(0.001)	(0.003)
Age		−0.021***	−0.036***	0.002	−0.003
		(0.001)	(0.002)	(0.004)	(0.014)
Urban		0.011***	0.014***	0.003	0.013
		(0.001)	(0.002)	(0.003)	(0.007)
Cluster		0.018***	0.025***	0.005	−0.022
		(0.004)	(0.005)	(0.006)	(0.014)
Know-how		0.014***	0.015***	0.008*	0.008
		(0.002)	(0.003)	(0.004)	(0.010)
Proprietary		−0.037***	−0.029***	−0.047***	−0.080***
		(0.004)	(0.005)	(0.006)	(0.014)
Industry effects		Yes	Yes	Yes	Yes
State effects		Yes	Yes	Yes	Yes
Constant	0.177***	0.548***	0.600***	0.434***	0.511***
	(0.001)	(0.014)	(0.019)	(0.026)	(0.069)
N	109506	109506	76934	32572	5243
R^2	0.000	0.047	0.047	0.053	0.104

Source: Authors' estimates.

Note: (a) Standard errors in parentheses; (b) * $p < 0.05$, ** $p < 0.01$, *** $p < 0.001$; and (c) Young firms = Age < 10 years, Mature firms = 10 =<Age< 20 years and Oldest firms = Age => 20 years.

Finance and growth: robustness tests

We perform several robustness checks to verify the stability of our results. First, we estimate our baseline regressions on many different subsamples of the data. Second, in order to deal with causality and endogeneity problems influencing our core results, we employ an Instrumental Variable (IV) method, using a district-specific measure of financial depth as an IV. And lastly, we consider estimating these baseline specifications in a quantile regression framework so as to see the stability of our results for various quantiles.

Robustness check: subsample analysis

In this subsection, we validate the robustness of our results by splitting the dataset into subsamples based on sources of finance and firm size. First, the baseline regressions results of two subsamples of firms are compared with each other – firms that obtained a loan from non-institutional sources and firms that obtained loan from both institutional and non-institutional sources. This would help us to understand whether sources of finance matter for the growth of MSME firms. We also examine whether our results are sensitive to firms belonging to different size categories – micro, small, and medium. This would also help us to confirm the veracity of the argument, most often found in the literature, that the impact of finance on growth is most evident among smaller firms than larger ones. The results are presented in Table 5.6 for the subsamples based on sources of finance and in Table 5.7 for the subsamples based on firm size. The estimates in Tables 5.6 and 5.7 largely reinforce the main finding that access to credit is crucial for firm growth. More importantly, they show that the source of credit and the

Table 5.6 Access to Finance and Firm Growth by Sources of Finance
Dependent Variable: Growth of Output

Variables	*(1)*	*(2)*
Non-institutional loan	0.007** (0.002)	
Institutional and non-institutional loan		-0.003 (0.003)
Size of the firm	-0.007*** (0.0002)	-0.009*** (0.0001)
Age of the firm	-0.017*** (0.0003)	-0.019*** (0.0003)
Rural area	0.016*** (0.0004)	0.013*** (0.0004)
Firm is part of a cluster	-0.008*** (0.001)	-0.001 (0.001)
Technological know-how	0.027*** (0.001)	0.014*** (0.001)
Proprietary ownership	-0.043*** (0.001)	-0.035*** (0.001)
Women-owned firm	-0.007*** (0.001)	-0.002** (0.001)
Industry effects	Yes	Yes
State effects	Yes	Yes
Constant	0.331*** (0.002)	0.387*** (0.003)
N	1113823	1113823
R^2	0.011	0.056

Source: Authors' estimates.

Note: (a) Standard errors in parentheses; and (b) * $p < 0.05$, ** $p < 0.01$, *** $p < 0.001$.

Table 5.7 Access to Finance and Firm Growth by Firm Size

Variables	*Micro*	*Small*	*Medium*
Loan	0.009***	0.009*	-0.048*
	(0.001)	(0.004)	(0.020)
Size of the firm	-0.012***	-0.012***	-0.012*
	(0.0001)	(0.001)	(0.006)
Age of the firm	-0.019***	-0.018***	-0.030**
	(0.0003)	(0.002)	(0.010)
Rural area	0.014***	0.005	0.009
	(0.0004)	(0.003)	(0.018)
Firm is part of a cluster	-0.002*	-0.001	0.002
	(0.001)	(0.002)	(0.012)
Technological know-how	0.014***	0.010*	0.005
	(0.001)	(0.004)	(0.014)
Proprietary ownership	-0.032***	-0.007**	-0.043***
	(0.001)	(0.002)	(0.011)
Women-owned firm	-0.004***	-0.001	-0.044
	(0.001)	(0.013)	(0.046)
Industry effects	Yes	Yes	Yes
State effects	Yes	Yes	Yes
Constant	0.419***	0.492***	1.016***
	(0.003)	(0.033)	(0.170)
N	1066254	45761	1808
R^2	0.056	0.099	0.279

Source: Authors' estimates.

Note: (a) Standard errors in parentheses; and (b) * $p < 0.05$, ** $p < 0.01$, *** $p < 0.001$.

size of the firm are important in determining the magnitude of this growth. These subsample analyses provide the evidence that the finance-growth nexus is stronger for firms that source their loans from non-institutional sources and for micro and small firms.

Robustness check: endogeneity correction

An important econometric issue associated with relating credit access to firm growth using micro-data is the presence of selection bias in estimates. The selection bias is likely to occur due to two reasons: self-selection and non-random replacement. The first, self-selection bias, might arise because firms with certain characteristics may decide to apply for formal finance as compared to other eligible firms in the dataset. This bias tends to exaggerate the relationship between credit access and firm growth as the estimated impact could be partly due to the differences in the unobserved characteristics between the firms that applied for formal finance and those who did not. Additionally, the observed relationship between access to finance and growth is also likely to be contaminated by non-random placement, where the factors specific to location are expected to influence firm growth. Reverse causality is another possible factor that could influence the baseline regression results as the high-growth firms are more likely to apply for formal finance as well as have a greater likelihood of being favoured by formal financial institutions. In the presence of these possible biases, we are likely to obtain biased estimates of access to finance on firm growth. We circumvent the possible endogeneity issues associated with the loan variable by employing the Heckman Two-Stage Estimation Method with a district-specific measure of financial depth – the number of bank branches per 10000 population – and the efficient use of capital – the ratio of fixed assets to total assets – as instruments for the loan, and estimate the full specification with controls and industry and state effects. We also introduce some variables as controls in the regression model to further correct for the location effects. The results of our IV estimations are presented in Table 5.8.

Table 5.8 Access to Finance and Firm Growth: Instrumental Variable (IV) Estimates

Variables	*Model 1*		*Model 2*	
	Second Stage: Dependent Variable: Growth of Output	*First Stage: Dependent Variable: Loan*	*Second Stage: Dependent Variable: Growth of Output*	*First Stage: Dependent Variable: Loan*
Loan	0.010***		0.141***	
	(0.001)		(0.004)	
Size of the firm	-0.009***	0.123***	-0.015***	0.199***
	(0.0001)	(0.003)	(0.0002)	(0.001)
Age of the firm	-0.019***	-0.0538***	-0.015***	-0.154***
	(0.0003)	(0.007)	(0.0003)	(0.003)
Rural area	0.013***	-0.044***	0.016***	-0.146***
	(0.0004)	(0.011)	(0.0004)	(0.004)
Firm is part of a cluster	-0.001	0.079***	-0.001	0.087***
	(0.001)	(0.019)	(0.001)	(0.007)
Technological know-how	0.014***	0.082***	0.014***	0.003
	(0.001)	(0.014)	(0.001)	(0.005)
Proprietary ownership	-0.034***	-0.152***	-0.028***	-0.173***
	(0.001)	(0.016)	(0.001)	(0.006)
Women-owned firm	-0.002**	-0.516***	-0.002**	-0.046***
	(0.001)	(0.016)	(0.001)	(0.007)
Collateral		4.925***		
		(0.016)		

(*Continued*)

Table 5.8 (Continued)

Variables	*Model 1*		*Model 2*	
	Second Stage: Dependent Variable: Growth of Output	*First Stage: Dependent Variable: Loan*	*Second Stage: Dependent Variable: Growth of Output*	*First Stage: Dependent Variable: Loan*
Bank density				-0.016*** (0.002)
Industry effects	Yes	Yes	Yes	Yes
State effects	Yes	Yes	Yes	Yes
Inverse Mills Ratio (IMR)	-0.003* (0.001)		-0.072*** (0.002)	
Constant	0.404*** (0.003)	-4.008*** (0.082)	0.443*** (0.004)	-3.259*** (0.027)
N	1113823	1113821	1113823	1113821
R^2	0.056		0.057	

Source: Authors' estimates.

Note: (a) Standard errors in parentheses; and (b) * $p < 0.05$, ** $p < 0.01$, *** $p < 0.001$.

The IV two-stage least squares estimates reinforce the main findings based on OLS estimates. The coefficient of the *Loan* is positive and significant at the 1 percent level, suggesting that credit access is an important factor determining the growth of firms in the MSME sector. Our results are thus robust to concerns arising from endogeneity of the loan variable and highlight the positive role of access to finance on firm growth.

Robustness check: quantile regressions

We carry out one more robustness check to test the stability of our results. As mentioned, one of the drawbacks of estimating model specifications using the robust OLS technique is that it ignores extreme values of outliers and does not include them in the estimation. We circumvent this issue by estimating the model specifications in a quantile regression framework. By applying the quantile regression method with bootstrapped standard errors, we will be able to assess whether the impact of access to finance on firm growth remains the same across the different quantiles of the conditional distribution of the dependent variable. We estimate the full model with controls and state and industry effects and concentrate on five representative quantiles, namely, 10 percent, 25 percent, 50 percent, 75

Table 5.9 Access to Finance and Firm Growth: Quantile Regression Estimates
Dependent Variable: Growth of Output

Variables	*All Firms*	*All Firms*	*Young Firms*	*Mature Firms*	*Oldest Firms*
Loan	0.021***	0.010***	0.016***	-0.007*	0.002
	(0.0001)	(0.002)	(0.002)	(0.004)	(0.009)
Size of the firm		-0.019***	-0.023***	-0.014***	-0.011***
		(0.0005)	(0.001)	(0.001)	(0.002)
Age of the firm		-0.010***	-0.016***	-0.001	0.008
		(0.001)	(0.001)	(0.003)	(0.010)
Rural area		0.003**	0.004**	0.0001	0.008
		(0.001)	(0.001)	(0.002)	(0.005)
Firm is part of a cluster		0.015***	0.019***	0.011*	-0.002
		(0.003)	(0.003)	(0.005)	(0.010)
Technological know-how		0.005**	0.006**	0.003	0.005
		(0.002)	(0.002)	(0.003)	(0.007)
Proprietary ownership		-0.017***	-0.010**	-0.027***	-0.039***
		(0.003)	(0.003)	(0.005)	(0.009)
Industry effects	No	Yes	Yes	Yes	Yes
State effects	No	Yes	Yes	Yes	Yes
Constant	0.143***	0.425***	0.471***	0.332***	0.312***
	(0.001)	(0.011)	(0.014)	(0.020)	(0.047)
N	1113823	109506	76934	32572	5243
Psuedo R^2	0.000	0.026	0.027	0.028	0.062

Source: Authors' estimates.

Note: (a) Standard errors in parentheses; and (b) * $p < 0.05$, ** $p < 0.01$, *** $p < 0.001$; and (c) Young firms = Age < 10 years, Mature firms = 10 =<Age< 20 years and Oldest firms = Age => 20 years.

percent and 90 percent. Tables 5.9 and 5.10 present the results from the quantile regression. In Table 5.9, we present the median values of the coefficients and in Table 5.10 we present the estimates of the finance variable for the five quantiles: 10 percent, 25 percent, 50 percent, 75 percent and 90 percent. The results of our quantile regression exercise, too, endorse the positive relationship between access to finance and firm growth. The coefficient value of finance variable in Table 5.9 yields the same sign and significance as in our OLS estimates. The results reported in Table 5.10 also suggest that the coefficients vary across quantiles and exhibit a heterogeneous pattern. The coefficients of all quantiles, except for the bottom ones, are positive and are increasing in magnitude as we move from the bottom to top quantiles. Our results broadly indicate that the finance-growth nexus is highly evident for high-growth firms and point to the significant role of finance for such firms. These results withstand scrutiny even after we correct for the possible endogeneity of the loan variable.

Table 5.10 Access to Finance and Firm Growth: Quantile Regression Estimates by Quintiles

Dependent Variable: Growth of Output

Quantile	*Coefficients*
10 percent	–0.061*** (0.002)
25 percent	–0.016*** (0.0005)
50 percent	0.017*** (0.001)
75 percent	0.056*** (0.001)
90 percent	0.117*** (0.003)
Number of Observations	1132098

Source: Authors' estimates.

Note: (a) Standard errors in parentheses; and (b) * $p < 0.05$, ** $p < 0.01$, *** $p < 0.001$.

Table 5.11 Access to Finance and Firm Growth: Instrumental Variable (IV) Quantile Regression Estimates

Dependent Variable: Growth of Output

Quantile	*Coefficients*
10 percent	–0.012*** (0.001)
25 percent	0.003*** (0.001)
50 percent	–5.74e-07 (0.0003)
75 percent	0.006*** (0.001)
90 percent	0.012*** (0.002)
Number of Observations	1113823

Source: Authors' estimates.

Note: (a) Standard errors in parentheses; and (b) * $p < 0.05$, ** $p < 0.01$, *** $p < 0.001$.

This is substantiated by the IV quantile estimates presented in Table 5.11. We repeated the same exercise for the subsample of female-owned firms (Table 5.12). We observe that the results are similar which again underlines the importance of credit.

Table 5.12 Access to Finance and Firm Growth for Women-Owned Enterprises: Quantile Regression Estimates

Dependent Variable: Growth of Output

Variables	*All Firms*	*All Firms*	*Young Firms*	*Mature Firms*	*Oldest Firms*
Loan	0.004* (0.002)	0.010*** (0.002)	0.016*** (0.002)	-0.007* (0.004)	0.002 (0.009)
Size of the firm		-0.019*** (0.001)	-0.023*** (0.001)	-0.014*** (0.001)	-0.011*** (0.002)
Age of the firm		-0.010*** (0.001)	-0.016*** (0.001)	-0.001 (0.003)	0.008 (0.010)
Rural area		0.003** (0.001)	0.004** (0.001)	0.0001 (0.002)	0.008 (0.005)
Firm is part of a cluster		0.015*** (0.003)	0.019*** (0.003)	0.011* (0.005)	-0.002 (0.010)
Technological know-how		0.005** (0.002)	0.006** (0.002)	0.002 (0.003)	0.005 (0.007)
Proprietary ownership		-0.017*** (0.003)	-0.010** (0.003)	-0.027*** (0.005)	-0.039*** (0.010)
Industry effects	Yes	Yes	Yes	Yes	Yes
State effects	Yes	Yes	Yes	Yes	Yes
Constant	0.143*** (0.001)	0.425*** (0.011)	0.471*** (0.014)	0.332*** (0.020)	0.312*** (0.047)
N	109506	109506	76934	32572	5243
Psuedo R^2	0.000	0.026	0.027	0.028	0.062

Source: Authors' estimates.

Note: (a) Standard errors in parentheses; and (b) * $p < 0.05$, ** $p < 0.01$, *** $p < 0.001$; and (c) Young firms = Age < 10 years, Old firms = 10 =<Age< 20 years and Oldest firms = Age => 20 years.

Conclusion

There is ample literature on the importance of financial constraints on firm growth. Most of these studies focus on large firms, and there is a dearth of studies that explore the role of finance on the growth of small firms. Another limitation of this abundant literature corresponds to its exclusive focus on developed markets. In the case of India, there are not many studies that have studied the relationship between access to finance and firm growth. In this chapter, we addressed this obvious gap in the literature and examined the role of access to finance in promoting small firm growth in India.

Our analysis unambiguously shows that access to credit and output growth are positively related. We also find that the finance-growth nexus is more striking in the case of young firms as compared to the oldest firms. In line with the evidence available in the literature, our results also point to the fact that firms owned and managed by women grow at a slower rate than male-owned firms. The study, however, shows that credit access makes a larger impact on the growth of female-owned firms as compared to the growth of an average firm in the MSME sector. Our results are robust to concerns arising from the endogeneity of finance variable and also to alternate methods and specifications.

Notes

1 The construction of these variables is explained later in the chapter.

2 Though this chapter discusses the role of credit access on firm growth, we have also examined the relationship between credit access and other measures of performance such as size (proxied using output, gross value added, fixed assets and employment) and efficiency (proxied using labour productivity). The results are in line with our expectations, which unambiguously suggest that access to finance fosters firm performance significantly. The baseline regression results of these estimations are presented in Table 5A.1 in Appendix I.

3 We arrived at this estimate as follows. The SD of natural log of output is 1.699 (see Table 5.2) and the coefficient value of the same variable is -0.009 (column 2, Table 5.4). A 1 SD change in log of output changes the dependent variable by $1.699 \times -0.009 = -0.015291$. As our dependent variable is log_e(*growth rate*), the current change in the dependent variable to -0.015291 is analogous to a growth rate of -0.01517 (given that $e^{-0.015291} - 1 = -0.01517$), which then can be rounded off to -1.52%.

6

GENDER, SMALL FIRM OWNERSHIP AND CREDIT CONSTRAINTS

Introduction

It is well recognised that small firms are the engine of innovation and economic growth (Acs and Armington, 2006; Baumol, 2002). The Organisation for Economic Co-operation and Development (OECD) (2016) reports that in emerging economies SMEs contribute up to 45 percent of the total employment and 33 percent of the GDP. According to a recent study from the International Finance Corporation (International Finance Corporation, 2017a, 2017b), SMEs account for more than half of all formal jobs worldwide, and their share of aggregate employment is comparable to that of large firms. The re-evaluation of the role of small firms is related to a renewed attention to the role of entrepreneurship as it can create new economic opportunities for women and contribute to overall inclusive growth. GEM (2013) observes that the share of entrepreneurs remains relatively stagnant over the years and female entrepreneurs face gender biases due to various socio-economic factors.[1]

A related question of great policy importance on gender, entrepreneurship and firm performance is therefore to analyse the performance of female-owned firms compared to the ones owned by males and examine the differences in the observed performance. Using firm-level data from OECD countries, Watson (2002), Robb and Fairlie (2007, 2009), and Robb and Watson (2012) demonstrate that the performance of female-owned businesses on key parameters, such as profit, size and productivity, is lower than that of male-owned businesses. But the findings differ across countries, types of firms and the control that has been used, and are also subject to criticism due to their small sample size. Sabarwal and Terrell (2008), using data from Eastern ECA, document that female-owned enterprises are smaller in both size of assets and employment. The findings have been echoed by Coleman (2007) in the case of the 1998 US Survey of Small Business Finances. Using the WBES data, Bardasi et al. (2011) document the absence of a gender differential in value added per worker and Total Factor Productivity (TFP) while holding constant the industry in which they work. However, Bardasi et al. (2011) show that female-owned firms are less efficient in both Eastern ECA and LA but not in SSA.

Using the WBES data for the Sub-Saharan African region, Aterido et al. (2013) indicate a significant gender gap in the labor coefficient and a 12 percent productivity gap between male- and female-owned firms.

Various factors have been put forward in the literature to explain the underperformance of female entrepreneurs: disproportionate concentration in more competitive industries or in industries with lower productivity, asymmetric access to capital and discriminatory access to finance. Coleman (2007) shows that the women are concentrated in more competitive sectors such as retail and service sectors, thus getting less opportunities for growth and performance. Watson (2002) documents that the poor performance of female-owned enterprises in Australia is due to lower initial start-up capital.

Although access to formal finance is often highlighted as the most pressing obstacle to the growth of SMEs irrespective of the gender of the entrepreneur, existing literature highlights the fact that women-owned enterprises particularly suffer from difficulty in obtaining credit from formal sources (Berger and Udell, 2006).[2] Previous literature also highlights that women-owned firms have lower loan approval rates from formal sources, indicating credit market discrimination (Muravyev et al. 2009). Using cross-country data from the Business Environment and Enterprise Performance Survey (BEEPS), Muravyev et al. (2009) observe that females face a lower probability of receiving loans and have to pay higher interest rates. As a result, women are dissuaded from entrepreneurship and running a business on an efficient scale. However, Bardasi et al. (2011) do not find evidence of gender-based discrimination in access to formal finance. Apart from the credit market discrimination aspect, women-owned businesses face difficulty in the form of cultural and institutional barriers, concentration of business in low-productivity sectors and small size of the business, and these barriers widen the performance gap between women- and men-led enterprises (Klapper and Parker, 2011; Tlaiss, 2014). Even though both male-owned and female-owned businesses face barriers in access to formal financial services, the obstacles are bigger for women-led businesses.

Although there exists some work on OECD countries, research using data on small firms in developing countries including India is growing. For example, Coad and Tamvada (2012), using firm-level data from the third census of registered small-scale firms, showed that firms headed by females grow slower after controlling for other factors. De and Nagaraj (2014) also use data from Indian manufacturing firms to show that firms with better liquidity turn out to be the most productive. Deshpande and Sharma (2013) highlighted the ethical and racial disparity in the indicators of business performance.

This chapter contributes to the growing body of literature on ownership and firm performance and access to finance in the following ways. First, most of the studies were confined to the experience of developed countries and these findings cannot be easily generalised to the context of developing economies. Second, in this chapter, we use a unique large dataset of Indian

MSMEs in analysing gender differences in obtaining formal finance. As mentioned in Chapter 3, policy makers in India after independence emphasised the need to promote MSMEs and provided favorable treatment to such firms in the form of credit concessions, reservation of certain products exclusively for MSMEs and tax concessions (Tendulkar and Bhavani, 1997). With the onset of economic reforms, new policy initiatives led to the de-reservation of various items reserved for MSMEs and preference for such firms in government purchase procurements. Despite the preferential treatment of the MSME sector in India, such firms are plagued by several obstacles. Among the set of constraints faced by these firms, access to finance is reported to be the most pressing obstacle (Sharma, 2014). In this context, policy makers have realised the need to provide a helping hand to this sector and have undertaken a host of initiatives such as credit guarantee schemes, promotion of women entrepreneurship and marketing assistance for accelerating the growth of this sector. Third, the dataset that we use is rich in terms of detailed information about the presence of females in the ownership and management of enterprises. Finally, a recent study noted that empirical studies on the gender gap in access to finance will provide better insight into credit market functioning, if the details of different measures of female participation in the firms are taken into account (Presbitero et al., 2014). Since our dataset contains information about different measures of female participation regarding the ownership and management of firms and credit access, we are able to investigate the presence of a gender gap in access to financial instruments along with a decomposition analysis applicable to non-linear models.

The rest of the chapter is organised as follows. We present descriptive statistics in the second section. The third section presents details of the methodology. Discussion of the results obtained from the empirical analysis is reported in the fourth section followed by concluding remarks.

Descriptive statistics

Table 6.1 compares the mean values of our main variables of interest by gender of the owner. It is clearly evident from the table that there exist considerable differences in firm characteristics between male-owned and female-owned firms. Compared to the male-owned firms, the average production is considerably lower in female-owned firms. The average log of output for male-owned firms is 12.633 and for female-owned firms is 11.250. The female-owned firms are younger and smaller in size and mostly located in urban areas as compared to male-owned firms. As regards loan availability, male business owners are more likely to obtain credit (12 percent) than women (8 percent). Looking at the firms' presence in the export market, male business owners are highly more likely to enter the export market than women-run businesses. Thus, in terms of raw averages, female-owned firms clearly perform much worse than male-owned firms.

Table 6.1 Descriptive Statistics

Variables	*Male Owned*		*Female Owned*		*p-value*
	Mean	*Standard Deviation (SD)*	*Mean*	*SD*	
Log of Output	12.633	1.722	11.250	1.306	0.000
Log of Employment	1.091	0.920	0.514	0.701	0.000
Age	13.156	9.030	8.772	6.364	0.000
Loan Dummy (Yes=1)	0.118	–	0.078	–	0.000
Institutional Loan Dummy (Yes=1)	0.099	–	0.070	–	0.000
Account Maintenance Dummy (Yes=1)	0.332	–	0.148	–	0.000
Location (Rural/Urban)	0.545	–	0.422	–	0.000
Unit a Part of Cluster Dummy	0.080	–	0.038	–	0.000
Has a Quality Certificate Dummy	0.040	–	0.025	–	0.000
Export Dummy	0.034	–	0.012	–	0.000
Knowledge of Technology Dummy	0.121	–	0.108	–	0.000
Log of Net Worth	12.142	1.808	10.866	1.514	0.000
Single Ownership Dummy	0.905	–	0.963	–	0.000

Source: Authors' estimates.

Note: p-value is for the two-sample t-test with unequal variances. For the binary variable, we do not report the SD.

Methodology

Difference in performance of male- and female-owned firms

We employ a number of indicators to capture the gaps in performance between male-owned and female-owned firms. These indicators include output, employment and capital stock (proxies for firm size), growth of output (proxy for firm growth) and labour productivity and TFP (proxies for firm efficiency). To measure the performance gap, we regress each of the indicators of performance/efficiency on three different dummies: dummy for female owner, dummy for female manager and, finally, a dummy for female in dual role as owner and manager (*Female*).

Gender gap in access to finance: baseline specification

In order to analyse whether businesses with female ownership participation are less likely to use a formal financing channel (loan), we test the following empirical model:

$$Y_i = f\,(\textit{female, size, age, agesq, exporter, account, quality certification, net worth, industry dummy, state dummy}) \tag{6.1}$$

where Y_i is a dummy variable indicating that the firm has access to external finance (loan). *Female* is a dummy variable which equals 1 indicating female ownership (owner/manager) participation and 0 otherwise. We also include a set of usual control variables and *industry* and *state dummies*. Since our dependent variable is a binary variable, we employ a logit model for the empirical analysis. Details of the explanatory variables are presented in Table 6A.1 in Appendix I.

Blinder-Oaxaca decomposition

In order to disentangle the role of various factors in determining the gender gap in access to finance, we use a decomposition technique to understand the extent to which our results are influenced by observable and unobservable components which will indicate the extent of discrimination. Decomposition techniques allow us to explain the gap in the access to credit for the two groups of firms. The gap is decomposed into that part which is due to the group differences in predictors, i.e. the part of the gap due to the differences in the average characteristics based on the gender of the owner (the "endowment effects") and group differences in the coefficients, where the latter are sometimes called the unexplained part of the gender gap. We adopted the Oaxaca-Blinder (1973) decomposition technique modified for a non-linear model. When the outcome of interest is binary, i.e. loan status, the estimation of outcome equations is based on logit or probit models. Therefore, differencing in means for non-linear models is not feasible. We use the method suggested by Fairlie (2006) for the decomposition[3] of non-linear models. Technical details of the decomposition are given in Appendix II.

Selection bias

It is highlighted by the earlier studies on access to finance that firms often self-select not to apply for a loan (Bardasi et al., 2011). Self-selection for not applying for loan may arise due to the absence of the need for external finance and some of the applicants may perceive the fear of rejection. What we observe in our dataset is the set of firms who self-selected to receive formal finance. Therefore, it is essential to correct for the self-selection problem in our empirical analysis. Our empirical strategy to overcome the self-selection problem involves identifying firms as "constrained" and "unconstrained" with credit demand (Bigsten et al., 2003). We classify sample firms as constrained if they reported a shortage of capital and as unconstrained if they reported to have received a loan but did not report a capital shortage. To address the selection issue, we employ a two-step Heckman probit (Van de Ven and Van Praag, 1981) procedure analogous to Heckman's (1979) approach. This approach requires an exclusion restriction for identification purposes. We use two variables for the purpose of exclusion restrictions[4]

(Cameron and Trivedi, 2009) and improve identification, i.e. (a) growth of annual output growth and (b) efficient use of capital which influences the selection but not the outcomes. We include these two variables since they are likely to influence the demand for credit but not the final outcome.

Ownership, credit constraint and firm performance: propensity score matching (PSM)

To compare the effects outcome of access to finance, we employ a non-parametric matching method. This approach enables us to match enterprises which are constrained by finance with the unconstrained firms in terms of their performance. The idea behind this approach is to match by gender with similar observable characteristics and to compare the average engagement behavior for the two subsamples of individuals. Compared to the traditions least squares approach, Propensity Score Matching (PSM) provides flexibility in terms of the absence of rigid functional form restrictions and assumes that selection is based on observables. Further, it is argued that regression techniques lead to biased estimates when the distribution of covariates differs across two groups of observations and the magnitude of the bias depends on the difference in the covariate distribution of two groups (Rubin, 1973).

We rely on the widely applied PSM introduced by Rosenbaum and Rubin (1983) using reweighting on the propensity score. The matching estimator is based on the following formulation: let T be the treatment (an indicator of the enterprise being constrained); let $Y_i(1)$ be the outcome for the treated enterprise (i.e. the firm performance in terms of labour productivity and value added); and let $Y_i(0)$ be the outcome of the non-treated individual. What we are interested in measuring is the mean effect on the firm performance of constrained firms vis-à-vis unconstrained firms. We classify firms as constrained (treated) if they report a working capital shortage as an obstacle. For firm i, we denote the treatment indicator $D_i = 1$, and the outcome of the treatment is the measure of firm performance w_{1i}. If the firm is unconstrained (does not report a working capital shortage), it is denoted as a control firm and the treatment indicator $D_i = 0$ and the outcome of the treatment is the measure of firm performance w_{0i}. The treatment effect for firm i is therefore the difference in the firm performance with and without treatment. Formally, it can be represented as $A_i = w_{1i} - w_{0i}$. Since we observe only the post-treatment effect, counterfactual is not observed, i.e. it is impossible to observe the value of $Y_i(1)$ and $Y_i(0)$ for the same firm. Even though we can estimate $E[Y_i(1) \mid D = 1]$ but we cannot estimate $E[Y_i(0) \mid D = 1]$. Therefore, the standard approach is to estimate the Average Treatment Effect on the Treated (ATT) given:

$$\text{ATT} = E\,(A_i \mid D_i = 1)$$
$$\text{ATT} = E\,(w_{1i} \mid D_i = 1) - (E\,(w_{0i} \mid D_i = 1)$$

PSM is based on the idea of constructing a comparison group as a control group, which are identical to the treatment group. Matching is carried out using propensity scores $P(X)$ conditioned on the vector of observables X. The propensity score can be interpreted as the predicted probability of participating in a program. A critical factor associated with the matching process is the Conditional Independence Assumption (CIA). It means that there is no issue of selection; potential outcomes are independent of the treatment assignment and there is no unobserved heterogeneity (Heckman and Robb, 1985). Further, PSM requires a common support assumption, i.e. units with the same X values have a positive probability of being both treated and non-treated (Heckman et al., 1999). Following Rosenbaum and Rubin's (1983) theorem, the PSM procedure involves two steps. In the first step, we estimate the propensity score $Pr(D = 1|X)$ using the standard binary discrete choice model (probit). In the second step, we build weights as $1/Pr(D = 1|X)$ for the treated observations and $1/(1-(Pr(D = 1|X))$ for the untreated observations;[5] and then in the final step, we estimate the treatment effects by using a weighted regression.

Findings

Gender of the owner and performance

In this section, we begin by discussing the results of the difference in performance between male- and women-led businesses. As highlighted previously, there is already a large body of literature highlighting the significant differences in performance between male and female entrepreneurs. Many of these studies point to the prevalence of substantial gender-specific barriers to entrepreneurship that constrain the performance of female entrepreneurs (Bardasi et al., 2011). These barriers also explain the lesser participation of women into entrepreneurship. Available evidence shows that female entrepreneurs are a minority in developing countries as well as in high-income countries including the US and the UK (Bardasi et al., 2011). This chapter though does not probe the reasons behind the lower participation of women in entrepreneurship (female entrepreneurs constitute only 15 percent in our dataset), locating the constraints that could explain the observed gaps in performance between male and female entrepreneurs can provide some new insights into the lower female participation rate in entrepreneurial activities. We begin our empirical analysis by first exploring the relationship between the gender of the owner and gaps in performance. In other words, our intention is to see whether there exists any significant difference in performance between firms owned by males and females in the MSME sector in India.

Our estimation results are presented in Table 6.2. In all cases, we estimate three specifications based on the extent and involvement of women in the ownership and management of firms, i.e. *women as owner*, *women as manager*, *women as owner and manager*: without any controls (column 1), controlling for state effects (column 2) and controlling for state and industry effects (column 3). Our results clearly suggest that there exists a significant gap in performance between firms owned by males and those owned by females. Across all specifications, all measures of performance and all measures of female entrepreneurship, male entrepreneurs do perform better than female entrepreneurs.[6] Controlling for industry and state effects, the annual production of an average female-owned firm is 41 percent less than the annual production for an average male-owned firm. The gap is much larger for *women as manager* (65 percent) and *women as owner and manager* (72 percent). Using the number of workers as a proxy for firm size, we find an average female-owned firm to be 5/6th of the size of an average male-owned firm. In terms of capital investment too, female-run firms are smaller in size as compared to their male counterparts. These findings are robust to our alternate measures of women entrepreneurship and the gaps are found to be much larger for these alternate measures. However, based on output growth as a measure of performance, we do not observe strong evidence to confirm significant differences in performance between male and female entrepreneurs, since the coefficients of women in all our specifications are not significant (though they have the expected negative sign).

Further, we proceed to examine whether female-run enterprises are less productive than those operated by males. To capture the productivity differences, we rely on two standard measures: (a) Labour productivity (defined as the ratio of gross value added (GVA) to number of workers); and (b) TFP. Following Bardasi et al. (2011), we compute TFP by estimating a Cobb-Douglas production function from firm level data. The function takes the following form:

$$lnY_{jis} = \beta_0 + \beta_k lnK_{jis} + \beta_l lnL_{jis} + \beta_f F_{jis} + \gamma_i + \delta_s + \varepsilon_{jis} \quad (6.2)$$

where Y_{jis} stands for GVA of firm *j* operating in industry *i* and in state *s*. *K* and *L* are capital input and labour input, respectively. Real gross fixed assets are used to represent the capital input; the number of workers employed by the firm is used as the variable for the labour input. *F* is our variable of interest which takes the value 1 for female entrepreneur and 0 for male entrepreneur. γ_i are industry-fixed effects and δ_s are state-fixed effects. We transform all the variables (output, capital and labour) into their natural logarithmic values. The estimated coefficient (β_f) of *F* in the equation captures gender differences in TFP.

The results obtained from productivity measures, (labour productivity and TFP), are presented in the lower panel of Table 6.2 (see the panel under the sub-heading "efficiency"). Results for all specifications and for alternate measures of women entrepreneurship clearly indicate that female-run firms are less efficient than male-run firms. Controlling for state and industry effects, the

Table 6.2 Gender of the Owner and Performance Gaps

Variable	*Woman as Owner*			*Woman as Manager*			*Woman as Owner and Manager*		
	(1)	*(2)*	*(3)*	*(1)*	*(2)*	*(3)*	*(1)*	*(2)*	*(3)*
Size									
a. Ln(output)									
Female	−0.868***	−0.704***	−0.411***	−1.231***	−1.014***	−0.652***	−1.330***	−1.103***	−0.720***
	(0.005)	(0.004)	(0.004)	(0.005)	(0.005)	(0.005)	(0.005)	(0.005)	(0.005)
Number of observations	1157961	1157961	1157961	1157961	1157961	1157961	1157961	1157961	1157961
R-squared	0.03	0.17	0.25	0.05	0.19	0.25	0.05	0.19	0.26
b. Ln(employment)									
Female	−0.359***	−0.305***	−0.177***	−0.530***	−0.463***	−0.301***	−0.577***	−0.509***	−0.338***
	(0.002)	(0.002)	(0.002)	(0.003)	(0.003)	(0.003)	(0.003)	(0.003)	(0.003)
Number of observations	1157961	1157961	1157961	1157961	1157961	1157961	1157961	1157961	1157961
R-squared	0.02	0.11	0.19	0.03	0.12	0.20	0.03	0.12	0.20
c. Ln(capital)									
Female	−1.074***	−0.784***	−0.414***	−1.416***	−1.085***	−0.627***	−1.515***	−1.183***	−0.696***
	(0.005)	(0.005)	(0.005)	(0.006)	(0.005)	(0.005)	(0.006)	(0.005)	(0.005)
Number of observations	1157961	1157961	1157961	1157961	1157961	1157961	1157961	1157961	1157961
R-squared	0.03	0.37	0.44	0.05	0.38	0.44	0.05	0.38	0.44
Growth									
d. Output growth									
Female	−3.131	−7.177	−0.337	−0.969	−4.419	4.505	−4.928	−8.732	0.043
	(15.458)	(16.025)	(16.978)	(16.854)	(17.452)	(18.859)	(17.801)	(18.432)	(19.964)
Number of observations	1157961	1157961	1157961	1157961	1157961	1157961	1157961	1157961	1157961
R-squared	0.0001	0.0002	0.0002	0.0001	0.0002	0.0002	0.0001	0.0002	0.0002

(*Continued*)

Table 6.2 (Continued)

Efficiency									
e. Gross value added (GVA) per worker (labour productivity)									
Female	−0.509***	−0.399***	−0.234***	−0.700***	−0.550***	−0.351***	−0.753***	−0.594***	−0.382***
	(0.003)	(0.003)	(0.003)	(0.003)	(0.003)	(0.003)	(0.004)	(0.003)	(0.004)
Number of observations	1157961	1157961	1157961	1157961	1157961	1157961	1157961	1157961	1157961
R-squared	0.02	0.15	0.19	0.04	0.16	0.20	0.04	0.16	0.20
f. Total Factor Productivity (TFP)									
Female	−0.114***	−0.103***	−0.112***	−0.170***	−0.121***	−0.135***	−0.196***	−0.133***	−0.150***
	(0.003)	(0.003)	(0.003)	(0.003)	(0.003)	(0.003)	(0.004)	(0.003)	(0.004)
Number of observations	1156855	1156855	1156855	1156855	1156855	1156855	1156855	1156855	1156855
R-squared	0.52	0.60	0.60	0.53	0.60	0.60	0.53	0.60	0.60

Source: Authors' estimates based on Fourth All India Census of Micro, Small and Medium Enterprises (MSMEs), 2006–2007.

Note: Female variable stands for dummy for female as owner, female as manager and female as both owner and manager. In model 2 and model 3, we include state-fixed effects and state- and industry-fixed effects, respectively. No effects are included in model 1. *** significant at 1 percent.

"male-female entrepreneurial" gap in labour productivity is 23 percent and the gap in TFP is 11 percent. These gaps in efficiency are significantly higher when we use *women as manager* and *women as owner and manager* as measures of women entrepreneurship. On the whole, our findings point to the underperformance of female entrepreneurs in indicators pertaining to size, growth and efficiency of MSME firms. Based on the results of the preceding analysis, we seek to probe further into the underperformance of female-led firms in the MSME. More importantly, why women-owned firms are significantly smaller and less efficient than the firms operated by male entrepreneurs. Therefore, in the next section, an attempt is made to map the possible factors constraining the growth of female entrepreneurial activities in India.

Constraints to growth of women-owned firms

We explore here various possible explanations for the significant "male-female differential" in the performance of firms in the MSME sector in India. Previous studies provide several explanations for the prevalence of gender-based gaps in entrepreneurial performance. Given the data constraints, our objective is to provide explanations for the following: (a) Whether the gender differences in firm age explain the observed gender gaps in performance; (b) Whether the observed differences in performance are due to the smaller size of their concerns; (c) Whether the observed gap in performance is due to the crowding of female firms in specific industrial sectors with low productivity; and (d) Are gender gaps in performance driven by gender differences in access to credit?

Differences in firm age and gaps in performance

One possibility is that the differences in the age of the firm owned by males and females could explain the observed gaps in the performance of male and female entrepreneurs. This argument emanates from the realisation that women are increasingly engaging in entrepreneurial activities; hence their ventures will be much younger than the ones operated by their male counterparts. Their having less experience in managing entrepreneurial concerns might well explain their underperformance as entrepreneurs.[7] Female-owned firms in our dataset are indeed much younger than the male-owned firms (Table 6.3). The average age of women-owned enterprises in our data is around nine years. One can observe from the figures that firms operated by male entrepreneurs are on average four years older than the female-owned firms.

To examine the possibility that differences in firm age may be driving the male-female gaps in performance, we re-estimate regressions shown in Table 6.2, controlling for the age of the firm. Results for the complete specification with industry and fixed effects are presented in Table 6.4. For each measure of women

Table 6.3 Average Firm Age by Gender of the Owner

	Woman as Owner	*Woman as Manager*	*Woman as Owner and Manager*
Male-run firms	13.15	13.18	13.15
Female-run firms	9.99	9.12	8.77
Difference	3.16	4.06	4.38
t-statistic	131.40	155.35	158.83
Significant?	Yes	Yes	Yes

Source: Authors' estimates based on Fourth All India Census of Micro, Small and Medium Enterprises (MSMEs), 2006–2007.

entrepreneurship, we present two columns: one without age as a control variable (column 1) and one with age as a control variable (column 2). We find that the results are unaffected even after controlling for the influence of the age of the firm. The size and sign of the estimated coefficient of *Female* (women owner, manager and owner-manager) hardly vary when we introduce *age* as a control variable (compare columns 1 and 2 in Table 6.4). Our results thus show that firm *age* does not account for the observed gender differences in firm performance, and the reason for gender gaps in performance therefore has to be found elsewhere.

Dominance of smaller firms

Women entrepreneurship is largely skewed towards smaller-sized firms, and this gap in firm size, at least partially, explains the existence of a gender gap in firms' performance (Sabarwal and Terrell 2008).[8] It is argued that the majority of women entrepreneurs are often in business because running a small enterprise allows them to bring in additional income with little additional effort and they are unlikely to expand or invest in their businesses. Some studies also show that women tend to display greater risk aversion, which leads women to restrict investment in their business concerns thereby limiting the growth of their firms (Barber and Odean, 2001; Dohmen et al., 2005). However, the differences in firm size may also be an outcome of the differences in the survival rate of male- and female-owned enterprises. If the female-owned firms do not survive at the same rate as male-owned firms, we would expect the female-owned enterprises to be more skewed towards smaller-sized firms. Though our dataset does not permit us to explore these two questions, it is, however, possible to analyse whether the differences in firm size explain the gender gap in firm performance. In our dataset too, about 97 percent of firms owned by women entrepreneurs are micro enterprises as against 85 percent for male-owned firms.

Table 6.4 Gender of the Owner and Performance Gaps, Controlling for Age of the Firm

Variable	*Woman as Owner*		*Woman as Manager*		*Woman as Owner and Manager*	
	(1)	*(2)*	*(1)*	*(2)*	*(1)*	*(2)*
Size						
a. Ln(output)						
Female	−0.411***	−0.402***	−0.652***	−0.642***	−0.720***	−0.709***
	(0.004)	(0.004)	(0.005)	(0.005)	(0.005)	(0.005)
Number of observations	1157961	1157961	1157961	1157961	1157961	1157961
R-squared	0.25	0.25	0.25	0.26	0.26	0.26
b. Ln(employment)						
Female	−0.177***	−0.174***	−0.301***	−0.298***	−0.338***	−0.335***
	(0.002)	(0.002)	(0.003)	(0.003)	(0.003)	(0.003)
Number of observations	1157961	1157961	1157961	1157961	1157961	1157961
R-squared	0.19	0.19	0.20	0.20	0.20	0.20
c. Ln(capital)						
Female	−0.414***	−0.404***	−0.627***	−0.615***	−0.696***	−0.683***
	(0.005)	(0.004)	(0.005)	(0.005)	(0.005)	(0.006)
Number of observations	1157961	1157961	1157961	1157961	1157961	1157961
R-squared	0.44	0.44	0.44	0.44	0.44	0.44
Growth						
d. Output growth						
Female	−0.337	-7.020	4.505	-3.888	0.043	-9.180
	(16.978)	(17.022)	(18.859)	(18.923)	(19.964)	(20.038)
Number of observations	1157961	1157961	1157961	1157961	1157961	1157961
R-squared	0.0002	0.0002	0.0002	0.0002	0.0002	0.0002

(*Continued*)

Table 6.4 (Continued)

Variable	*Woman as Owner*		*Woman as Manager*		*Woman as Owner and Manager*	
	(1)	*(2)*	*(1)*	*(2)*	*(1)*	*(2)*
Efficiency						
e. Gross value added (GVA) per worker (labour productivity)						
Female	–0.234***	–0.228***	–0.351***	–0.344***	–0.382***	–0.374***
	(0.003)	(0.003)	(0.003)	(0.003)	(0.004)	(0.004)
Number of observations	1157961	1157961	1157961	1157961	1157961	1157961
R-squared	0.19	0.19	0.20	0.20	0.20	0.20
f. Total Factor Productivity (TFP)						
Female	–0.112***	–0.110***	–0.135***	–0.132***	–0.150***	–0.146***
	(0.003)	(0.003)	(0.003)	(0.003)	(0.004)	(0.004)
Number of observations	1156855	1156855	1156855	1156855	1156855	1156855
R-squared	0.60	0.60	0.60	0.60	0.60	0.60

Source: Authors' estimates based on Fourth All India Census of Micro, Small and Medium Enterprises (MSMEs), 2006–2007.

Note: Female stands for dummy for female as owner, female as manager and female as both owner and manager. Model 1 corresponds to model 3 in Table 6.2. In model 2, we also include age of the firm and square of age of the firm. *** significnt at 1 percent.

To account for potential differences in performance that can emerge from differences in firm size, we re-estimate regressions shown in Table 5.2, controlling for the size of the firm. We do this by introducing three different dummy variables for micro, small and medium firms. The results of our re-estimation are reported in Table 6.5. Our results clearly show that differences in firm size explain only marginal differences in performance between male- and female-owned firms. The estimated coefficient of *female* is still large in magnitude and negative when we introduce firm size dummies as control variables (compare columns 1 and 2 in Table 6.5). Our results are also robust to alternate measures of women entrepreneurship. As a robustness test, we re-estimate model 3 in Table 6.2 separately for micro, small and medium firms. Barring a few exceptions the coefficients are still negative and significant though lesser in magnitude, confirming that one has to search for alternate explanations for the underperformance of women entrepreneurs in the MSME sector in India (Table 6.6).

Higher concentration of female entrepreneurs in industrial sectors with low productivity

Another explanation cited in the literature related to the underperformance of female entrepreneurs is their higher concentration in low performing and less productive industries. This issue has been previously addressed by Bardasi et al. (2011) for three developing regions: Eastern ECA, LA and SSA. We proceed as follows. First, we investigate whether female-owned firms are heavily concentrated in few industrial sectors. This is done by computing a concentration index at the industry level. We then compare the performance of firms in these industries (industries where the female entrepreneurs are more concentrated) with those in other industrial sectors. Finally, we examine the relative performance of male- and female-owned businesses in female-dominated (FD) and male-dominated sectors.

The distribution of women entrepreneurs across industrial sectors presented in Figure 6.1 shows that women-owned enterprises are present in all industrial sectors. The same result holds even when we use alternate measures of entrepreneurship (Figure 6.2). However, very few women entrepreneurs are found in industrial sectors such as transport equipment and parts (automobiles) and electronics. Our estimates suggest that wearing apparel, textiles and food products are the dominant industries for women entrepreneurs. These industries together accommodate 72 percent of total women entrepreneurs in the MSME sector. Among them, wearing apparel alone constitutes about half of the women-owned firms. Using an index of concentration, we find out whether there is a large concentration of women entrepreneurs in few sectors. Following Bardasi et al. (2011), we define the index of concentration for a sector as the ratio of the percentage of female entrepreneurs to total entrepreneurs in that sector to

Table 6.5 Gender of the Owner and Performance Gaps, Controlling for Firm Size

Variable	*Woman as Owner*		*Woman as Manager*		*Woman as Owner and Manager*	
	(1)	*(2)*	*(1)*	*(2)*	*(1)*	*(2)*
Size						
a. Ln(output)						
Female	–0.411***	–0.340***	–0.652***	–0.558***	–0.720***	–0.615***
	(0.004)	(0.004)	(0.005)	(0.004)	(0.005)	(0.005)
Number of observations	1157961	1157961	1157961	1157961	1157961	1157961
R-squared	0.25	0.44	0.25	0.45	0.26	0.45
b. Ln(employment)						
Female	–0.177***	–0.142***	–0.301***	–0.256***	–0.338***	–0.287***
	(0.002)	(0.002)	(0.003)	(0.002)	(0.003)	(0.003)
Number of observations	1157961	1157961	1157961	1157961	1157961	1157961
R-squared	0.19	0.36	0.20	0.37	0.20	0.37
c. Ln(capital)						
Female	–0.414***	–0.328***	–0.627***	–0.514***	–0.696***	–0.569***
	(0.005)	(0.004)	(0.005)	(0.004)	(0.005)	(0.005)
Number of observations	1157961	1157961	1157961	1157961	1157961	1157961
R-squared	0.44	0.62	0.44	0.63	0.44	0.63
Growth						
d. Output growth						
Female	–0.337	1.697	4.505	7.272	0.043	3.160
	(16.978)	(16.985)	(18.859)	(18.871)	(19.964)	(19.978)
Number of observations	1157961	1157961	1157961	1157961	1157961	1157961
R-squared	0.0002	0.0001	0.0002	0.0001	0.0002	0.0001

Efficiency						
e. Gross value added (GVA) per worker (labour productivity)						
Female	−0.234***	−0.198***	−0.351***	−0.303***	−0.382***	−0.327***
	(0.003)	(0.003)	(0.003)	(0.003)	(0.004)	(0.003)
Number of observations	1157961	1157961	1157961	1157961	1157961	1157961
R-squared	0.19	0.30	0.20	0.30	0.20	0.31
f. Total Factor Productivity (TFP)						
Female	−0.112***	−0.124***	−0.135***	−0.157***	−0.150***	−0.175***
	(0.003)	(0.003)	(0.003)	(0.003)	(0.004)	(0.004)
Number of observations	1156855	1156855	1156855	1156855	1156855	1156855
R-squared	0.60	0.61	0.60	0.61	0.60	0.61

Source: Authors' estimates based on Fourth All India Census of Micro, Small and Medium Enterprises (MSMEs), 2006–2007.

Note: Female stands for dummy for female as owner, female as manager and female as both owner and manager. Model 1 corresponds to model 3 in Table 6.2. In model 2, we also include dummy variables for micro, small and medium firms. *** significant at 1 percent.

Table 6.6 Gender of the Owner and Performance Gaps by firm type

Variables	*Woman as Owner*				*Woman as Manager*				*Woman as Owner and Manager*			
	Overall	*Micro*	*Small*	*Medium*	*Overall*	*Micro*	*Small*	*Medium*	*Overall*	*Micro*	*Small*	*Medium*
Size												
a. Ln(output)												
Female	−0.411*** (0.004)	−0.328*** (0.004)	−0.102*** (0.017)	−0.195** (0.098)	−0.652*** (0.005)	−0.523*** (0.004)	−0.311*** (0.023)	−0.002 (0.145)	−0.720*** (0.005)	−0.573*** (0.004)	−0.409*** (0.029)	−0.211 (0.222)
Number of observations	1157961	1010055	139815	4916	1157961	1010055	139815	4916	1157961	1010055	139815	4916
R-squared	0.25	0.24	0.51	0.35	0.25	0.25	0.51	0.35	0.26	0.25	0.51	0.35
b. Ln(employment)												
Female	−0.177*** (0.002)	−0.127*** (0.002)	−0.001 (0.010)	0.022 (0.079)	−0.301*** (0.003)	−0.226*** (0.002)	−0.099*** (0.014)	0.038 (0.119)	−0.338*** (0.003)	−0.254*** (0.002)	−0.138*** (0.018)	−0.195 (0.179)
Number of observations	1157961	1010055	139815	4916	1157961	1010055	139815	4916	1157961	1010055	139815	4916
R-squared	0.19	0.19	0.42	0.17	0.20	0.20	0.42	0.17	0.20	0.20	0.42	0.17
c. Ln(capital)												
Female	−0.414*** (0.005)	−0.312*** (0.004)	−0.065*** (0.011)	−0.013 (0.017)	−0.627*** (0.005)	−0.477*** (0.004)	−0.107*** (0.016)	−0.044* (0.025)	−0.696*** (0.005)	−0.524*** (0.005)	−0.147*** (0.019)	−0.057 (0.037)
Number of observations	1157961	1010055	139815	4916	1157961	1010055	139815	4916	1157961	1010055	139815	4916
R-squared	0.44	0.40	0.04	0.04	0.44	0.40	0.04	0.03	0.44	0.40	0.04	0.04
Growth												
d. Output growth												
Female	−0.337 (16.978)	4.096 (6.268)	−69.414 (200.93)	−2.913 (10.023)	4.505 (18.859)	7.994 (6.901)	−63.374 (277.797)	−6.605 (15.030)	0.043 (19.964)	2.410 (7.273)	−45.572 (342.075)	−1.184 (22.612)
Number of observations	1157961	1010055	139815	4916	1157961	1010055	139815	4916	1157961	1010055	139815	4916
R-squared	0.0002	0.001	0.0002	0.012	0.0002	0.001	0.0002	0.012	0.0002	0.001	0.0002	0.013

Efficiency												
e. Gross value added (GVA) per worker (labour productivity)												
Female	−0.234*** (0.003)	−0.201*** (0.003)	−0.101*** (0.014)	−0.216*** (0.088)	−0.351*** (0.003)	−0.296*** (0.003)	−0.212*** (0.019)	−0.040 (0.132)	−0.382*** (0.004)	−0.319*** (0.003)	−0.270*** (0.024)	−0.015 (0.198)
Number of observations	1157961	1010055	139815	4916	1157961	1010055	139815	4916	1157961	1010055	139815	4916
R-squared	0.19	0.17	0.30	0.27	0.20	0.17	0.30	0.27	0.20	0.17	0.30	0.27
f. Total Factor Productivity (TFP)												
Female	−0.112*** (0.003)	−0.149*** (0.003)	−0.067*** (0.017)	−0.232*** (0.094)	−0.135*** (0.003)	−0.186*** (0.003)	−0.198*** (0.024)	0.120 (0.140)	−0.150*** (0.004)	−0.206*** (0.003)	−0.272*** (0.029)	−0.073 (0.211)
Number of observations	1156855	1009135	139643	4909	1156855	1009135	139643	4909	1156855	1009135	139643	4909
R-squared	0.60	0.49	0.61	0.30	0.60	0.49	0.61	0.30	0.60	0.49	0.61	0.30

Source: Authors' estimates based on Fourth All India Census of Micro, Small and Medium Enterprises (MSME), 2006–2007.

Note: Micro = enterprises where the investment in plant and machinery does not exceed 25 lakh rupees; Small = enterprises where the investment in plant and machinery is more than 25 lakh rupees but does not exceed 5 crore rupees; Medium= enterprises where the investment in plant and machinery is more than 5 crore rupees but does not exceed 10 crore rupees; Female variable stands for dummy for female as owner, female as manager and female as both owner and manager. In model 2 and model 3, we include state-fixed effects and state- and industry-fixed effects, respectively. The estimated model corresponds to model 3 in Table 6.2. ***, ** and * indicate level of significance at 1 percent, 5 percent and 10 percent, respectively.

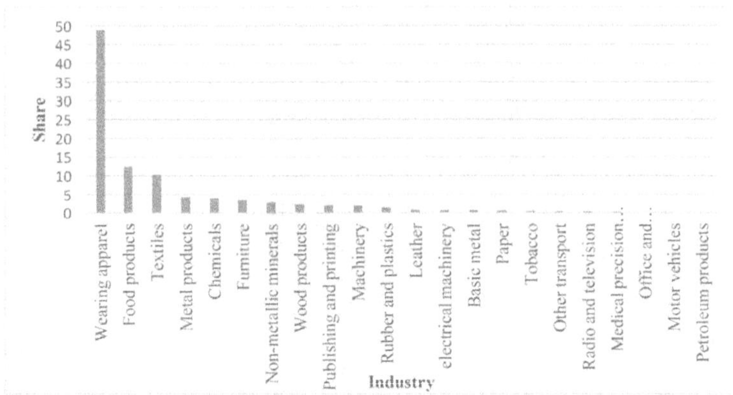

Figure 6.1 Distribution of Female Firms Across Industries (Percent, Value Sum to 100)

Source: Authors' estimates based on Micro, Small and Medium Enterprise (MSME) dataset.

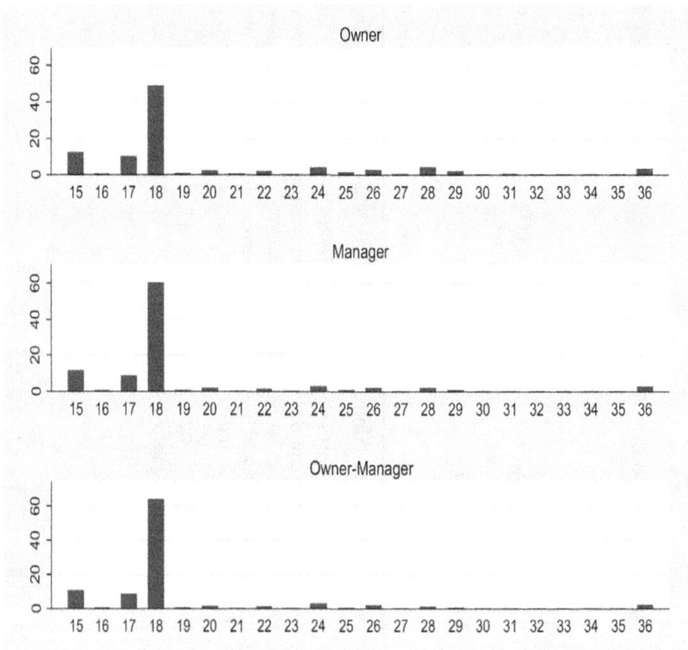

Figure 6.2 Distribution of Female Firms by Owner/Manager Attributes Across Industries (Percent, Value Sum to 100)

Source: Authors' estimates based on Micro, Small and Medium Enterprise (MSME) dataset.

Note: Industries are represented using National Industrial Classification codes to save space. Table 6A.2 in Appendix I presents industry names against industry codes.

percentage of female entrepreneurs to total entrepreneurs in the MSME sector. Symbolically, the index of concentration is $(I_c) = \frac{F_s}{F_T}$, where F_s is the share of female entrepreneurs to total entrepreneurs in a sector and F_T is the share of female entrepreneurs to total entrepreneurs in the MSME sector. If the value of the index of concentration is greater than one in a sector, it implies that the female entrepreneurs are overrepresented in that sector in comparison with their representation in the sector as a whole. We report the index of concentration for all industrial sectors and for all measures of women entrepreneurship in Figure 6.3. Our findings indicate that the concentration ratio is greater than one in just three industrial sectors, namely wearing apparel, textiles and tobacco products. In these three sectors, there is an overrepresentation of women entrepreneurs. The main idea emerges from Figure 6.1 and Figure 6.3 that women are heavily concentrated in few sectors while men are more or less proportionately distributed across industrial sectors.[9]

Given that women-owned firms tend to concentrate in few sectors, it may be possible that the observed underperformance of women enterprises is due to the below average performance of sectors where women entrepreneurs are overrepresented. We now examine this issue. For this, we need to compare the relative performance of female-owned firms in the FD industries with those industries where they are not overrepresented. One drawback of such a comparison is the presence of endogeneity, as it is possible

Figure 6.3 Index of Concentration of Female Entrepreneurs by Industry

Source: Authors' estimates.

Figure 6.3 (Continued)

that the lower performance of female-owned enterprises may be explaining the lower performance of sectors where they are overcrowded. In order to overcome this, we measure the relative performance by analysing the performance of male-owned firms. In other words, what we are attempting here is to verify whether the performance of male-owned firms in FD industries is lower than the performance of male-owned firms in other industries (where females are not overrepresented). To implement this, we first group the industrial sectors into two categories: one category for FD industrial sectors (sectors with $I_c > 1$) and another for male-dominated sectors (sectors with $I_c < 1$). In the next step, we employ the following specification to examine the relative performance of male- and female-owned firms:

$$lnY_{jis} = \beta_0 + \pi F_{jis} + \gamma FD_{is} + \theta F_{jis} * FD_{is} + \delta_s + \varepsilon_{jis} \tag{6.3}$$

where Y_{jis} stands for the GVA of firm *j* operating in industry *i* and in state *s*. *F* is a dummy variable which takes the value 1 for female entrepreneur and 0 for male entrepreneur. The estimated π coefficient of *F* indicates the overall performance of female firms in our dataset. *FD* is the dummy variable for female-dominated sectors and its coefficient, γ, enables us to capture the differences in performance between firms in FD and male-dominated sectors. The estimated θ coefficient of the interaction term *F*FD* yields the additional effect associated with female-owned firms operating in a FD sector. δ_s stands for state-fixed effects. It is clearly evident that equation (6.3) helps us to differentiate between two implicit hypotheses of the lower performance of the industries and the lower performance of women entrepreneurs within these industries.

The results are presented in Table 6.7. The table reports the results for two measures of performance: log of output and value added per worker. The estimations are performed for all three measures of women entrepreneurship (*women as owner*, *women as manager* and *women as owner and manager*). In all cases, we report the results for two specifications of regression equation: (a) Without industry and state dummies; and (b) With industry and state dummies. Is the overrepresentation of women in sectors that are underperforming actually constraining the performance of women-owned firms? Our findings do confirm that the partial explanation for the underperformance of female entrepreneurs can be derived from our concentration story. Across all estimations, the estimates of coefficients *F*, *FD* and *F*FD* are negative and significant. These results point to the fact that firms operating in FD sectors are significantly smaller and less efficient compared to firms operating in male-owned sectors. In other words, our results unambiguously indicate that women do concentrate in sectors where firms are on average smaller.

Though these results offer a partial explanation for the underperformance of women entrepreneurs in the MSME sector, what it fails to explain is why female-owned firms indeed would like to be based in sectors which are poorly performing. An interesting policy question is whether women entrepreneurs are entering into sectors with smaller and less efficient firms by "choice" or by "force". If it is by choice, what are the key factors that make them attractive towards these sectors? If they are forced to work in these sectors, what are the key elements that exclude them from the other sectors? Our dataset, however, does not permit us to undertake an analytical exercise for searching answers for these questions. We are indeed able

Table 6.7 Gender of the Owner and Gaps in Performance: Whether Operating in Female-Dominant Sectors Is a Justification?

Variables	*Ln(Output)*						*Value Added Per Worker (labour productivity)*					
	Woman as Owner		*Woman as Manager*		*Woman as Owner and Manager*		*Woman as Owner*		*Woman as Manager*		*Woman as Owner and Manager*	
	(1)	*(2)*	*(1)*	*(2)*	*(1)*	*(2)*	*(1)*	*(2)*	*(1)*	*(2)*	*(1)*	*(2)*
Female	−0.068*** (0.008)	−0.030*** (0.007)	−0.526*** (0.009)	−0.410*** (0.008)	−0.662*** (0.010)	−0.523*** (0.009)	−0.092*** (0.005)	−0.068*** (0.005)	−0.362*** (0.006)	−0.283*** (0.006)	−0.444*** (0.007)	−0.348*** (0.006)
Female-dominant sector	−0.155*** (0.004)	−0.136*** (0.004)	−0.349*** (0.004)	−0.309*** (0.004)	−0.370*** (0.004)	−0.325*** (0.004)	−0.168*** (0.003)	−0.147*** (0.002)	−0.270*** (0.003)	−0.236*** (0.003)	−0.281*** (0.003)	−0.245*** (0.003)
Female* Female-dominant sector	−1.130*** (0.010)	−0.967*** (0.009)	−0.758*** (0.011)	−0.666*** (0.010)	−0.638*** (0.012)	−0.573*** (0.011)	−0.535*** (0.007)	−0.425*** (0.006)	−0.291*** (0.007)	−0.229*** (0.007)	−0.215*** (0.008)	−0.169*** (0.008)
Constant	12.572*** (0.002)	12.745*** (0.015)	12.626*** (0.002)	12.754*** (0.015)	12.626*** (0.002)	12.753*** (0.015)	11.488*** (0.001)	11.855*** (0.010)	11.512*** (0.001)	11.851*** (0.010)	11.511*** (0.001)	11.850*** (0.010)
Number of observations	1157961	1157961	1157961	1157961	1157961	1157961	1157961	1157961	1157961	1157961	1157961	1157961
Industry effects	N	Y	N	Y	N	Y	N	Y	N	Y	N	Y
State effects	N	Y	N	Y	N	Y	N	Y	N	Y	N	Y
R-squared	0.05	0.19	0.07	0.20	0.07	0.20	0.04	0.16	0.05	0.17	0.05	0.17

Source: Authors' estimates based on Fourth All India Census of Micro, Small and Medium Enterprises (MSMEs), 2006–2007.

Note: Female is a dummy variable for women-owned enterprises. Female-dominant sectors are those where the index of concentration is larger or equal to 1 (the index of concentration represents the ratio between the percentage of women entrepreneurs in a specific industrial sector and the percentage of women entrepreneurs in the dataset). *** significant at 1 percent.

to investigate, in the following section, whether their decision to operate in these sectors is constrained by their access to credit.

Are gender gaps in performance driven by gender differences in access to credit?

The significance of credit access for the subsequent growth and performance of firms is well documented in the literature (Binks and Ennew, 1996; Rajan and Zingales, 1998; Oliveira and Fortunato, 2006). A large number of studies carried out in the recent past have focused on the question of whether the financial constraints facing entrepreneurs differ with respect to demographic characteristics, including gender. Some of these studies revealed that female-owned firms tend to have less access to formal credit than male-owned firms (Carter and Rosa, 1998; Coleman, 2007). If there is a clear discrimination in access to credit, female entrepreneurs are less likely to invest in fixed assets, and in the process finding it difficult to penetrate into industries that require large investments. In other words, women entrepreneurs are more likely to crowd into industries requiring lesser investments, in the presence of discrimination in credit access. This is clearly evident from our dataset as female-owned firms are heavily concentrated in industries requiring lesser investments (Table 6.8). Nearly 70 percent of female entrepreneurs in the MSME sector are in industries that are labor intensive and require fewer investments in fixed capital. More importantly, the explanation for the observed gender differences in performance can be perhaps found in this gender gap in access to credit. In order to investigate the relationship between the gender of entrepreneurs and their access to a formal financing channel (loan), we test the following empirical model:

$$Y_{jis} = \beta_0 + \pi F_{jis} + \delta X_{jis} + \gamma_i + \delta_s + \varepsilon_{jis} \tag{6.4}$$

where Y_{jis} is a dummy variable which takes the value 1 if the firm j operating in industry i and in state s has obtained external finance (loan) and 0 otherwise. F is the dummy for a female entrepreneur which takes the value 1 for female entrepreneur and 0 for male entrepreneur. As in other estimations, we use three alternate measures of female entrepreneurship: *women as owner*, *women as manager* and *women as owner and manager*. X is a vector of firm-specific attributes that could influence the probability of obtaining a loan. These firm-specific characteristics are also important from the lender's point of view as they reflect the creditworthiness and resources of a firm that the lender will consider while making the decision to grant a loan. To be specific, we include three measures of firm performance or how well the firm is run (measured by performance variables such as profit, labour productivity and net worth of the firms), a measure of export opportunities (a dummy indicating whether or not a firm exports), the financial literacy and ability of the entrepreneur (whether or not the firm is maintaining an account and

Table 6.8 Are Female Entrepreneurs Entering More Into Industries Requiring Lesser Investments?

Industry	*Capital Intensive?*	*Share of Women Entrepreneurs*
Food products	N	12.5
Tobacco	N	0.6
Textiles	Y	10.3
Wearing apparel	N	49.0
Leather	N	0.9
Wood products	N	2.3
Paper	Y	0.6
Publishing and printing	Y	2.2
Petroleum products	Y	0.1
Chemicals	Y	4.0
Rubber and plastics	Y	1.4
Non-metallic minerals	N	3.0
Basic metal	Y	0.8
Metal products	Y	4.4
Machinery	Y	2.1
Office and computing machinery	Y	0.2
electrical machinery	Y	0.8
Radio and television (TV)	Y	0.4
Medical precision and opticals	Y	0.4
Motor vehicles	Y	0.2
Other transport	N	0.4
Furniture	Y	3.5

Source: Authors' estimates based on Fourth All India Census of Micro, Small and Medium Enterprises (MSMEs), 2006–2007.

Note: Labour-intensive industries are those industries whose capital-labour ratio (CLR) falls below the median value of CLR. Those industries whose CLR is above the median value are classified as capital-intensive industries. N = not capital intensive and Y = capital intensive.

whether the firm has a quality certificate), a measure of ownership (whether the firm has a single owner or multiple owners), a measure to capture the possible effects of participating in networks (whether the firm is part of a cluster), the stability of the firm (captured by age and age squared) and the size of the firm (measured by two proxies: employment and the amount of sales two years before the current period). To control for the environments in which firms operate, we include a dummy for location, which takes the value 1 if the firms are operating from rural areas and 0 if they operate from urban areas. γ_i are industry-fixed effects and δ_s are state-fixed effects.

The main estimation results are reported in Table 6.9. The table presents the estimates for a number of specifications. In all these specifications, the

Table 6.9 Gender of the Owner and Access to Credit

Dependent Variable: Whether or Not Obtained Loan (Obtained = 1)

Variables	*(1)*	*(2)*	*(3)*	*(4)*	*(5)*	*(6)*	*(7)*	*(8)*	*(9)*	*(10)*	*(11)*	*(12)*	*(13)*
Female	−0.187***	−.0324***	−0.186***	−0.223***	−0.172***	−0.178***	−0.191***	−0.192***	−0.154***	−0.140***	−0.169***	−0.131***	−0.155***
	(0.009)	(0.009)	(0.010)	(0.010)	(0.010)	(0.010)	(0.010)	(0.010)	(0.010)	(0.010)	(0.012)	(0.010)	(0.010)
Age of the firm				−0.039***	−0.037***	−0.037***	−0.038***	−0.037***	−0.039***	−0.038***	−0.042***	−0.040***	−0.039***
				(0.001)	(0.001)	(0.001)	(0.001)	(0.001)	(0.001)	(0.001)	(0.001)	(0.001)	(0.001)
Age square				0.001***	0.001***	0.001***	0.001***	0.001***	0.001***	0.001***	0.001***	0.001***	0.001***
				(0.000)	(0.000)	(0.000)	(0.000)	(0.000)	(0.000)	(0.000)	(0.000)	(0.000)	(0.000)
Firm size					0.551***	0.558***	0.441***	0.434***	0.234***	0.379***	0.324***		0.219***
					(0.003)	(0.003)	(0.004)	(0.004)	(0.005)	(0.004)	(0.005)		(0.005)
Location						−0.148***	−0.208***	−0.209***	−0.267***	−0.294***	−0.265***	−0.304***	−0.265***
						(0.007)	(0.007)	(0.007)	(0.007)	(0.007)	(0.008)	(0.007)	(0.007)
Firm is part of a cluster						0.434***	0.395***	0.394***	0.417***	0.390***	0.414***	0.402***	0.424***
						(0.012)	(0.012)	(0.012)	(0.012)	(0.012)	(0.013)	(0.012)	(0.012)
Firm maintains an account							0.395***	0.574***	0.434***	0.375***	0.507***	0.388***	0.417***
							(0.012)	(0.008)	(0.008)	(0.008)	(0.009)	(0.008)	(0.008)
Firm has a quality certificate							0.210***	0.180***	0.125***	0.094***	0.057***	0.116***	0.105***
							(0.014)	(0.014)	(0.014)	(0.014)	(0.016)	(0.014)	(0.014)
Firm is exporting								0.275***	0.209***	0.170***	0.211***	0.194***	0.191***
								(0.018)	(0.019)	(0.019)	(0.021)	(0.019)	(0.019)
Log of net worth of the firm									0.193***			0.107***	0.185***
									(0.003)			(0.003)	(0.003)
Value added per worker										0.267***			
										(0.003)			
Log of profit											0.126***		
											(0.003)		
Output two years ago												0.222***	
												(0.003)	
Firm has a single owner													−0.217***
													(0.010)
Constant	−2.023***	−2.127***	−2.034***	−1.647***	−2.163***	−2.132***	−2.171***	−2.175***	−4.354***	−5.259***	−3.370***	−5.889***	−4.030***
	(0.003)	(0.033)	(0.033)	(0.034)	(0.035)	(0.035)	(0.035)	(0.035)	(0.047)	(0.049)	(0.046)	(0.045)	(0.049)
State effects	N	Y	Y	Y	Y	Y	Y	Y	Y	Y	Y	Y	Y
Industry effects	N	N	Y	Y	Y	Y	Y	Y	Y	Y	Y	Y	Y
Number of observations	1157961	1157959	1157959	1157959	1157959	1157959	1157959	1157959	1151271	1157959	814066	1151271	1151271
Pseudo R^2	0.0005	0.10	0.11	0.11	0.15	0.15	0.16	0.16	0.16	0.17	0.16	0.17	0.17

Source: Authors' estimates based on Fourth All India Census of Micro, Small and Medium Enterprises (MSMEs), 2006–2007.

coefficient on variable *F*, which is our variable of interest, is negative and statistically significant. Controlling for firm performance and other firm characteristics representing creditworthiness, this suggests that female-owned firms in the MSME sector are less likely to obtain a loan as compared to male-owned firms. According to the estimates, female entrepreneurs have about a 15–20 percent lower probability of obtaining a loan than male entrepreneurs. Considering the smaller proportion of firms that receive loans in the MSME sector, this is a fairly large number, indicating the presence of a substantial gender difference in financial constraints. As conjectured, our estimation results also lend evidence in support of greater difficulties faced by smaller firms, firms that are located in rural areas and firms that have a single owner in securing external finance. Exporting firms and those that are part of a cluster have a higher probability of loan approval, which implies that lenders consider it less risky to lend to those firms that market their product abroad and that are part of a larger network. Consistent with our prior expectations, we also find that entrepreneurial ability and financial literacy do matter in eliciting a positive response from the lender. Our proxies for ability and literacy (account maintenance and possessing a quality certificate) have yielded positive coefficients, signifying the fact that lenders' satisfaction on entrepreneurial abilities increases the likelihood of loan approval. There is also a clear direction from our results that the probability of obtaining a loan is significantly higher among firms that throw up a better performance in terms of profitability and productivity, as the coefficients of all measures of firm performance are positive and significant across all our specifications.

Furthermore, our results are also robust to alternate measures of women entrepreneurship. If we focus on the variable identifying the gender of the manager rather than female participation in ownership (Table 6.10), the results again show evidence of gender-based discrimination in the credit market, once we condition for firms' characteristics. The same result holds even when we use the variable capturing the dual role of women as owner and manager (Table 6.11).

Our dataset does provide rich information on firm-specific characteristics; however, it provides very little information on the characteristics of owners and managers operating the firm. Previous research has shown that while deciding on the loan applications, lenders tend to look at attributes of entrepreneurs such as education and personal wealth. Hence it is very much possible that the results of our study may be biased due to the omission of such entrepreneurial characteristics. Following Blanchflower et al. (2003) and Muravyev (2009), we implement a number of sample splits that can take care of these differences in entrepreneurial characteristics and then we compare the regression results. To be specific, we use net worth of the firm, size of the firm and source of credit to perform an analysis based on sample splits. The net worth of the firm can be considered as a proxy to represent the wealth of the entrepreneur, especially in the case of MSME firms, which are our units of analysis. The idea behind splitting the sample based on size

Table 6.10 Gender of the Manager and Access to Credit

Dependent Variable: Whether or Not Obtained Loan (Obtained = 1)

Variables	*(1)*	*(2)*	*(3)*	*(4)*	*(5)*	*(6)*	*(7)*	*(8)*	*(9)*	*(10)*	*(11)*	*(12)*	*(13)*
Female	−0.366***	−0.429***	−0.216***	−0.267***	−0.129***	−0.126***	−0.125***	−0.125***	−0.076***	−0.053***	−0.089***	−0.047***	−0.081***
	(0.010)	(0.011)	(0.012)	(0.012)	(0.012)	(0.012)	(0.012)	(0.012)	(0.012)	(0.012)	(0.014)	(0.012)	(0.012)
Age of the firm				−0.039***	−0.037***	−0.037***	−0.037***	−0.037***	−0.038***	−0.038***	−0.042***	−0.040***	−0.039***
				(0.001)	(0.001)	(0.001)	(0.001)	(0.001)	(0.001)	(0.001)	(0.001)	(0.001)	(0.001)
Age square				0.001***	0.001***	0.001***	0.001***	0.001***	0.001***	0.001***	0.001***	0.001***	0.001***
				(0.000)	(0.000)	(0.000)	(0.000)	(0.000)	(0.000)	(0.000)	(0.000)	(0.000)	(0.000)
Firm size					0.550***	0.558***	0.441***	0.434***	0.234***	0.379***	0.323***		0.218***
					(0.003)	(0.003)	(0.004)	(0.004)	(0.005)	(0.004)	(0.005)		(0.005)
Location						−0.149***	−0.209***	−0.210***	−0.268***	−0.294***	−0.267***	−0.305***	−0.266***
						(0.007)	(0.007)	(0.007)	(0.007)	(0.007)	(0.008)	(0.007)	(0.007)
Firm is part of a cluster						0.428***	0.389***	0.388***	0.413***	0.387***	0.410***	0.399***	0.419***
						(0.012)	(0.012)	(0.012)	(0.012)	(0.012)	(0.013)	(0.012)	(0.012)
Firm maintains an account							0.570***	0.572***	0.431***	0.373***	0.504***	0.386***	0.415***
							(0.008)	(0.008)	(0.008)	(0.008)	(0.009)	(0.008)	(0.008)
Firm has a quality certificate							0.208***	0.179***	0.123***	0.091***	0.054***	0.114***	0.103***
							(0.014)	(0.014)	(0.014)	(0.014)	(0.016)	(0.014)	(0.014)
Firm is exporting								0.271***	0.207***	0.167***	0.207***	0.191***	0.188***
								(0.018)	(0.019)	(0.019)	(0.021)	(0.019)	(0.019)
Log of net worth of the firm									0.194***			0.108***	0.186***
									(0.003)			(0.003)	(0.003)
Value added per worker										0.268***			
										(0.003)			
Log of profit											0.127***		
											(0.003)		
Output two years ago												0.223***	
												(0.003)	
Firm has a single owner													−0.218***
													(0.010)
Constant	−2.011***	−2.170***	−2.060***	−1.675***	−2.191***	−2.160***	−2.201***	−2.205***	−4.393***	−5.302***	−3.410***	−5.927***	−4.067***
	(0.003)	(0.033)	(0.033)	(0.034)	(0.035)	(0.035)	(0.035)	(0.035)	(0.047)	(0.049)	(0.046)	(0.045)	(0.049)
State effects	N	Y	Y	Y	Y	Y	Y	Y	Y	Y	Y	Y	Y
Industry effects	N	N	Y	Y	Y	Y	Y	Y	Y	Y	Y	Y	Y
Number of observations	1157961	1157959	1157959	1157959	1157959	1157959	1157959	1157959	1151271	1157959	814066	1151271	1151271
Pseudo R^2	0.002	0.10	0.11	0.11	0.15	0.15	0.16	0.16	0.16	0.17	0.16	0.17	0.17

Source: Authors' estimates based on Fourth All India Census of Micro, Small and Medium Enterprises (MSMEs), 2006–2007.

Table 6.11 Gender of the Manager Cum Owner and Access to Credit

Dependent Variable: Whether or Not Obtained Loan (Obtained = 1)

Variables	*(1)*	*(2)*	*(3)*	*(4)*	*(5)*	*(6)*	*(7)*	*(8)*	*(9)*	*(10)*	*(11)*	*(12)*	*(13)*
Female	−0.458***	−0.518***	−0.292***	−0.350***	−0.192***	−0.189***	−0.189***	−0.188***	−0.134***	−0.110***	−0.143***	−0.104***	−0.138***
	(0.011)	(0.012)	(0.013)	(0.013)	(0.013)	(0.013)	(0.013)	(0.013)	(0.013)	(0.013)	(0.015)	(0.013)	(0.013)
Age of the firm				−0.039***	−0.038***	−0.037***	−0.038***	−0.037***	−0.039***	−0.038***	−0.042***	−0.040***	−0.039***
				(0.001)	(0.001)	(0.001)	(0.001)	(0.001)	(0.001)	(0.001)	(0.001)	(0.001)	(0.001)
Age square				0.001***	0.001***	0.001***	0.001***	0.001***	0.001***	0.001***	0.001***	0.001***	0.001***
				(0.000)	(0.000)	(0.000)	(0.000)	(0.000)	(0.000)	(0.000)	(0.000)	(0.000)	(0.000)
Firm size					0.549***	0.556***	0.440***	0.433***	0.233***	0.379***	0.322***		0.218***
					(0.003)	(0.003)	(0.004)	(0.004)	(0.005)	(0.004)	(0.005)		(0.005)
Location						−0.149***	−0.210***	−0.210***	−0.268***	−0.295***	−0.267***	−0.305***	−0.267***
						(0.007)	(0.007)	(0.007)	(0.007)	(0.007)	(0.008)	(0.007)	(0.007)
Firm is part of a cluster						0.428***	0.389***	0.388***	0.412***	0.386***	0.409***	0.398***	0.419***
						(0.012)	(0.012)	(0.012)	(0.012)	(0.012)	(0.013)	(0.012)	(0.012)
Firm maintains an account							0.570***	0.572***	0.431***	0.373***	0.504***	0.386***	0.415***
							(0.008)	(0.008)	(0.008)	(0.008)	(0.009)	(0.008)	(0.008)
Firm has a quality certificate							0.208***	0.179***	0.123***	0.092***	0.055***	0.114***	0.103***
							(0.014)	(0.014)	(0.014)	(0.014)	(0.016)	(0.014)	(0.014)
Firm is exporting								0.270***	0.206***	0.167***	0.206***	0.190***	0.188***
								(0.018)	(0.019)	(0.019)	(0.021)	(0.019)	(0.019)
Log of net worth of the firm									0.194***			0.108***	0.185***
									(0.003)			(0.003)	(0.003)
Value added per worker										0.267***			
										(0.003)			
Log of profit											0.126***		
											(0.003)		
Output two years ago												0.223***	
												(0.003)	
Firm has a single owner													−0.218***
													(0.010)
Constant	−2.008***	−2.172***	−2.062***	−1.674***	−2.188***	−2.157***	−2.197***	−2.202***	−4.383***	−5.289***	−3.402***	−5.913***	−4.057***
	(0.003)	(0.033)	(0.033)	(0.034)	(0.035)	(0.035)	(0.035)	(0.035)	(0.047)	(0.049)	(0.046)	(0.045)	(0.049)
State effects	N	Y	Y	Y	Y	Y	Y	Y	Y	Y	Y	Y	Y
Industry effects	N	N	Y	Y	Y	Y	Y	Y	Y	Y	Y	Y	Y
Number of observations	1157961	1157959	1157959	1157959	1157959	1157959	1157959	1157959	1151271	1157959	814066	1151271	1151271
Pseudo R^2	0.002	0.10	0.11	0.11	0.15	0.15	0.16	0.16	0.16	0.17	0.16	0.17	0.17

Source: Authors' estimates based on Fourth All India Census of Micro, Small and Medium Enterprises (MSMEs), 2006–2007.

of firms is that larger firms in our dataset are less likely to rely on owners' funds to repay loan obligations. We also split the sample based on the source of credit, institutional or non-institutional, which we believe also captures the ability of the entrepreneur. The regression results based on source of loan, net worth and firm size are presented in Tables 6.12, 6.13 and 6.14, respectively. In the subsample analysis, our variable of interest, F, retains the same sign and significance thereby strengthening our earlier finding that the probability of obtaining a loan crucially depends on the gender of the entrepreneur. In other words, we find that a female entrepreneur in the MSME sector has a lower probability of obtaining a loan as compared to a male entrepreneur in the same sector.

Robustness tests

To validate our core results, we carry out three robustness checks.

Self-selection bias: bivariate probit regressions

Since applying for formal credit is voluntary, it is argued that owners self-select into the loan market (Blanchard et al., 2008). In the dataset, therefore, loan status indicating 0 may be due to the denial, discouragement and absence of the need for credit. This introduces a potential selection bias. Following Asiedu et al. (2012), we employ a bivariate probit model to correct for the selection bias. Results of our bivariate probit regression estimations after correcting for the self-section bias are reported in Table 6.15. The various test statistics show that the bivariate probit regressions work well for our estimations. The Wald test of independent equations rejects the null hypothesis (H0: $\rho = 0$), validating our model specification. The results are in line with our expectations. The coefficient of our variable of interest *female* is negative and significant, suggesting that the likelihood of receiving a bank loan is higher among male entrepreneurs as compared to female entrepreneurs. Other controls have maintained more or less the same sign and significance as the results for our baseline econometric specification. Our findings are thus essentially robust with regard to concerns arising from self-selection bias, and we are quite confident to conclude that there exists clear evidence to support the existence of gender-based discrimination in the credit market.

Modified Blinder-Oaxaca decomposition

In Table 6.16, we report the results of the modified version of the Blinder-Oaxaca decomposition technique to explain the gender gap in access to formal finance. As explained previously, we use the Fairlie (2006) method since our empirical specification is non-linear. The decomposition technique is a kind of

Table 6.12 Gender of the Owner and Access to Credit: Sample Split Based on Source of Finance

Dependent Variable: Whether or Not Obtained Loan (Obtained = 1)

	Institutional Loan						*Non-Institutional Loan*					
Variables	*(1)*	*(2)*	*(3)*	*(4)*	*(5)*	*(6)*	*(1)*	*(2)*	*(3)*	*(4)*	*(5)*	*(6)*
Female	−0.130***	−0.109***	−0.098***	−0.130***	−0.090***	−0.109***	−0.590***	−0.542***	−0.532***	−0.510***	−0.529***	−0.549***
	(0.011)	(0.011)	(0.011)	(0.012)	(0.011)	(0.011)	(0.035)	(0.035)	(0.035)	(0.040)	(0.035)	(0.035)
Age of the firm		−0.042***	−0.041***	−0.046***	−0.043***	−0.042***		−0.009***	−0.009***	−0.007***	−0.010***	−0.010***
		(0.001)	(0.001)	(0.001)	(0.001)	(0.001)		(0.002)	(0.002)	(0.003)	(0.002)	(0.002)
Age square		0.001***	0.001***	0.001***	0.001***	0.001***		0.001***	0.0001***	0.0001**	0.0002***	0.0002***
		(0.000)	(0.000)	(0.000)	(0.000)	(0.000)		(0.000)	(0.000)	(0.000)	(0.000)	(0.000)
Firm size		0.216***	0.338***	0.297***		0.209***		0.108***	0.202***	0.141***		0.075***
		(0.005)	(0.004)	(0.005)		(0.005)		(0.013)	(0.010)	(0.014)		(0.013)
Location		−0.275***	−0.295***	−0.287***	−0.306***	−0.274***		−0.059***	−0.076**	0.048**	−0.079***	−0.055***
		(0.007)	(0.008)	(0.009)	(0.008)	(0.008)		(0.021)	(0.021)	(0.024)	(0.021)	(0.021)
Firm is part of a cluster		0.459***	0.437***	0.472***	0.448***	0.462***		0.186***	0.167***	0.050	0.174***	0.197***
		(0.012)	(0.012)	(0.014)	(0.012)	(0.012)		(0.035)	(0.035)	(0.042)	(0.035)	(0.035)
Firm maintains an account		0.432***	0.387***	0.492***	0.402***	0.425***		0.230***	0.191***	0.305***	0.194***	0.191***
		(0.009)	(0.008)	(0.010)	(0.009)	(0.009)		(0.024)	(0.024)	(0.027)	(0.024)	(0.025)
Firm has a quality certificate		0.043***	0.018	−0.009	0.041***	0.033**		0.414***	0.388***	0.315***	0.397***	0.370***
		(0.015)	(0.015)	(0.017)	(0.015)	(0.015)		(0.035)	(0.035)	(0.040)	(0.035)	(0.035)
Firm is exporting		0.098***	0.066***	0.095***	0.093***	0.090***		0.157***	0.131***	0.139**	0.141***	0.125***
		(0.020)	(0.020)	(0.023)	(0.020)	(0.020)		(0.049)	(0.049)	(0.057)	(0.049)	(0.049)
Log of net worth of the firm		0.163***			0.099***	0.159***		0.125***			0.061***	0.107***
		(0.003)			(0.003)	(0.003)		(0.008)			(0.009)	(0.008)
Value added per worker			0.218***						0.175***			
			(0.003)						(0.008)			
Log of profit				0.101***						0.084***		
				(0.003)						(0.008)		
Output two years ago					0.184***						0.135***	
					(0.003)						(0.009)	
Firm has a single owner						−0.099***						−0.458***
						(0.011)						(0.028)
Constant	−2.136***	−4.007***	−4.699***	−3.110***	−5.348***	−3.859***	−5.191***	−6.876***	−7.489***	−6.307***	−7.690***	−6.187***
	(0.035)	(0.049)	(0.051)	(0.048)	(0.047)	(0.051)	(0.142)	(0.170)	(0.174)	(0.171)	(0.164)	(0.174)
State Effects	Y	Y	Y	Y	Y	Y	Y	Y	Y	Y	Y	Y
Industry Effects	Y	Y	Y	Y	Y	Y	Y	Y	Y	Y	Y	Y
Number of observations	1157959	1157959	1157959	814066	1151271	1151271	1156080	1149399	1156080	812356	1149399	1149399
Pseudo R^2	0.11	0.15	0.15	0.14	0.15	0.15	0.04	0.06	0.06	0.06	0.06	0.06

Source: Authors' estimates based on Fourth All India Census of Micro, Small and Medium Enterprises (MSMEs), 2006–2007.

Dependent Variable: Whether or Not Obtained Loan (Obtained = 1)

	Net Worth > Median						*Net Worth < Median*					
Variables	*(1)*	*(2)*	*(3)*	*(4)*	*(5)*	*(6)*	*(1)*	*(2)*	*(3)*	*(4)*	*(5)*	*(6)*
Female	−0.077***	−0.086***	−0.073***	−0.113***	−0.068***	−0.084***	−0.253***	−0.272***	−0.224***	−0.257***	−0.211***	−0.273***
	(0.012)	(0.013)	(0.013)	(0.014)	(0.013)	(0.013)	(0.017)	(0.018)	(0.018)	(0.021)	(0.018)	(0.018)
Age of the firm		−0.037***	−0.036***	−0.038***	−0.038***	−0.037***		−0.044***	−0.044***	−0.056***	−0.046***	−0.044***
		(0.001)	(0.001)	(0.001)	(0.001)	(0.001)		(0.002)	(0.002)	(0.002)	(0.002)	(0.002)
Age square		0.001***	0.001***	0.001***	0.001***	0.001***		0.001***	0.001***	0.001***	0.001***	0.001***
		(0.000)	(0.000)	(0.000)	(0.000)	(0.000)		(0.000)	(0.000)	(0.000)	(0.000)	(0.000)
Firm size		0.184***	0.306***	0.272***		0.168***		0.399***	0.500***	0.324***		0.397***
		(0.005)	(0.004)	(0.006)		(0.005)		(0.010)	(0.010)	(0.012)		(0.010)
Location		−0.305***	−0.332***	−0.320***	−0.337***	−0.304***		−0.247***	−0.309***	−0.287***	−0.298***	−0.248***
		(0.009)	(0.009)	(0.010)	(0.009)	(0.009)		(0.013)	(0.013)	(0.015)	(0.013)	(0.013)
Firm is part of a cluster		0.458***	0.432***	0.429***	0.443***	0.465***		0.242***	0.221***	0.322***	0.225***	0.242***
		(0.013)	(0.013)	(0.015)	(0.013)	(0.013)		(0.026)	(0.026)	(0.030)	(0.027)	(0.026)
Firm maintains an account		0.459***	0.385***	0.483***	0.414***	0.437***		0.261***	0.197***	0.264***	0.240***	0.257***
		(0.009)	(0.009)	(0.010)	(0.009)	(0.009)		(0.018)	(0.018)	(0.020)	(0.018)	(0.018)
Firm has a quality certificate		0.158***	0.144***	0.098***	0.156***	0.138***		0.004	−0.035	−0.054	−0.001	−0.0002
		(0.015)	(0.015)	(0.017)	(0.015)	(0.015)		(0.038)	(0.038)	(0.045)	(0.039)	(0.038)
Firm is exporting		0.320***	0.297***	0.321***	0.307***	0.304***		−0.426***	−0.408***	−0.326***	−0.403***	−0.428***
		(0.020)	(0.020)	(0.023)	(0.020)	(0.020)		(0.055)	(0.055)	(0.064)	(0.056)	(0.055)
Log of net worth of the firm		0.180***			0.097***	0.163***		0.085***			0.016**	0.085***
		(0.004)			(0.004)	(0.004)		(0.007)			(0.007)	(0.007)
Value added per worker			0.225***						0.286***			
			(0.003)						(0.007)			
Log of profit				0.098***						0.104***		
				(0.003)						(0.006)		
Output two years ago					0.183***						0.349***	
					(0.004)						(0.007)	
Firm has a single owner						0.168***						−0.103***
						(0.005)						(0.033)
Constant	−1.604***	−3.969***	−4.485***	−2.789***	−5.095***	−3.503***	−2.954***	−3.552***	−5.856***	−3.437***	−6.652***	−3.456***
	(0.039)	(0.061)	(0.059)	(0.054)	(0.057)	(0.065)	(0.070)	(0.105)	(0.108)	(0.098)	(0.117)	(0.110)
State Effects	Y	Y	Y	Y	Y	Y	Y	Y	Y	Y	Y	Y
Industry Effects	Y	Y	Y	Y	Y	Y	Y	Y	Y	Y	Y	Y
Number of observations	580050	580050	580050	429229	580050	580050	572766	570775	572766	381368	570775	570775
Pseudo R^2	0.10	0.15	0.15	0.14	0.15	0.15	0.11	0.13	0.13	0.12	0.13	0.13

Source: Authors' estimates based on Fourth All India Census of Micro, Small and Medium Enterprises (MSMEs), 2006–2007.

Table 6.14 Gender of the Owner and Access to Credit: Sample Split Based on Size of the Firm

Dependent Variable: Whether or Not Obtained Loan (Obtained = 1)

Variables	*Micro*			*Small*			*Medium*		
	Female as Owner	*Female as Manager*	*Female as Owner and Manager*	*Female as Owner*	*Female as Manager*	*Female as Owner and Manager*	*Female as Owner*	*Female as Manager*	*Female as Owner and Manager*
Female	−0.162***	−0.082***	−0.137***	−0.013	0.291***	0.349***	−0.326*	0.012	−0.015
	(0.011)	(0.013)	(0.014)	(0.032)	(0.047)	(0.059)	(0.011)	(0.290)	(0.445)
Age of the firm	−0.043***	−0.043***	−0.043***	−0.019***	−0.019***	−0.019***	−0.006	−0.006	−0.006
	(0.001)	(0.001)	(0.001)	(0.002)	(0.002)	(0.002)	(0.009)	(0.009)	(0.009)
Age square	0.001***	0.001***	0.001***	0.0002***	0.0002***	0.0002***	0.00001	0.00001	0.00001
	(0.000)	(0.000)	(0.000)	(0.000)	(0.000)	(0.000)	(0.0001)	(0.0001)	(0.0001)
Firm size	0.257***	0.256***	0.255***	0.101***	0.101***	0.101***	0.003	0.003	0.003
	(0.006)	(0.006)	(0.006)	(0.010)	(0.010)	(0.010)	(0.042)	(0.043)	(0.043)
Location	−0.278***	−0.279***	−0.279***	−0.346***	−0.345***	−0.345***	−0.036	−0.033	−0.033
	(0.008)	(0.008)	(0.008)	(0.019)	(0.019)	(0.019)	(0.098)	(0.098)	(0.098)
Firm is part of a cluster	0.462***	0.458***	0.458***	0.163***	0.164***	0.163***	−0.552***	−0.550***	−0.550***
	(0.014)	(0.014)	(0.014)	(0.026)	(0.026)	(0.026)	(0.145)	(0.145)	(0.145)
Firm maintains an account	0.329***	0.326***	0.327***	0.467***	0.470***	0.468***	0.782***	0.784***	0.784***
	(0.009)	(0.009)	(0.009)	(0.027)	(0.027)	(0.009)	(0.195)	(0.195)	(0.195)
Firm has a quality certificate	−0.034*	−0.035*	−0.035*	0.388***	0.385***	0.386***	0.282**	0.281**	0.280***
	(0.018)	(0.018)	(0.018)	(0.024)	(0.024)	(0.024)	(0.102)	(0.102)	(0.102)
Firm is exporting	0.003	−0.001	−0.001	0.407***	0.405***	0.405***	0.599***	0.594***	0.594***
	(0.027)	(0.027)	(0.027)	(0.030)	(0.030)	(0.030)	(0.115)	(0.115)	(0.115)
Log of net worth of the firm	0.204***	0.205***	0.204***	−0.030***	−0.028***	−0.028***	−0.001	0.001	0.001
	(0.003)	(0.003)	(0.003)	(0.007)	(0.007)	(0.007)	(0.035)	(0.035)	(0.035)
Firm has a single owner	−0.145***	−0.146***	−0.146***	−0.360***	−0.363***	−0.364***	−0.710***	−0.702***	−0.702***
	(0.013)	(0.013)	(0.013)	(0.018)	(0.018)	(0.017)	(0.103)	(0.103)	(0.103)
Constant	−4.409***	−4.447***	−4.435***	0.195	0.156	0.161	0.369	0.320	0.320
	(0.057)	(0.056)	(0.057)	(0.144)	(0.144)	(0.144)	(0.741)	(0.740)	(0.740)
State Effects	Y	Y	Y	Y	Y	Y	Y	Y	Y
Industry Effects	Y	Y	Y	Y	Y	Y	Y	Y	Y
Number of observations	1003820	1003820	1003820	139394	139394	139394	4890	4890	4890
Pseudo R^2	0.15	0.15	0.15	0.26	0.27	0.27	0.32	0.31	0.31

Table 6.15 Probit Model With Sample Selection

Variables	*Bivariate Probit Regression*		*Seemingly Unrelated Bivariate Probit Regression*	
	Coefficients	*Robust Standard Errors*	*Coefficients*	*Robust Standard Errors*
Outcome: Loan				
Female	-0.083***	0.005	-0.007***	0.001
Age of the firm	-0.019***	0.000	-0.001***	0.000
Age square	0.0002***	0.0000	0.00001***	0.00000
Firm size	0.127***	0.003	0.004	0.001
Firm has a single owner	-0.144***	0.006	0.002***	0.001
Location	-0.135***	0.004	-0.005***	0.001
Firm is part of a cluster	0.199***	0.006	-0.011***	0.002
Firm maintains an account	0.214***	0.004	0.008***	0.001
Firm has a quality certificate	0.074***	0.008	-0.005***	0.002
Firm is exporting	0.103***	0.010	0.003	0.002
Log of net worth of the firm	0.093***	0.001	0.007***	0.000
Constant	-2.207***	0.026	-1.316***	0.018
State effects?	Y		Y	
Industry effects?	Y		Y	
Selection: Credit Demand				
Female	-0.078***	0.005		
Age of the firm	-0.018***	0.000		
Age square	0.0002***	0.0000		
Firm size	0.126***	0.002		
Firm has a single owner	-0.147***	0.006		
Location	-0.133***	0.004		
Firm is part of a cluster	0.216***	0.006		
Firm maintains an account	0.211***	0.004		
Firm has a quality certificate	0.080***	0.008		
Firm is exporting	0.102***	0.010		
Log of net worth of the firm	0.089***	0.001		
Output growth			7.57E-09*	4.32E-09
Constant	-2.094***	0.025	-1.171***	0.017
Athrho	5.385***	0.070	4.880***	0.024
State Effects	Y		Y	
Industry effects	Y		Y	
Rho	0.999		0.999	
Wald test (Rho = 0): Chi^2 (1)	5904.58		40211.80	
Prob > Chi^2	0.0000		0.0000	
Number of observations	1151273		1151273	
Log pseudolikelihood	-384906.59		-406680.49	

Source: Authors' estimates based on Fourth All India Census of Micro, Small and Medium Enterprises (MSMEs), 2006–2007.

Table 6.16 Non-Linear Decomposition of Gender Discrimination in Access to Credit Using Modified Blinder-Oaxaca Decomposition Method

Gender Discrimination Due to Differences in Group Characteristics (by Variables) and Group Processes		*Contribution of Group Characteristics to Gender Inequality*	*Standard Error*	*95 percent CI*	*Percent Contribution of Group Differences to Gender Discrimination*
Age of the firm		–0.0126328***	0.000396	–0.013408–0.011858	–70.2
Age square		0.0061830***	0.000321	0.005554–0.006812	34.4
Firm size		0.0047012***	0.000098	0.004509–0.004894	26.1
Firm has a single owner		0.0008910***	0.000040	0.000812–0.000970	5.0
Location		–0.0024200***	0.000074	–0.002566–0.002274	–13.4
Firm is part of a cluster		–0.0008670***	0.000028	–0.000921–0.000813	–4.8
Firm maintains an account		0.0021692***	0.000054	0.002063–0.002276	12.1
Firm has a quality certificate		0.0000309***	0.000004	0.000024–0.000038	0.2
Firm is exporting		–0.0000307***	0.000003	–0.000037–0.000025	–0.2
Log of net worth of the firm		0.0056083***	0.000116	0.005382–0.005835	31.2
State effects?		Y			
Industry effects?		Y			
Contribution to gender discrimination explained by differences in group characteristics*	without industry and state dummies	0.004			20.2
	with industry and state dummies	0.002			11.11
Contribution to gender discrimination explained by differences in group processes		0.016			88.89
Total inequality		0.018			100
Observations		1151273			

Source: Authors' estimates based on Fourth All India Census of Micro, Small and Medium Enterprises (MSMEs), 2006–2007.

Note: *Total contribution from all variables including industry dummies and regional dummies. CI stands for confidence interval. Our results are robust to alternate measures of women ownership (women managers and women as owners and managers). Results are obtained using the Stata routine Fairlie (Jann, 2006).

matching where two groups are matched on a one-to-one basis. This decomposition technique helps in providing an answer to the extent to which differences in observable group characteristics can explain the gender gap in access to credit. The extent to which one may attribute the gender gap in credit access will depend on the choice of the reference group. The standard practice is to use the relatively more advantaged group as the reference (male-owned firms in our case) and show discrimination against the less advantaged female-led firms.

From the results of the decomposition, it is evident that the differences in observable group characteristics explain a small percentage (11.11 percent) while 88.89 percent is attributed to differences in group processes of the gender gap. While one may attribute the 88.89 percent indicating discrimination, caution might be exercised in interpreting this number solely to the discrimination aspect since our dataset is cross-sectional and the number of factors included in the analysis influences the interpretation of the decomposition estimates. All the estimates from the decomposition are statistically significant contributors to the part of the gender gap attributed to group characteristics. Within the component of the gender gap in credit gap access, group differences in size contributed 26.1 percent, differences in net worth contributed 31.2 percent and maintaining accounts contributed 12.1 percent.

Impact of credit and firm performance: propensity score matching

In order to further strengthen the results, we employ PSM to examine the effect of the credit access gap and firm performance by gender. We estimate three models treating (a) women as owners, (b) women as managers and (c) financially constrained firms (firms reporting shortage of financial capital). We use a logit model to estimate the propensity score and bootstrap the standard errors with 100 replications. Table 6.17 reports the obtained results using a kernel matching estimator. The set of covariates remain the same as in the other models that we have estimated so far. We used three indicators of firm performance: labour productivity (output per worker), value added per worker and profitability. We observe that in terms of the all of the outcome variables, women as owners/managers increase the outcome significantly; for example, the profitability increases by 10.8 (28.7) percentage points when women are owners (managers).

The productivity is lower by 8.3 percentage points and profitability is lower by 28.5 percentage points for credit-constrained micro enterprises compared to unconstrained firms. We provide our results based on the disaggregation based on the gender of the owner. In terms of output per worker and value added per worker, credit constraints are more pronounced. Among the female-owned

Table 6.17 Results From the Propensity Score Matching (PSM) Estimates

Outcome Variable	*Coefficient*	*Standard Error*	*p-Value*
	Women as Owners		
Log of Labour Productivity	0.251	0.007	0.000
Log of Gross Value Added (GVA)	0.186	0.006	0.000
Log of Profit	0.108	0.009	0.000
	Women as Managers		
Log of Labour Productivity	0.452	0.015	0.000
Log of GVA	0.370	0.018	0.000
Log of Profit	0.287	0.023	0.000
	Financially Constrained Firms		
Log of Labour Productivity	−0.083	0.007	0.000
Log of GVA	−0.079	0.006	0.000
Log of Profit	−0.285	0.012	0.000

Source: Authors' estimates based on Fourth All India Census of Micro, Small and Medium Enterprises (MSMEs), 2006–2007.

firms which are credit constrained, the difference in output per worker and value added per worker is lower even further. We end this with the comment that female owners/managers actually enhance productivity but the financial constraint impedes the performance of the micro enterprises in India.

Conclusion

This chapter presents new evidence on whether the gender of the owner influences firm performance and credit access from institutional sources. Our findings are broadly in line with the previous studies on women entrepreneurship in developed and emerging economies. In the first part of the empirical analysis, we attempt to measure the gender gaps in performance in terms of output, employment, labour productivity and TFP. We observe significant differences in the performance gap between male- and female-owned enterprises even after controlling for size, age and industry and state differences. We also observe that there is a concentration of women enterprises in a few sectors which are typically considered "feminine occupations". Taking this into account, we test whether the performance differential arises due to the concentration of women enterprises in certain sectors. We find that female-run firms operating in female-dominant sectors are significantly smaller and less efficient than those that operate in male-dominated sectors, thereby suggesting that the partial explanation for the underperformance of female entrepreneurs can be derived from the concentration story. However, the large and significant difference in the performance of male-owned and female-owned firms, and their size, even after controlling for the choice of the sector of operation shows that the concentration story does not seem to explain fully the underperformance of firms owned by women entrepreneurs.

As several studies have highlighted the severe impediments that women-owned firms face in obtaining credit, we investigate whether significant gender discrimination exists against women entrepreneurs for formal credit in the small-firm credit market. Our econometric exercise points out unambiguously that irrespective of the extent of women's involvement in the firms, women-led businesses are less likely to obtain formal finance. Various robustness tests that we undertook support the existence of gender-based discrimination in the credit market. The findings are thus consistent with the fact that women-owned firms are disadvantaged in the market for small-business credit, which would be traditionally attributed to discrimination, and any attempt to bridge the gender gap in performance should focus on addressing the gender discrimination in the small-business credit market.

Notes

1 The total early-stage entrepreneurial activity (defined as the percentage of either nascent entrepreneurs or owner-managers of new businesses in the 18–64 age group of the population) in India has remained stagnant – 10.09% in 2006 and 9.88% in 2013 – whereas the ratio of female to male in the same category has declined from 0.79 in 2006 to 0.49 in 2013 (source: http://gemconsortium.org/data/key-aps).

2 Numerous studies have confirmed the role of the availability of capital in promoting the growth of small firms (Banerjee and Duflo, 2010; De Mel et al., 2009).

3 The decomposition was implemented with the "fairlie" package provided by Jann (2008) for Stata.

4 Exclusion restriction means a variable that affects the selection equation but does not affect the outcome equation (Cameron and Trivedi, 2009). Those variables should be correlated with the firm's demand for credit. However, those variables should not be correlated with the firm's loan status.

5 The weighting scheme is based on the inverse probability regression (Robins et al., 2000; Brunell and Dinardo, 2004).

6 The only exception is with respect to output growth where the coefficient is negative but not significant.

7 It needs to be stated that the relatively lesser age of firms owned by females may be a result of underperformance of women entrepreneurs, as we observed in this chapter. If the survival rate of women-owned firms are lower than that of male-owned firms, it is very much possible that the female-owned firms are on average younger than male-owned firms. Our data does not permit us to examine this hypothesis; however, it is safer to assume that younger firms are on average less experienced than older firms (Bardasi et al., 2011).

8 In India, almost 98 percent of women-owned firms are micro enterprises, and approximately 90 percent of women-owned enterprises are in the informal sector (International Finance Corporation, 2017).

9 Our computations show that the index of concentration is greater than one for men in many sectors.

7

CASTE, FINANCE AND FIRM PERFORMANCE

Introduction

In the context of India, social group affiliation (caste) deeply influences economic outcomes. Previous studies have shown that caste is an important factor affecting the availability of inputs like capital and labour (Banerjee and Munshi, 2004). Among India's socially disadvantaged groups, SCs and STs remain socially excluded from the mainstream due to the persistence of caste and other forms of social discrimination and are much more likely to face barriers to access to credit and human capital acquisition (Raj and Sen, 2015). Though there exists some evidence and debate on the issue of whether entrepreneurs from socially disadvantaged groups face discrimination in accessing formal credit (Jodhka, 2010), a serious and much deeper examination on the role of caste in determining access to formal credit in the small-business credit markets using nationally representative data is lacking.

Of the existing studies on the role of caste in determining access to credit, Kumar's (2013, 2016) approach is closest to the question we are addressing in this chapter. The results of these studies provide empirical evidence in support of discrimination by cooperative banks against lower caste communities in the case of agricultural credit. Another study which is of interest in the present context is Sarap (1990), who reports that farmers belonging to lower castes face barriers in access to formal credit institutions. Based on a survey of SC/ST businesses in six states, Prakash (2010) finds difficulty in obtaining institutional credit by SC/ST entrepreneurs. Due to their lower social status and capital unavailability, SC/ST-owned firms operate on a small scale. Deshpande and Sharma (2016) argue that

> *businesses owned by low-caste owners, face discrimination at the hands of customers, suppliers and lenders, since their caste status is easily identifiable and salient, unlike in large businesses with complex ownership and management structures, where observing the caste of the owners might be less straightforward.*
>
> (p. 326)

On the whole, these studies suggest that socially disadvantaged groups face constraints in entering and running businesses and in obtaining credit from institutional sources.

As evident from the review of literature discussed in detail in Chapter 2, existing studies focusing on caste affiliation and access to formal credit in India are mostly confined to the farm sector. There is a dearth of studies which analyse the role of caste in influencing institutional credit in the context of the industrial sector in India, with specific focus on MSMEs. Therefore, unlike the prior studies, the novelty of this chapter is our focus on firms spanning the entire spectrum of the Indian MSME sector. Given that the major chunk of firms in India are small in size and a significant share of the socially disadvantaged population in India is dependent on these firms for their livelihood, probing the potential interaction between caste affiliation and credit access has serious implications for the larger policy agenda of reducing poverty and achieving financial inclusion. Further, since small businesses already face significant barriers in accessing formal credit, the existence of caste discrimination in the small-business credit market can be doubly disadvantageous to the firms owned by those belonging to socially disadvantaged categories. Therefore, in this chapter, we examine the question of the prevalence of caste discrimination in the credit market for small businesses, which in turn can aid in suggesting suitable policy measures to improve access to institutional credit for small business owners, especially those belonging to socially disadvantaged categories.

The rest of the chapter has the following structure. In the second section, we present the summary statistics for the whole sample and for the sample of SC/ST and non-SC/ST firms separately. The third section discusses the econometric methods employed for the empirical analysis. We present the results of our empirical analysis in the fourth section. The last section is the conclusion.

Descriptive statistics

As already mentioned, we employ unit-level data from the Fourth round of the Indian MSMEs Census data.[1] For the empirical analysis in this chapter, the dependent variable is the loan status, i.e. whether a firm has taken a loan or not. Our main variable of interest is the social group affiliation of the owner, whether the owner belongs to a disadvantaged background or not (in our case SC/ST). In our dataset, about 11 percent of enterprises are owned by those belonging to SC and ST communities. Variables on firm characteristics include firm size, age, location (rural or urban), whether it is part of a cluster, whether it maintains an account, whether it possesses a quality certificate, whether it is an exporting firm and whether it is a single-owner firm, in addition to the variables that control for its size and performance such as profit, net worth of the firm and labour productivity. The description of main variables (both dependent and independent variables) used in the empirical analysis are provided in Table 7A.1 in Appendix I.

Table 7.1 Mean and Standard Deviations (SDs) of the Variables by Social Group Affiliation of the Owner

Variable	*All Firms*		*Scheduled Caste Scheduled Tribe (SC/ST) Firms*		*Non-SC/ST Firms*	
	Mean	*Standard Deviation (SD)*	*Mean*	*SD*	*Mean*	*SD*
Proportion of owners with loan	0.11	0.32	0.10	0.30	0.12	0.32
Firm size	1.04	0.22	1.01	0.15	1.05	0.23
Firm age	12.73	8.90	11.89	8.48	12.83	8.94
Loan amount (in Rs)	2524703	30500000	1355706	13000000	2648882	31800000
Proportion of firms that maintain an account	0.31	0.46	0.17	0.38	0.33	0.47
Proportion of urban firms	0.53	0.50	0.35	0.48	0.55	0.50
Proportion of firms that are part of a cluster	0.08	0.26	0.06	0.24	0.08	0.27
Proportion of firms with quality certificate	0.04	0.19	0.04	0.19	0.04	0.19
Proportion of exporting firms	0.03	0.18	0.02	0.14	0.03	0.18
Proportion of single-owner firms	0.91	0.29	0.95	0.22	0.91	0.29
Profit (in lakhs)	12.12	392.57	7.86	434.26	12.58	387.97
Net worth (in lakhs)	22.09	464.98	11.23	333.78	23.36	478.01
Labour productivity (in lakhs)	3.04	110.14	2.06	120.67	3.15	108.88

Source: Authors' estimates based on the Micro, Small and Medium Enterprise (MSME) dataset.

Table 7.1 presents the summary statistics for the whole sample and for the sample of SC/ST and non-SC/ST firms separately.[2] It is clearly evident from the table that there exist considerable differences in firm characteristics between SC/ST firms and non-SC/ST firms. Compared to the non-SC/ST firms, a lesser proportion of SC/ST firms have received credit through formal sources. They are younger and smaller in size as compared to non-SC/ST firms. A much smaller number of SC/ST firms maintained accounts, and they are mostly located in rural areas. In terms of performance too the non-SC/ST firms fared much better than SC/ST firms, as is evident from the

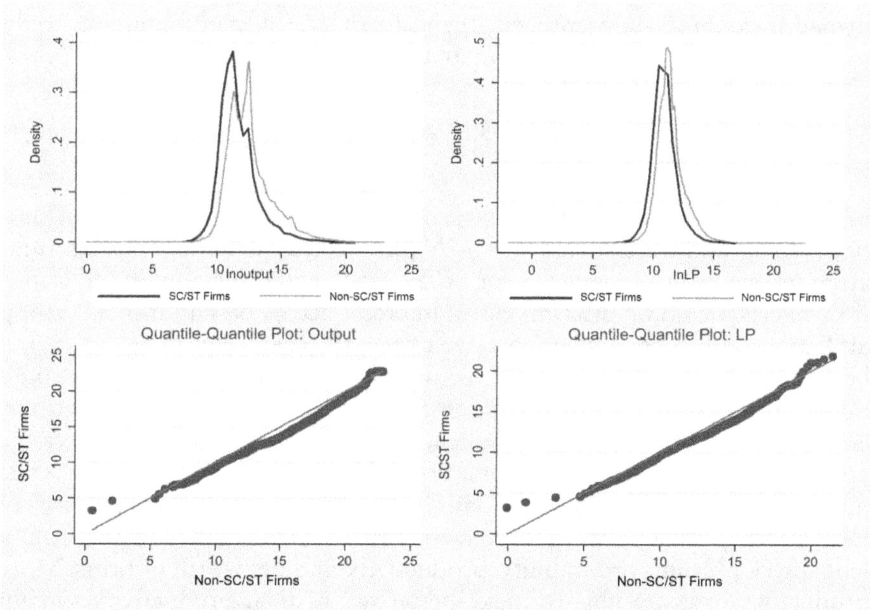

Figure 7.1 Social Group Affiliation of the Firm Owner and Firm Performance

Source: Authors' estimates based on the Micro, Small and Medium Enterprises (MSME) dataset.

Note: Figures in the upper panel present the size (output) and productivity (LP) distribution of firms, depending on whether the firm is an SC/ST firm or not. Epanechnikov kernel. Figures in the lower panel show the distribution of size and productivity for SC/ST firms in comparison with non-SC/ST firms.

productivity and profitability indicators. This difference in performance is also clearly evident from Figure 7.1 which displays the kernel density distribution of logged values of output and labour productivity for SC/ST and non-SC/ST firms (upper panel of Figure 7.1). The distribution of output and labour productivity of non-SC/ST firms lies distinctly to the right of the SC/ST firms. The lower panel also clearly shows that firms with SC/ST owners are smaller in size and less productive as compared to firms owned by non-SC/STs.

Baseline model

In order to investigate the relationship between the social group affiliation of entrepreneurs and their access to a financing channel (loan), we model the probability with which a firm owned by certain social groups, such as SC and ST, obtain a loan by employing a probit model. We fit to the data several specifications of the probit model to analyse the probability of a firm owned by an SC/ST entrepreneur (henceforth, *SC/ST* firm) obtaining credit from formal institutions. We estimate the following binary probit model:

$$\Pr(y_i = 1 | \text{a set of covariates}) = \Phi\left(\alpha_0 + \alpha_1 SCST_i + \sum_{p>1} \alpha_p Z_i + \delta_i + \mu_s + \varepsilon_i\right) \quad (7.1)$$

where y_i is the probability that firm has access to a formal credit (institutional loan) and we assume that $\varepsilon_i \sim N[0, 1]$. *SC/ST* denotes the caste affiliation of the business owner (1 for SC/ST firms and 0 for non-SC/ST firms). If obstacles including discrimination in credit access based on social group affiliation of the firm owner exist, we expect the coefficient of *SC/ST* (α_1) to be negative and significant. Z is a vector of firm-specific attributes that could influence the likelihood of obtaining a loan. These firm-specific characteristics are also important from the lender's point of view as they reflect the creditworthiness and resources of a firm that the lender may consider while making the decision to grant a loan. In particular, vector Z contains three measures capturing how well the firm is run, which is a key factor from a lender's view point: profitability, productivity and net worth of firms. More productive firms are able to make better use of their productivity to gain external finance than their respective counterparts (Chen, 2013). It is also argued that highly profitable firms are more likely to obtain external finance due to their lower level of debt. Bigsten et al. (2003) tested this proposition and reported that greater profits are associated with greater access to credit. In addition, the lender's decision to grant a loan crucially depends on the associated risk and the ability of a firm to secure its debt. Our dataset, however, does not capture them directly, and hence we proxy them with a number of variables. The financial literacy and ability of the entrepreneur is captured using two indicators: *acmaint* and *qualitycert*. *Acmaint* is a binary variable for account maintenance by firms which takes the value 1 for firms that maintain an account and 0 for those that do not. As argued by Stiglitz and Weiss (1981), maintenance of financial accounts is an indicator of better financial performance of small firms and is also an instrument for lenders to distinguish them from bad borrowers. According to Sacerdoti (2005), the availability of financial information about the firm reduces the risk of the lenders and increases the reputation of the borrower. *Qualitycert* is another binary variable for the possession of a quality certificate by firms. Recent studies report the increasing adoption of quality certification issued by an international standards organization as the signal of a potential high quality firm to the lender that reduces its financial constraints (Minard, 2016). To control for the possible effects of participating in networks, which may help in easing the financial constraints, we use a variable *cluster*. *Cluster* is a binary variable for firm's participation in a cluster. There is enough evidence to show that network participation helps firms in gaining credible information on training opportunities and access to new markets (Muravyev et al., 2009). According to Verheul and Thurik (2001), networking helps in lowering barriers associated with obtaining bank loans.

Consistent with earlier studies, we include a measure of export opportunities (*export*) in vector *Z*. *Export* is a binary variable for firms that export. We also include a measure of ownership (*ownership*), age of the firm (*age*), age squared (*age2*), size of the firm (*size*) and location of the firm (*location*). Bigger and older firms tend to enjoy better reputations, credit histories and longer sustained relationships with formal credit institutions than small and younger ones (Muravyev et al., 2009). *Location* is a dummy for firms that are located in rural areas and is expected to control for the environment in which these firms operate.[3] δ is the random error term. While estimating the model, we also control for industry- and region-specific influences by introducing industry (δ_i) and state-level dummies (μ_s). The model is estimated using the maximum likelihood function.

Results

Caste affiliation of the firm owner and access to formal credit: baseline results

Table 7.2a and Table 7.2b present the probit regression results for the model described in equation 7.1 for the entire sample of firms. We report the coefficients for a number of specifications in Table 7.2a and the marginal effects estimated around mean points in Table 7.2b.[4] Following the standard procedure based on the previous studies, we carry out the empirical verification by introducing the social group affiliation variable initially. Then we add, step-by-step, a set of control variables. We also control for regional and sectoral effects in all specifications, except for the first specification in Tables 7.2a and 7.2b. The coefficient of variable *SC/ST*, which is our main variable of interest, is negative and significant at the 1 percent level across all specifications. Controlling for firm performance and other firm characteristics representing creditworthiness, this result is consistent with the hypothesis that SC/ST-managed firms have a lower propensity to receive a loan. In particular, SC/ST-managed businesses appear to have about 1 to 2 percent lower probability of obtaining a needed loan as compared to businesses run by non-SC/ST entrepreneurs. This is a fairly large number, considering the smaller proportion of firms that receive loans in the MSME sector, and it points to the presence of substantial caste-related differences in securing formal credit.

Estimation results also indicate that large firms are likely to have lower credit constraints. This result is in line with Gertler and Gilchrist (1994) and Muravyev et al. (2009) who show that small firms face greater financial difficulties in obtaining credit from formal financial institutions than

Table 7.2a Probit Model Estimations

Variables	*(1)*	*(2)*	*(3)*	*(4)*	*(5)*	*(6)*	*(7)*	*(8)*	*(9)*	*(10)*	*(11)*	*(12)*
Scheduled Caste Scheduled Tribe (SC/ST)	−0.173*** (0.010)	−0.248*** (0.011)	−0.180*** (0.011)	−0.196*** (0.011)	−0.166*** (0.011)	−0.167*** (0.011)	−0.077*** (0.011)	−0.076*** (0.011)	−0.082*** (0.012)	−0.073*** (0.012)	−0.075*** (0.011)	−0.076*** (0.011)
Age				−0.038*** (0.001)	−0.038*** (0.001)	−0.038*** (0.001)	−0.038*** (0.001)	−0.038*** (0.001)	−0.040*** (0.001)	−0.040*** (0.001)	−0.038*** (0.001)	−0.038*** (0.001)
Age squared				0.001*** (0.000)	0.001*** (0.000)	0.001*** (0.000)	0.001*** (0.000)	0.001*** (0.000)	0.001*** (0.000)	0.001*** (0.000)	0.001*** (0.000)	0.001*** (0.000)
Firm size					1.082*** (0.012)	1.076*** (0.012)	0.721*** (0.012)	0.692*** (0.012)	0.681*** (0.013)	0.509*** (0.013)	0.684*** (0.013)	0.691*** (0.012)
Location						−0.030*** (0.007)	−0.155*** (0.007)	−0.158*** (0.007)	−0.163*** (0.007)	−0.171*** (0.007)	−0.158*** (0.007)	−0.158*** (0.007)
Firm is part of a cluster						0.447*** (0.012)	0.377*** (0.012)	0.376*** (0.012)	0.378*** (0.012)	0.398*** (0.012)	0.379*** (0.012)	0.376*** (0.012)
Firm maintains an account							0.875*** (0.007)	0.873*** (0.007)	0.852*** (0.008)	0.769*** (0.008)	0.874*** (0.007)	0.872*** (0.007)
Firm has a quality certificate							0.357*** (0.013)	0.306*** (0.014)	0.293*** (0.014)	0.231*** (0.014)	0.303*** (0.014)	0.306*** (0.014)
Firm is exporting								0.462*** (0.018)	0.473*** (0.018)	0.410*** (0.019)	0.461*** (0.018)	0.462*** (0.018)
Log of profit									0.00001*** (0.00000)	0.00001 (0.00000)		
Firm has a single owner										−0.530*** (0.010)		
Log of net worth of the firm											0.00002*** (0.00000)	
Value added per worker												0.0001*** (0.0000)
Constant	−2.029*** (0.003)	−2.161*** (0.033)	−2.053*** (0.033)	−1.677*** (0.034)	−2.810*** (0.037)	−2.802*** (0.037)	−2.659*** (0.037)	−2.646*** (0.037)	−2.577*** (0.038)	−1.881*** (0.040)	−2.637*** (0.037)	−2.645*** (0.037)
State Effects	N	Y	Y	Y	Y	Y	Y	Y	Y	Y	Y	Y
Industry Effects	N	N	Y	Y	Y	Y	Y	Y	Y	Y	Y	Y
Number of observations	1157296	1157294	1157294	1157294	1154536	1154536	1154536	1154536	1048224	1048224	1149881	1154536
Pseudo R^2	0.0004	0.10	0.11	0.11	0.12	0.12	0.14	0.14	0.15	0.15	0.15	0.14

Source: Authors' estimates based on the Micro, Small and Medium Enterprise (MSME) dataset.

Note: Figures in parentheses are robust standard errors. *** and ** indicate significance at 1 percent and 5 percent levels, respectively.

Table 7.2b Probit Model Estimations (Marginal Effects)

Dependent Variable: Whether or Not Obtained Loan (Obtained = 1)

Variables	*(1)*	*(2)*	*(3)*	*(4)*	*(5)*	*(6)*	*(7)*	*(8)*	*(9)*	*(10)*	*(11)*
Scheduled Caste Scheduled Tribe (SC/ST)	–0.017*** (0.001)	–0.014*** (0.001)	–0.015*** (0.001)	–0.012*** (0.001)	–0.012*** (0.001)	–0.005*** (0.001)	–0.005*** (0.001)	–0.005*** (0.001)	–0.005*** (0.001)	–0.005*** (0.001)	–0.005*** (0.001)
Age			–0.003*** (0.000)	–0.003*** (0.000)	–0.003*** (0.0000)	–0.003*** (0.0001)	–0.003*** (0.0001)	–0.003*** (0.001)	–0.003*** (0.0001)	–0.003*** (0.0001)	–0.003*** (0.0001)
Age2			0.00004*** (0.0000)	0.00004*** (0.0000)	0.00004*** (0.0000)	0.00004*** (0.000)	0.00004*** (0.000)	0.00004*** (0.000)	0.00004*** (0.000)	0.00004*** (0.000)	0.00004*** (0.000)
Size				0.092*** (0.001)	0.090*** (0.001)	0.058*** (0.001)	0.055*** (0.001)	0.055*** (0.001)	0.041*** (0.001)	0.054*** (0.001)	0.055*** (0.001)
Location					–0.001** (0.001)	–0.011*** (0.001)	–0.012*** (0.001)	–0.012*** (0.001)	–0.013*** (0.001)	–0.012*** (0.001)	–0.012*** (0.001)
Cluster					0.034*** (0.001)	0.026*** (0.001)	0.027*** (0.001)	0.027*** (0.001)	0.029*** (0.001)	0.027*** (0.001)	0.027*** (0.001)
Acmaint						0.071*** (0.001)	0.071*** (0.001)	0.071*** (0.001)	0.063*** (0.001)	0.071*** (0.001)	0.071*** (0.001)
Qualitycert						0.032*** (0.001)	0.027*** (0.001)	0.027*** (0.001)	0.021*** (0.001)	0.027*** (0.001)	0.027*** (0.001)
Export							0.039*** (0.001)	0.041*** (0.002)	0.035*** (0.002)	0.039*** (0.001)	0.039*** (0.001)
Profitability								1.49e-6*** (0.000)	8.92e-7* (0.000)		
Ownership									–0.048*** (0.001)		
Net Worth										2.36e-06*** (0.000)	
Productivity											6.71e-06*** (0. 000)

Source: Authors' estimates based on the Micro, Small and Medium Enterprise (MSME) dataset.

Note: Figures in parentheses are robust standard errors. *** and ** indicate significance at 1 percent and 5 percent levels, respectively.

large firms. Results also show that the location of firms is of significant importance in determining access to credit. According to our findings, rural firms experience larger credit constraints as compared to urban firms. Our estimates also point to the larger difficulties faced by firms with a single owner in obtaining credit from formal institutions as compared to firms with multiple owners (Beck et al., 2005). Exporting firms and firms located in a cluster have a higher probability of loan approval, implying that lenders consider it less risky to lend to those firms that market their product abroad and are part of a larger network. Consistent with our prior expectations, we also find that ability and financial literacy of entrepreneurs matters a lot in eliciting a positive response from an institutional lender. Our proxies for ability and financial literacy (account maintenance and possessing a quality certificate) have yielded positive coefficients signifying the fact that lenders' satisfaction on entrepreneurial abilities increases the likelihood of loan approval.[5] There is also a clear direction from our results that the probability of obtaining a loan is significantly higher among well-run firms, as the coefficients of profit, productivity and net worth are positive and significant across all our specifications.[6]

Robustness checks

To check the sensitivity of our main findings, we conducted a battery of robustness checks.

Self-selection bias: bivariate probit regressions

Studies by Blanchard et al. (2008) and Asiedu et al. (2012) highlight that results of the studies analysing the role of ethnicity and race on access to finance are likely to suffer from potential biases due to selection bias. It is likely that firms' very often self-select not to apply for a loan (Bardasi et al., 2011). This situation may arise mainly due to: (a) The absence of need of external finance; and (b) The fear of rejection of application. In our dataset, what we observe is a set of firms who have self-selected to receive formal finance.[7] Hence, our estimates based on the binary probit model may suffer from selection bias, and it is essential to correct for its likely influence on our baseline results.

Our empirical strategy to overcome the self-selection problem involves identifying firms as "constrained" and "unconstrained" with credit demand (Bigsten et al., 2003). We classify sample firms as "constrained" if they reported a shortage of capital and as "unconstrained" if they obtained a loan and did not report a capital shortage. To address the selection issue, we employ a two-step Heckman probit (Van de Ven and Van Praag, 1981) procedure analogous to the Heckman (1979) approach. This approach requires an exclusion restriction for identification purposes. Following Cameron and Trivedi (2009) and Presbitero and Rabellotti (2016), we use the growth of the annual output (Output Growth) for the purpose of exclusion restrictions and to improve identification. This variable is expected to influence the demand for credit but not the final outcome, actual loan access. We believe that the annual change in output is expected to influence the demand for credit, being a proxy for the firm's level of economic activity (Presbitero and Rabellotti, 2016).[8] This approach is implemented using two different models: a bivariate probit model and a seemingly unrelated bivariate probit regression model. While we assume that the same set of variables is likely to influence the dependent variable (actual loan access and credit demand) in both the stages in the bivariate probit model, the exclusion restriction is introduced in the seemingly unrelated bivariate probit regression model. More technical details on the method are presented in Appendix II.

Results of both estimations are presented in Table 7.3.[9] The various test statistics reported in the table are in line with our expectations. The Wald test of independent equations rejects the null hypothesis (H0; $\rho = 0$), thereby validating our model specification. It is clearly evident from Table 7.3 that the coefficient of *SC/ST* maintains the same sign and significance in both models, suggesting that the likelihood of receiving a bank loan is significantly higher among non-SC/ST entrepreneurs as compared to SC/ST entrepreneurs. Other controls have maintained more or less the same sign and significance as the results for our univariate probit specification. Our findings are thus essentially robust to concerns arising from self-selection bias, and these results unequivocally highlight the importance of caste affiliation of the firm owner in influencing the lender's decision to approve a loan application.

In addition, as an additional robustness check, we also employ a recently developed methodology to deal with situations in the absence of IVs in the dataset or the presence of weak instruments (Lewbel, 2012). In this chapter, we implement this method to ensure robustness of our baseline results since we suspect some of our controls like profits, net worth and labour productivity may be endogenous. In this approach, identification is achieved through the assumption that exogenous regressors are uncorrelated with the product of heteroskedastic errors. Since we do not have external multiple instruments to deal with this issue, we rely on the Lewbel's (2012) two-staged least squares (2SLS) method of constructing additional instruments from each of the exogenous regressors in the model.[10] Table 7.4 presents the results for three different specifications. Our results turn out to be insensitive to the possible endogeneity bias and they confirm our findings are qualitatively similar to the baseline estimations.

Table 7.3 Probit Models With Sample Selection

Variables	*Bivariate Probit Regression*			*Seemingly Unrelated Bivariate Probit Regression*		
	Coefficients	*Robust Standard Errors*	*Marginal Effects*	*Coefficients*	*Robust Standard Effects*	*Marginal Effects*
			Outcome: Loan			
Scheduled Caste Scheduled Tribe (SC/ST)	−0.049***	0.005	−0.009 (0.001)	−0.003**	0.001	−0.0006 (0.0003)
Age	−0.016***	0.0004	−0.003 (0.0001)	−0.001***	0.000	−0.0003 (0.00002)
Age2	0.0003***	8.41e-06	0.00005 (1.61e-06)	0.00002***	1.97e-06	2.88e-06 (3.78e-07)
Size	0.211***	0.007	0.039 (0.001)	0.016***	0.001	0.003 (0.0002)
Location	−0.301***	0.003	−0.055 (0.001)	−0.005***	0.001	−0.001 (0.0001)
Cluster	0.079***	0.006	0.014 (0.001)	−0.016***	0.001	−0.003 (0.0003)
Acmaint	0.504***	0.004	0.092 (0.001)	0.026***	0.001	0.005 (0.0002)
Qualitycert	0.272***	0.007	0.050 (0.001)	−0.001	0.001	−0.0001 (0.0003)
Export	0.041***	0.008	0.007 (0.002)	0.007***	0.002	0.001 (0.0003)
Net Worth	0.00004***	4.85e-06	6.82e-06 (8.91e-07)	5.89e-07	5.24e-07	1.13e-07 (1.00e-07)
Constant	−1.350***	0.008		−1.218***	0.002	
State Effects	Y			Y		
Industry Effects	Y			Y		

			Selection: Credit Demand			
Scheduled Caste Scheduled Tribe (SC/ST)	–0.047***	0.005	–0.005 (0.002)			
Age	–0.015***	0.0004	–0.003 (0.0002)			
Age2	0.0003***	8.20e-06	0.00003 (3.83e-06)			
Size	0.197***	0.006	0.029 (0.002)			
Location	–0.299***	0.003	–0.011 (0.001)			
Cluster	0.098***	0.006	–0.029 (0.003)			
Acmaint	0.484***	0.003	0.046 (0.001)			
Qualitycert	0.276***	0.007	0.0009 (0.002)			
Export	0.034***	0.008	0.011 (0.003)			
Net Worth	0.00004***	4.86e-06	1.45e-06 (4.27e-07)			
Output Growth				2.83e-09	2.82e-09	4.73e-12 (5.12e-12)
Constant	–1.306***	0.007		–1.171***	0.015	
Athrho	5.908***	0.141		5.437***	0.055	
State Effects	Y			Y		
Industry Effects	Y			Y		
Rho	0.99			0.99		
Wald Test (Rho = 0): Chi^2 (1)	1759.58			9670.54		
Prob > Chi^2	0.0000			0.0000		
Number of Observations	1149883			1149883		
Log Pseudolikelihood	–435830.09			–453230.41		

Source: Authors' estimates based on the Micro, Small and Medium Enterprise (MSME) dataset.

Note: *** and ** indicate significance at 1 percent and 5 percent levels, respectively. Figures in the parentheses are robust standard errors.

Table 7.4 Instrumental Variable (IV) Estimation: Lewbel Method

Variables	*(1)*	*(2)*	*(3)*
Scheduled Caste Scheduled tribe (SC/ST)	-0.013***	-0.009***	-0.012***
	(0.001)	(0.001)	(0.001)
Age	-0.004***	-0.004***	-0.004***
	(8.51e-05)	(8.01e-05)	(8.00e-05)
Age2	5.42e-05***	5.05e-05***	5.03e-05***
	(1.96e-06)	(1.86e-06)	(1.86e-06)
Size	0.079***	0.077***	0.081***
	(0.002)	(0.002)	(0.002)
Location	-0.015***	-0.017***	-0.014***
	(0.00)	(0.001)	(0.001)
Cluster	0.023***	0.023***	0.022***
	(0.001)	(0.001)	(0.001)
Acmaint	0.086***	0.080***	0.087***
	(0.001)	(0.001)	(0.001)
Qualitycert	0.046***	0.046***	0.046***
	(0.002)	(0.002)	(0.002)
Export	0.058***	0.056***	0.058***
	(0.002)	(0.002)	(0.002)
Profitability	2.24e-06*		
	(1.24e-06)		
Net Worth		0.023***	
		(0.002)	
Productivity			6.84e-06*
			(3.97e-06)
Constant	0.117***	0.103***	0.114***
	(0.0003)	(0.001)	(0.0002)
State effects	Y	Y	Y
Industry effects	Y	Y	Y
Observations	1048226	1149883	1154538
R-Squared (Centred)	0.103	0.103	0.099
R-Squared (Uncentred)	0.209	0.206	0.202

Source: Authors' estimates.

Note: Robust standard errors in parentheses. *** $p < 0.01$, ** $p < 0.05$, * $p < 0.1$.

Double-hurdle model for loan amounts

Further, we analyse whether the caste affiliation of the owner determines the loan amount by modeling loan amounts together with the probability of obtaining a loan using double-hurdle models. This is important as formal credit institutions can also discriminate by providing smaller amounts of loans to borrowers from certain caste-groups (Kumar and Venkatachalam, 2016). Table 7.1 points to this possibility as we observe significant caste-wise differences in loan amounts. Many firms in our dataset did not receive a loan, which makes our data left-censored due to a large proportion of observations at zero. Given the left-censored nature of the current dataset, we employ an empirical method that accounts for the probability of non-occurrence of the event. The standard practice in the literature is to estimate a Tobit (Tobin, 1958) model. However, a Tobit model assumes the same data-generating process determines both the binary outcome variable (in the present case loan status) and the continuous dependent variables (in the present case loan amount). The double-hurdle model pioneered by Cragg (1971) has proven superior to the Tobit model for models where the participation decision is different from the level of participations (Jones, 1989), even though they are independent, sequential decisions. Therefore, we estimate a double-hurdle model to deal with this situation. As implied by the name, under the double-hurdle model, the firms have to cross two hurdles. The first hurdle needs to be crossed in order to be a "*potential*" borrower. Given that a firm is a "*potential*" borrower, its current circumstances like market environment, characteristics of the firm owner and firm attributes determine the optimal amount to borrow – this is the "second hurdle" (Moffatt, 2005; Engel and Moffatt, 2014).[11]

The estimation results are presented in Table 7.5. For the purpose of interpretation of the results, we take the case of the general model including industry and state dummies (Model 2). Along the expected lines, in the propensity to access (decision) equation, our main variable of interest, the caste affiliation of the firm owner (*SC/ST*), has the expected negative sign and is highly significant. Similarly, in the loan amount equation too, we observe that the coefficient of the *SC/ST* variable is negative and significant at the 1 percent level. Results from the double-hurdle model indicate that caste plays a significant role in access to credit for MSME firms, and the influence of caste is evident not only in getting institutional credit but caste discrimination by formal credit institutions extends to the amount of the loan sanctioned as well.

Modified Blinder-Oaxaca composition

We perform an additional empirical exercise to check the robustness of our baseline results. We use the Blinder-Oaxaca method that decomposes the differences in credit access between SC/ST entrepreneurs and non-SC/ST entrepreneurs into two fractions, a fraction that is attributable to differences in firm characteristics (also known as "explained component" or "composition effect" since it reflects differences in the distribution of the

Table 7.5 Estimates of Double-Hurdle Model for Loan Amounts
Dependent Variable: Log of Total Loan Amount

Variables	*Model 1*		*Model 2*	
	Decision	*Amount*	*Decision*	*Amount*
Scheduled Caste Scheduled tribe (SC/ST)	-0.765*** (0.014)	-1.067*** (0.108)	-0.614*** (0.014)	-0.659*** (0.106)
Age	-0.033*** (0.001)	-0.332*** (0.008)	-0.028*** (0.001)	-0.362*** (0.008)
Age2	0.001*** (0.000)	0.006*** (0.000)	0.0005*** (0.000)	0.005*** (0.000)
Size	2.170*** (0.014)	4.892*** (0.126)	2.072*** (0.014)	6.950*** (0.123)
Location	0.224*** (0.009)	-6.005*** (0.068)	0.296** (0.009)	-1.375*** (0.067)
Cluster	-0.056*** (0.014)	1.532*** (0.112)	-0.162*** (0.015)	3.031*** (0.114)
Acmaint	1.681*** (0.009)	10.497*** (0.073)	1.461*** (0.009)	8.826*** (0.073)
Qualitycert	0.610*** (0.017)	5.382*** (0.143)	0.536*** (0.016)	3.261*** (0.135)
Export	0.582*** (0.022)	1.074*** (0.176)	0.723*** (0.021)	4.689*** (0.174)
Net Worth	0.0001*** (0.0000)	0.001*** (0.000)	0.0001*** (0.000)	0.0003*** (0.000)
State effects	N	N	Y	Y
Industry effects	N	N	Y	Y
Constant	9.116*** (0.018)	-28.362*** (0.166)	1.367*** (0.003)	-28.141*** (0.356)
N	1149883		1149883	
$Chi^2(10)$	1.1e+05		1.4e+05	
Prob > Chi^2	0.0000		0.0000	

Source: Authors' estimates based on Micro, Small and Medium Enterprise (MSME) dataset.

Note: We carried out a double-hurdle estimation using dhreg developed by Engel and Moffatt (2014). We used the probit option that estimates the equation for outer hurdle with just the intercept.

Figures in parentheses are standard errors. *** and ** indicate significance at 1 percent and 5 percent levels, respectively.

predictors between the two groups) and a residual fraction that represent the differences in returns to these endowments (also known as "unexplained component" or "coefficients effect"). As the coefficient's effect arises because one group (in our case non-SC/ST) is more favorably treated than the other (in our case SC/ST) given the same individual characteristics, it can be attributed to caste discrimination. One needs to exercise caution as the "unexplained part" also subsumes the effects of group differences in unobserved predictors (Jann, 2008). It also needs to be stated that the differences in characteristics between SC/ST and non-SC/ST firm owners could be also an outcome of pre-market discrimination, and hence the explained component also tends to capture the effects of past discrimination (Deshpande and Sharma, 2016). Hence, the coefficient effects may be considered as approximate estimates of discrimination, not as exact estimates. The choice of reference group is important in this matching exercise, and the general practice is to treat the more privileged group as the reference category (in our case non-SC/ST entrepreneurs) and show discrimination against the less privileged ones.[12] More technical details on the method are presented in Appendix II.

Results of our decomposition exercise are presented in Table 7.6. While endowment effects explain 56 percent of the gap in credit access, a significant 44 percent goes as unexplained in the gap. In other words, 44 percent may be due to the existence of caste discrimination in the credit market, though this needs to be corroborated with further evidence since we use a cross-sectional dataset and the predictors incorporated in the model influences interpretation of decomposition estimates. We find that all variables are significant predictors to the part of the gap ascribed to group characteristics. Our finding that the SC/ST entrepreneurs are largely discriminated against when compared to the non-SC/ST entrepreneurs in the credit market is broadly consistent across all our estimations.

Conclusion

In this chapter, we investigate whether social group affiliation matters in obtaining credit from institutional sources. We employed a unique enterprise-level dataset for the registered and unregistered MSMEs, drawn from the fourth survey round on the Indian MSMEs carried out for the period 2006–2007. Results of the empirical analysis unambiguously suggest that firms owned by socially disadvantaged categories (SCs and STs) face impediments in obtaining credit that go beyond observable differences in their creditworthiness. The results are robust to alternate specifications, endogeneity and self-selection. Our findings are thus consistent with the fact that SC/ST-owned firms are disadvantaged in the market for small-business credit, which would be traditionally attributed to caste discrimination. Since the existing evidence points to the crucial role of access to external finance in fostering small-firm growth, the existence of credit market discrimination due to social background would put the SC/ST-owned firms at a double disadvantage.

Table 7.6 Non-Linear Decomposition of Discrimination by Social Group in Access to Credit Using Blinder-Oaxaca Decomposition Method

Caste Discrimination Due to Differences in Group Characteristics (by Variables) and Group Processes		*Contribution of Group Characteristics to Caste Gap*	*Standard Error*	*95 percent CI*	*Percent Contribution of Group Differences to Caste Discrimination*
Age		–0.0102446***	0.000309	–0.010851 to –0.009639	–64.0
Age2		0.0060639***	0.000259	0.005557 to 0.006571	37.9
Size		0.0021803***	0.000047	0.002089 to 0.002272	13.6
Location		–0.0032641***	0.000145	–0.003549 to –0.002980	–20.4
Cluster		0.0000707***	0.000007	0.000057 to 0.000084	0.4
Acmaint		0.0113752***	0.000115	0.011151 to 0.011600	71.1
Qualitycert		–0.0002327***	0.000012	–0.000256 to –0.000210	–1.5
Export		–0.0001154***	0.000005	–0.000126 to –0.000105	–0.7
Net Worth		0.0000256***	0.000005	0.000015 to 0.000036	0.2
State effects		Y			
Industry effects		Y			
Caste discrimination due to differences in group processes (Coefficients Effect)	with industry and state dummies	0.006			37.5
	without industry and state dummies	0.009			56.3
Caste discrimination due to differences in group characteristics* (Composition Effect)		0.007			43.8
Total discrimination in access to credit		0.016			100.0

Source: Authors' estimates based on the Micro, Small and Medium Enterprise (MSME) dataset.

Note: *Total contribution from all variables including industry dummies and regional dummies. CI stands for confidence interval. *** and ** indicate significance at 1 percent and 5 percent levels, respectively.

Notes

1 A detailed description of the database is given in Chapter 1.
2 SC/ST firms denote firms owned by entrepreneurs belonging to SC/ST while non-SC/ST firms are firms owned by others.
3 The description of variables is presented in Table 7A.1 in Appendix I.
4 The marginal effect, $\frac{\partial E(y)}{\partial x}$, equals $\varphi(\beta'x)\beta$, where $\varphi(.)$ is the probability density function of standard normal distribution. The marginal effects were calculated at the means of the explanatory variables.
5 The higher coefficient values of these two variables vis-à-vis the caste variable perhaps indicate the possibility of overcoming caste discrimination in the credit market through signaling mechanisms like maintenance of financial accounts and possession of a quality certificate.
6 Multicollinearity problems might exist between some of the independent variables since many similar variables are adopted at the same time, hence the baseline results are likely to be biased. The collinearity diagnostics that we undertook, however, rule out any such possibility.
7 The dataset we employ does not provide the reasons for not applying for formal credit. Therefore, we are unable to account for those factors explicitly.
8 We do admit that the choice of this variable as exclusion restriction is debatable. However, on the issue of endogeneity of the exclusion restriction our results based on further robustness checks (after removing similar variables from specifications) too confirm the main findings.
9 We report both coefficient values and marginal effects in Table 3. Marginal effects were obtained following Greene (2003).
10 For a more complete discussion of this method, we refer the reader to Lewbel (2012). In the context of credit constraints, this methodology was previously adopted by Lin (2017) to show Chinese firms' decision to export directly or indirectly depending on the availability of finance.
11 More technical details on the method are presented in Appendix II.
12 The indicators of pre-market discrimination such as personal characteristics, assets and networks of firm owners are not available in the present dataset. Ideally these factors should be considered to decompose access to finance into explained and discriminatory components. Hence, the coefficient effects may be considered as approximate estimates of discrimination, not as precise estimates.

8
CONCLUSION

Introduction

Small firms account for the bulk of manufacturing enterprises in developing countries. In recent years, their importance in the development of the economy has been growing. However, these firms often lag behind large firms in terms of growth and performance. Existing literature highlighted various factors contributing to the performance gap between small and large firms. Among the set of factors identified for the poor performance of small firms, greater emphasis is accorded to the lack of access to institutional credit. Along with the credit availability, a growing set of studies points to the role of ownership characteristics, especially race, ethnicity and gender, in determining firms' access to credit. They maintain that, because of gender, racial and ethnic differences, the small firms owned by women and socially disadvantaged entrepreneurs might face more barriers in gaining access to formal financial systems and raising external finance. The sudden surge in these studies is aided by the substantial evidence supporting the large differences in firm formation, ownership rates, productivity levels and financing pattern of businesses among different demographic groups. Existing studies exploring this issue in a single country context are mostly confined to the experience of developed countries; most of them have very strong anti-discriminatory policies in place. Hence, the lessons drawn from these explorations might not be relevant to developing countries where caste and gender inequalities continue to be a pressing problem in the society. Even the limited studies that do exist on developing countries are mostly based on samples that are too small and are collected using ad hoc questionnaires.

In this book, our objective is to complement the thin literature on "finance-growth" nexus and credit market discrimination in developing countries. We began with a discussion of the alternate theoretical perspectives on credit market discrimination so as to understand their implication for discrimination in the small business credit market of India. We discussed the economic policies, including credit policies, enacted in India that have directly or indirectly impacted the MSME sector. Using a unique large-scale database on MSME firms in India, we then discussed the growth experience of the MSME sector in the aggregate and also by industry, region and different firm characteristics. Next, we investigated the role of access to finance on the growth of MSMEs in India. We also explored the issues relating to the female-owned and SC/ST-owned firms' access to finance, that is, whether firms owned by women, SCs and STs are discriminated against in lending markets. The main source of our data for the empirical analysis was drawn from the Fourth Census of the Registered MSMEs, obtained from the Ministry of MSME. The coverage of the survey includes firms belonging to manufacturing, repair and maintenance and services. We confined our analysis to over 1.3 million firms in the manufacturing sector. We empirically tested the objectives using an array of standard econometric methods, both linear and non-linear. Besides OLS, we also employed Logit and Bi-Probit models, non-linear decomposition techniques – Oaxaca-Blinder, PSM and quantile regression methods.

Key findings

Growth and structural change

In setting out the stylised facts about the MSME sector in India, we observed that the sector had witnessed quite noteworthy transformations over time, with the sector notching up a strong performance in output growth and productivity. The sector has also witnessed a considerable expansion of firm size, with the MSMEs in urban areas experiencing faster size expansion as compared to those in rural areas. The superior performance of firms located in urban areas is visible in labour productivity too, suggesting a clear urban bias in the performance of the MSME sector. Though the sector has seen a significant surge in growth and productivity in all states and industries, there has been a visible increase in inter-state and inter-industry variations too. Our analysis also yielded evidence on the clustering of firms in smaller size categories and the large productivity differences between small and larger firms, possibly suggesting the limited firm transition occurring within the sector. In terms of performance, medium firms outperform small firms and micro firms.

In the MSME sector, male-owned firms occupy a substantially larger share, though, as of late, the share of female-owned firms recorded a marginal increase. Only 10 percent of the firms in the sector are owned by SC/ST entrepreneurs and their share has even witnessed a decline between 2001 and 2006. The female-owned firms and SC/ST firms are found to be smaller in size and less productive as compared to their respective counterparts. Only 11 percent of the firms reported having had access to credit, and most of them relied on institutional sources of finance. Major beneficiaries of external funds are found to be male-owned firms and non-SC/ST firms. The visual examination suggests that firms with external funds are more productive and growth-oriented.

Finance and firm growth

Our investigation analysing the impact of financial constraints on firm growth unambiguously shows that financing constraints significantly obstruct firm growth. We found that the firm that finances its capital from external sources experiences an average growth rate of one percentage point more than a firm that has not obtained any financial support from external sources. Findings also suggest that financing constraints are significantly more harmful to younger firms than to older firms. There is also enough evidence to suggest that the gender of the owner is an important determinant of firm growth as we find firms owned and managed by women grow at a slower rate than male-owned firms. This gender gap in performance is likely to be worsened if the firms are credit constrained. This is evident from the fact that credit availability has a larger impact on the growth of female-owned firms as compared to an average firm in the MSME sector. Our results are robust to concerns arising from the endogeneity of finance variable and also to alternate methods and specifications.

Understanding gender discrimination in the small firm credit market

In the first part of the empirical analysis, our attempt was to confirm the existence of gender gaps in performance. We observed significant differences in the performance between male- and female-owned enterprises. Female-owned firms experienced a substantial underperformance in terms of size, growth and efficiency as compared to the firms owned and managed by males. Female-owned firms lag those owned by male entrepreneurs in productivity by a significant 23 percent, produce 41 percent less and are on an average 5/6ths the size of male-owned firms. While probing the reasons for this phenomenon, we found that the partial explanation for the underperformance of female entrepreneurs could be found in the concentration of female entrepreneurs in industrial sectors with low productivity.

In the second part of the analysis, we probed into the important question of gender-based discrimination in the small firm credit market. Using various measures of women involvement in the ownership and management of the enterprises, our econometric exercise pointed out unambiguously that irrespective of the extent of women's involvement in the firms, women-led businesses are less likely to obtain formal finance. The estimates suggest that female entrepreneurs have about a 15–20 percent lower probability of obtaining a loan than male entrepreneurs. Considering the smaller proportion of firms that receive loans in the MSME sector, this is a fairly large number, indicating the presence of a substantial gender difference in financial constraints. The various robustness tests that we undertook also supported the existence of gender-based discrimination in the credit market.

Social group affiliation and access to finance

As was the case with gender, our results also pointed to substantial differences in performance between SC/ST-owned firms and non-SC/ST-owned firms in size and efficiency. According to the estimates, SC/ST-owned firms lagged non-SC/ST-led firms in productivity by a significant 40 percent, produced 68 percent less and were on the average 3/4ths the size of non-SC/ST-owned firms. Our conjecture that the significant gap in performance between SC/ST and non-SC/ST firms could be found in caste-wise discrimination in credit access was duly supported by our findings. Our results unequivocally suggested that the caste affiliation of the firm owner played a crucial role in securing credit from institutional sources, and that firms owned by socially disadvantaged categories (SC and ST in our case) had about an 8 to 25 percent lower probability of obtaining formal credit.

Overall, our study of the MSME sector in India that focused on gender, caste and credit markets has thrown up interesting results. While the segment has seen a spurt in growth and productivity, we found that male-owned small enterprises grew at a faster clip compared to female-owned units, which often encountered difficulties in raising external finance. Similar to the female-owned units, which are smaller compared with male-owned ones, we observed that SC/ST-owned enterprises were also smaller and they, too, faced enormous constraints in obtaining external funds. It is unambiguously established, therefore, that the biggest beneficiaries of external funds in this sector were male-owned, non-SC/ST firms. We arrived at the conclusion that since the growth of small firms is directly linked to credit markets, gender and caste were major obstacles for enterprises belonging to the small scale sector to forge ahead.

Policy implications

A number of policy implications emanate from our study.

First, it is essential to keep in mind that MSME sector firms are not a homogenous group. There is considerable heterogeneity among the firms due to the presence of micro-, small- and medium-sized firms. As expected, in this study, we find that the impact of financial constraints significantly hamper the growth of small firms more than medium-sized firms. Therefore, the policy formulation exercise in the MSME sector should prescribe policies considering the heterogeneity of firms. Probably, an important consideration while prescribing policies which influence the growth trajectory of small firms is to understand the specific context in which these firms operate.

Instead of a top-down approach, a more suited policy making involves a decentralised approach in which policy making should be left to the regional and local bodies who may be more familiar with the nuances of the regions in which these firms are located.

Second, given that the small firms are most hurt by the presence of financial constraints, devising various financing schemes for start-up firms will enable small firms to commence operation with sufficient working capital. The reliance on internal sources and informal finance by most small firm owners to set-up businesses limits their operation and results in failures. As pointed out by Fanta et al. (2017) in the context of Southern African Development Community (SADC) region, formulating start-up financing techniques such as venture capital or government-backed guarantee schemes are likely to be successful in alleviating financial constraints that small business owners confront during the setting up of businesses.

Third, the results emanating from our detailed empirical analysis unambiguously point to the need to eliminate bias associated with the provision of credit to women-led and SC/ST-owned businesses so as to bridge the performance gap. Therefore, policy makers should formulate policies with an aim to include all stakeholders' credit needs. In this regard, we list the following policy recommendations:

(1) Since SC/ST-owned firms are survivalist in nature, there is a need to provide credit at affordable rates to these firms. Though the initiative of MUDRA bank is a positive step, efforts should be taken to enhance the spread of initiatives across the country. Policy measures should be introduced to improve the awareness of various special schemes to firm owners especially women and the socially disadvantaged. Respective industry associations can play a key role in this regard. Along the lines of the Global Banking Alliance (GBA) for Women, a consortium of financial institutions should be set up to promote credit support to women-led and SC/ST-led businesses.
(2) Due to inherent cultural barriers, women and SC/ST entrepreneurs may shy away from seeking formal credit. As suggested by Beck et al. (2013), appointment of special loan officers hailing from the same gender and social group may lessen the severity of bias in obtaining credit. In the meantime, existing loan officers should be given special training in evaluating women-led and SC/ST-led businesses.

Finally, we strongly feel the need to carry out an evaluation of the existing schemes targeted at women and socially disadvantaged entrepreneurs. Such an objective assessment will reveal the extent to which such programmes are able to fulfill the credit gap of such sections of society. There should be encouragement for female entrepreneurs to partner with male counterparts since such collaborations can exploit social networks. As mentioned previously, women face difficulty in obtaining formal finance due to the absence of collateral and rely more on informal sources. Initiatives like creating collateral registries can help in overcoming some of the hurdles in the credit market.

Suggestions for further research

Further rounds of the MSMEs census should collect detailed sources of loans, reasons behind not seeking formal credit, loan application status, education level of the entrepreneur, collateral and interest rate information and overdraft facility. In the absence of such information, a precise analysis of credit market participation of women and SC/ST entrepreneurs is akin to a glass half full or half empty.

APPENDIX I
Additional tables

Table 5A.1 Access to Finance and Firm Performance

Variable	*Model 1*	*Model 2*	*Model 3*
Size of the Firm			
Natural Log of Output (Three-year average)			
Loan	1.213***	1.169***	1.041***
	(0.005)	(0.005)	(0.005)
R-squared	0.049	0.201	0.284
Natural Log of Gross Value Added (GVA)			
Loan	1.207***	1.165***	1.040***
	(0.005)	(0.005)	(0.005)
R-squared	0.049	0.201	0.279
Natural Log of Fixed Assets			
Loan	0.958***	1.149***	1.006***
	(0.006)	(0.005)	(0.005)
R-squared	0.021	0.394	0.462
Natural Log of Employment			
Loan	0.563***	0.563***	0.497***
	(0.003)	(0.003)	(0.003)
R-squared	0.037	0.131	0.217
Efficiency			
Labour Productivity			
Loan	0.645***	0.602***	0.545***
	(0.00337)	(0.00322)	(0.00315)
R-squared	0.032	0.165	0.212
Number of Observations	1113823	1113823	1113823
Industry Effects	No	Yes	Yes
State Effects	No	No	Yes

Source: Authors' estimates.

Note: (a) Standard errors in parentheses; and (b) * $p < 0.05$, ** $p < 0.01$, *** $p < 0.001$

Table 6A.1 Description of the Variables

List of Variables	*Description*
Loan	This variable takes the value 1 if a firm has received credit from a formal source and 0 otherwise
Credit Demand	This variable takes the value 1 if a firm has received credit from a formal or informal source or those firms that reported they are short of working capital, 0 otherwise
Women owner	This takes the value 1 if the firm is owned by women and 0 otherwise
Women manager	This takes the value 1 if the firm is managed by women and 0 otherwise
Women owner manager	This takes the value 1 if the firm is owned and managed by women and 0 otherwise
Size	Measured as the total no. of employees
Account	This variable takes the value 1 if an enterprise maintained an account in written form and 0 otherwise
Exporter	This variable takes the value 1 if the firm is a direct or indirect exporter and 0 otherwise
Quality Certification	This variable takes the value 1 for firms that have a recognised quality certification and 0 otherwise
Net-worth	Difference between assets and liabilities

Table 6A.2 Name of Industries by National Industrial Classification Codes

NIC Code	*Industry*
15	Food Products
16	Tobacco
17	Textiles
18	Wearing Apparel
19	Leather
20	Wood Products
21	Paper
22	Publishing and Printing
23	Petroleum Products
24	Chemicals
25	Rubber and Plastics
26	Non-metallic Minerals
27	Basic Metal
28	Metal Products
29	Machinery
30	Office and Computing Machinery
31	Electrical Machinery
32	Radio and Television (TV)
33	Medical Precision and Opticals
34	Motor Vehicles
35	Other Transport
36	Furniture

Table 7A.1 Variable Definition

Variable Name	*Definition*
Output	Real output in 2004–2005 prices
Employment	Number of workers employed by the firm
Loan	Binary variable for loan obtained; 1 if the firm has a loan, 0 otherwise
SC/ST	Binary variable taking the value 1 if the firm owner is Scheduled Caste (SC) or Scheduled Tribe (ST), 0 otherwise
Age	The variable age represents the age of the firm, and is defined as the number of years elapsed since the establishment began its operations
Age2	Square of the age variable
Size	Ordered variable for size of the firm; 1 for micro firms, 2 for small firms and 3 for medium firms
Location	Dummy variable for urban firms (1 for rural firms and 0 for urban firms)
Cluster	Binary variable taking the value 1 if the firm is part of a cluster and 0 otherwise
Acmaint	Binary variable taking the value 1 if the firm is maintaining an account and 0 otherwise
Qualitycert	Dummy variable for firms that possess quality certificate (0 if they do not have one and 1 if they possess a quality certificate)
Export	Dummy variable for exporting firms (1 if the firm is an exporting firm and 0 otherwise)
Profitability	Real profit at 2004–2005 prices
Ownership	Binary variable taking the value 1 if the firm has a single owner and 0 otherwise
Net worth	Real net worth of the firm measured at 2004–2005 prices
Productivity	Ratio of real gross value added (GVA) to number of workers
Output Growth	(Real output in 2006–2007 - Real output in 2004–2005) / Real output in 2004–2005

APPENDIX II

Technical details on methods

Details of the Fairlie (2006) decomposition of non-linear models as follows:

$$\overline{Y}^M - \overline{Y}^F = \left[\sum_{i=1}^{N^M} \frac{F\left(X_i^M \hat{\beta}^M\right)}{N^M} - \sum_{i=1}^{N^F} \frac{F\left(X_i^F \hat{\beta}^M\right)}{N^F}\right] + \left[\sum_{i=1}^{N^F} \frac{F\left(X_i^F \hat{\beta}^M\right)}{N^F} - \sum_{i=1}^{N^F} \frac{F\left(X_i^F \hat{\beta}^F\right)}{N^F}\right]$$

where N denote the sample size for group, with Y^j as the average probability of being financially constrained for group j and $F(.)$ as the cumulative distribution function from the logistic distribution. F represents female-owned firms and M denotes male-owned firms. In this expression, male-owned firms are considered as the reference group since discrimination in the credit market is measured towards women-owned enterprises. Male coefficient estimates $\hat{\beta}^M$ are used as weights in the first term and female distributions of the explanatory variables X_i are used as weights in the second term. Fairlie (2005) shows that the equation holds exactly for a logit model including a constant term. In the equation, the first term on the right-hand side indicates the part of the gender gap in accessing formal finance due to group differences in distribution of X and the second term represents the part of the gap due to the differences in the group processes determining levels of Y. The second part or unexplained part is used to explain the role of unobservables (a proxy for discrimination). We obtain standard errors for the decomposition estimates based on methods employed by Oaxaca and Ransom (Fairlie, 2005; Oaxaca and Ransom, 1998).

Selection bias

Following Cameron and Trivedi (2009), we specify the following latent variable model:

$$y_{1j}^* = z_j'\alpha + \varepsilon_i$$

In this specification, y^*_{1j} depends on z'_j factors and the observed outcomes $y_{1j} = 1$ when $y^*_{1j} > 0$. Therefore, we can denote the outcome equation as:

$$y_{1j} = 1(z'\alpha + \varepsilon_{1j} > 0)$$

Since the dependent variable $y_1 j$ for the observation j is observed only if:

$$y_{2j} = 1(w'_j\beta + \tilde{\varepsilon}_{2j} > 0) \qquad \text{(selection equation)}$$

The model assumes that $\varepsilon \sim N(0,1)$, $\tilde{\varepsilon} \sim N(0,1)$ and corr $(\varepsilon, \tilde{\varepsilon}) = \rho$. The previous outcome and selection equation collapses to two separate probit models when $\rho = 0$.

We estimate the outcome equation by maximising the following log-likelihood function:

$$LogL(\alpha,\beta,\rho) = \sum_{y_{1j}=1;y_{2j}=1} \Phi_2(z'_j\alpha, w'_j\beta, \rho) + \sum_{y_{1j}=0;y_{2j}=1} \Phi_2(-z'_j\alpha, w'_j\beta, -\rho) + \sum_{y_{2j}=0} \Phi_1(w'_j\beta)$$

where $\phi(.)$ and $\phi_2(.)$ represent univariate and bivariate standard normal CDFs, respectively. In our empirical model, we observe a firm receiving formal finance (y_{1j} = 1 or y_{1j} = 0) only if they have a demand for external finance. In the outcome equation, the dependent variable is the same as defined previously in the case of the logit model.

Double hurdle model

The first decision, in our case, pertains to the decision to apply for formal credit; the second decision relates to how much the amount of the loan should be. The first equation in the double hurdle relates to the decision to access formal credit, and it can be represented as follows:

$$c^*_i = z'_i\gamma + \varepsilon_{1,i} \qquad \text{(propensity to access credit)}$$

Where

$$c_i = \begin{cases} 1, & \textit{if } c^*_i > 0 \\ 0, & \textit{otherwise} \end{cases}$$

In the previous equation, c^*_i is a latent variable representing firm i's propensity to access formal credit and c_i is the observed credit status of firm i where

c_i takes the value of 1 if the firm i has a credit and 0 otherwise. For firms that are potential borrowers, the latent variable y_i^* in the second hurdle models whether the loan amount is zero (no loan taken) or positive i.e. y_i takes a value 0 for non-borrowers and some positive values for the borrowers:

$$y_i^* = x_i'\beta + \varepsilon_{2,i} \qquad \text{(amount of credit)}$$

where

$$y_i = \begin{cases} y_i^*, & if\ y_i^* > 0\ and\ c_i = 1 \\ & 0,\ otherwise \end{cases}$$

and

$$\begin{pmatrix} \varepsilon_{1,i} \\ \varepsilon_{2,i} \end{pmatrix} \sim N\left[\begin{pmatrix} 0 \\ 0 \end{pmatrix}, \begin{pmatrix} 1 & 0 \\ 0 & \sigma^2 \end{pmatrix}\right]$$

The double hurdle model is developed under the assumption that error terms ($\varepsilon_{1,i}$, $\varepsilon_{2,i}$) of two hurdle models are independently distributed. In particular, we assume that the error terms $\varepsilon_{1,i}$ and $\varepsilon_{2,i}$ are distributed as a bivariate normal. Since the outcome of the first hurdle is binary, for identification purposes, the variance of the first error term is normalised to one. z_i' and x_i' denote vector of exogenous explanatory variables included in the first and second hurdles. We estimate the model by maximising the following log-likelihood using the Stata routine developed by Engel and Moffatt (2014) to obtain consistent estimates of the parameters γ, β and σ.

GLOSSARY AND ABBREVIATIONS

2SLS	Two-Staged Least Squares
AAPs	Annual Action Plans
ATT	Average Treatment effect on the Treated
BEEPS	Business Environment and Enterprise Performance Survey
CCS	Credit Cooperative Society
CDF	Cobb-Douglass Function
CGFMUs	Credit Guarantee Fund for Micro Units
CGS	Credit Guarantee Scheme
CGTMSEs	Credit Guarantee Fund Trust for Micro and Small Enterprises
CGTSIs	Credit Guarantee Fund Trust for Small Industries
CIA	Conditional Independence Assumption
CLCS-TU	Credit-Linked Capital Subsidy for Technology Upgradation
CLCSS	Credit-Linked Capital Subsidy Scheme
CRR	Cash Reserve Ratio
CRS	Constant Returns to Scale
DCMSME	Development Commissioner Micro, Small and Medium Enterprise
DCPs	District Credit Plans
DIC	District Industry Centers
ECA	Europe and Central Asia
EMS-ISO	Environmental Management System-International Organization for Standardisation
FD	Female Dominated
FEI	Female Entrepreneurship Index
FIN	Finance
GBA	Global Banking Alliance
GDP	Gross Domestic Product
GEM	Global Entrepreneurship Monitor
GEN	General
GOI	Government of India
GVA	Gross Value Added
HMDA	Home Mortgage Disclosure Act
IAT	Implicit Association Tests

IFC	International Finance Corporation
IMR	Inverse Mills Ratio
IV	Instrumental Variable
LA	Latin America
MFIs	Micro Finance Institutions
MLI	Member Lending Institution
MSMED	Micro, Small and Medium Enterprises Development
MSMEs	Micro, Small and Medium Enterprises
MUDRA	Micro Units Development and Refinance Agency
NA	Not Applicable
NABARD	National Bank for Agriculture and Rural Development
NBC	Net Bank Credit
NBFCs	Non-Banking Financial Companies
NGOs	Non-Governmental Organisations
NIC	National Industrial Classification
NSSBF	National Surveys of Small Business Finances
NSSO	National Sample Survey Office
OAMEs	Own Account Manufacturing Enterprises
OBC	Other Backward Class
OECD	Organisation for Economic Co-operation and Development
OLS	Ordinary Least Squares
PLIs	Primary Lending Institutions
PMMY	Pradhan Mantri Mudra Yojana
PSL	Priority Sector Lending
PSM	Propensity Score Matching
QMS-ISO	Quality Management System-International Organization for Standardisation
R&D	Research and Development
RBI	Reserve Bank of India
RMK	Rashtriya Mahila Kosh
RRBs	Regional Rural Banks
SADC	Southern African Development Community
SC	Scheduled Caste
SCBs	Scheduled Commercial Banks
SCLCSS	Special Credit-Linked Capital Subsidy Scheme
SD	Standard Deviation
SHG	Self-Help Group
SIDBI	Small Industries Development Bank of India
SIDO	Small Industries Development Organisation
SLR	Statutory Liquidity Ratio
SMEs	Small and Medium Enterprises
SSA	Sub-Saharan Africa
SSBF	Survey of Small Business Finances
SSIB	Small-Scale Industries Board

SSIs	Small Scale Industries
SSSBEs	Small-Scale Service and Business (industry-related) Enterprises
ST	Scheduled Tribe
TFP	Total Factor Productivity
TREAD	Trade-Related Entrepreneurship Assistance and Development
TV	Television
UK	United Kingdom
US	United States of America
UTs	Union Territories
WBES	World Bank Enterprise Survey
WEF	World Economic Forum

REFERENCES

Abildgren, K., Drejer, P. A. and Kuchler, A. (2013). Banks' Loan Rejection Rates and the Creditworthiness of the Banks' Corporate Customers, *Danish Journal of Economics*, 151(2): 207–224.

Acemoglu, D. and Cao, D. V. (2015). Innovation by Entrants and Incumbents, *Journal of Economic Theory*, 157: 255–294.

Acs, Z. J. and Armington, C. (2006). *Entrepreneurship, Geography, and American Economic Growth*, Cambridge, MA: Cambridge University Press.

Acs, Z. J. and Audretsch, D. B. (eds.) (1993). *Small Firms and Entrepreneurship: An East-West Perspective*, Cambridge, UK: Cambridge University Press.

Ahluwalia, M. S. (2002). Economic Reforms in India since 1991: Has Gradualism Worked? *Journal of Economic Perspectives*, 16: 67–88.

Alesina, A., Lotti, F. and Mistrulli, P. E. (2013). Do Women Pay More for Credit? Evidence from Italy, *Journal of European Economic Association*, 11: 45–66.

Allen, F., Carletti, E., Qian, J. and Valenzuela, P. (2013). Financial Intermediation, Markets, and Alternative Financial Sectors, in Constantinides, G., Harris, M. and Stulz, R. (eds.), *Handbook of the Economics of Finance*, Elsevier: Amsterdam.

Allen, F., Chakrabarti, R., De, S., Qian, J. Q. and Qian, M. (2012). Financing Firms in India, *Journal of Financial Intermediation*, 21(3): 409–415.

Allen, F. and Qian, J. (2010). Comparing Legal and Alternative Institutions in Finance and Commerce, in Heckman, J. and Nelson, R. (eds.), *Global Perspectives of Rule of Law*, New York: Routledge.

Allen, F., Qian, J. and Qian, M. (2005). Law, Finance, and Economic Growth in China, *Journal of Financial Economics*, 77: 57–116.

Altonji, J. and Blank, R. (1999). Race and Gender in the Labor Market, in Ashenfelter, O. and Card, D. (eds.), *Handbook of Labor Economics*, vol. 3C, Amsterdam: Elsevier.

Anyadike-Danes, M. and Hart, M. (2017). *High Performing Firms and Job Creation: A Longitudinal Analysis (1998–2013)*, ERC Insight Paper, Enterprise Research Centre, University of Warwick, UK. April. https://www.enterpriseresearch.ac.uk/wp-content/uploads/2017/04/ERC-InsightPap-HartDanes.pdf.

Aristei, D. and Gallo, M. (2016). Does Gender Matter for Firms' Access to Credit? Evidence from International Data, *Finance Research Letters*, 18: 67–75.

Arrow, K. (1972). Models of Job Discrimination. In Pascal, A. (ed.), *Racial Discrimination in Economic Life*, Lexington: Lexington Heath, pp. 83–102.

Arrow, K. (1998). What Has Economics to Say About Racial Discrimination, *Journal of Economic Perspectives*, 12(2): 91–100.

Aryeetey, E., Baah-Nuakoh, A., Duggleby, T., Hettige, H. and Steel, W. F. (1994). *Supply and Demand for Finance of Small Scale Enterprises in Ghana*, Discussion Paper No. 251, World Bank, Washington, DC.

Asiedu, E., Freeman, J. A. and Nti-Addae, A. (2012). Access to Credit by Small Businesses: How Relevant Are Race, Ethnicity, and Gender? *American Economic Review: Papers and Proceedings*, 102(3): 532–537.

Asiedu, E., Kalonda-Kanyama, I., Ndikumana, L. and Nti-Addae, A. (2013). Access to Credit by Firms in Sub-Saharan Africa: How Relevant Is Gender? *American Economic Review*, 103: 293–297.

Aterido, R., Beck, T. and Iacovone, L. (2013). Access to Finance in Sub-Saharan Africa: Is There a Gender Gap? *World Development*, 47: 102–120.

Athena Infonomics (2015). *Funds for SHE: A Study on Efficiency of Bank Loans for Women Entrepreneurs in the MSME Sector in India*, Deutsche Gesellschaft für Internationale Zusammenarbeit (GIZ) GmbH, New Delhi, India.

Audretsch, D. B. and Elston, J. A. (2002). Does Firm Size Matter? Evidence on the Impacts of Liquidity Constraints on Firm Investment Behavior in Germany, *International Journal of Industrial Organization*, 20: 1–17.

Ayyagari, M., Demirguc-Kunt, A. and Maksimovic, V. (2008). How Important Are Financing Constraints? The Role of Finance in the Business Environment, *World Bank Economic Review*, 22: 483–516.

Ayyagari, M., Demirgüç-Kunt, A. and Maksimovic, V. (2010). Formal versus Informal Finance: Evidence from China, *Review of Financial Studies*, 23: 3048–3097.

Ayyagari, M., Demirguc-Kunt, A. and Maksimovic, V. (2011). Firm Innovation in Emerging Markets: The Role of Finance, Governance, and Competition, *Journal of Financial and Quantitative Analysis*, 46(6): 1545–1580.

BalaSubrahmanya, M. H. (1995). Reservation Policy for Small Scale Industry: Has It Delivered the Goods?, *Economic and Political Weekly*, 30: M51–M54.

Bamiatzi, V. and Hall, G. (2009). Firm versus Sector Effects on Profitability and Growth: The Importance of Size and Interaction, *International Journal of the Economics of Business*, 16(2): 205–220.

Banerjee, A. V. and Duflo, E. (2010). Giving Credit Where It Is Due, *Journal of Economic Perspectives*, 24(3): 61–80.

Banerjee, A. V. and Duflo, E. (2014). Do Firms Want to Borrow More? Testing Credit Constraints Using a Directed Lending Program, *The Review of Economic Studies*, 81: 572–607.

Banerjee, A. V. and Munshi, K. (2004). How Efficiently Is Capital Allocated? Evidence from the Knitted Garment Industry in Tirupur, *Review of Economic Studies*, 71(1): 19–42.

Banerjee, B. and Knight, J. (1985). Caste Discrimination in the Indian Urban Labour Market, *Journal of Development Economics*, 17(3): 277–307.

Barber, B. M. and Odean, T. (2001). Boys Will Be Boys: Gender, Overconfidence, and Common Stock Investment, *Quarterly Journal of Economics*, 116(1): 261–292.

Bardasi, E., Sabarwal, S. and Terrell, K. (2011). How Do Female Entrepreneurs Perform? Evidence from Three Developing Regions, *Small Business Economics*, 37(4): 417–441.

Barron, D. N., West, E. and Hannan, M. T. (1994). A Time to Grow and a Time to Die: Growth and Mortality of Credit Unions in New York City, 1914–1990, *American Journal of Sociology*, 100: 381–421.

Baumol, W. J. (2002). *The Free-Market Innovation Machine: Analyzing the Growth Miracle of Capitalism*, Princeton, NJ: Princeton University Press.

Becchetti, L. and Trovato, G. (2002). The Determinants of Growth for Small and Medium Sized Firms: The Role of the Availability of External Finance, *Small Business Economics*, 19: 291–306.

Beck, T., Behr, P. and Guettler, A. (2013). Gender and Banking: Are Women Better Loan Officers?, *Review of Finance*, 17(4): 1279–1321.

Beck, T. and Demirguc-Kunt, A. (2006). Small and Medium-Size Enterprises: Access to Finance as a Growth Constraint, *Journal of Banking and Finance*, 30(11): 2931–2943.

Beck, T. and Demirguc-Kunt, A. (2008). Access to Finance: An Unfinished Agenda, *World Bank Economic Review*, 22: 383–396.

Beck, T., Demirgüç-Kunt, A., Laeven, L. and Levine, R. (2008a). Finance, Firm Size, and Growth, *Journal of Money, Credit and Banking*, 40(7): 1379–1405.

Beck, T., Demirgüç-Kunt, A. and Maksimovic, V. (2005). Financial and Legal Constraints to Firm Growth: Does Firm Size Matter? *Journal of Finance*, 60(1): 137–177.

Beck, T., Demirgüç-Kunt, A. and Maksimovic, V. (2008b). Financing Patterns Around the World: Are Small Firms Different?, *Journal of Financial Economics*, 89: 467–487.

Beck, T., Demirgüç-Kunt, A. and Peria M. S. M. (2008c). Banking Services for Everyone? Barriers to Bank Access and Use Around the World. *World Bank Economic Review*, 22(3): 397–430.

Beck, T., Lu, L. and Yang, R. (2015). Finance and Growth for Microenterprises: Evidence from Rural China, *World Development*, 67(4): 38–56.

Becker, G. (1957). *The Economics of Discrimination*, Chicago: University of Chicago Press.

Bellucci, A., Borisov, A. and Zazzaro, A. (2010). Does Gender Matter in Bank-Firm Relationships? Evidence from Small Business Lending, *Journal of Banking and Finance*, 34(12): 2968–2984.

Berger, A. and Udell, G. (1998). The Economics of Small Business Finance: The Roles of Private Equity and Debt Markets in the Financial Growth Cycle, *Journal of Banking & Finance*, 22(6): 613–673.

Berger, A. N. and Udell, G. F. (2006). A More Complete Conceptual Framework for SME Finance, *Journal of Banking and Finance*, 30: 2945–2966.

Bertrand, M., Chugh, D. and Mullainathan, S. (2005). Implicit Discrimination, *American Economic Review*, 95 (2): 94–98.

Bhaduri, S. and Shanmugam, K. R. (2002). Size, Age and Firm Growth in the Indian Manufacturing Firms, *Applied Economics Letters*, 9(9): 607–613.

Bhaduri, S. N. (2005). Investment, Financial Constraints and Financial Liberalization: Some Stylized Facts from a Developing Economy, India, *Journal of Asian Economics*, 16(4): 704–718.

Bharti, N. K. (2018). *Wealth Inequality, Class and Caste in India, 1961–2012*, World Inequality Database, Working Paper N° 2018/14, World Inequality Lab, Paris.

Bhue, G., Prabhala, N. R. and Tantri, P. (2019). Can Small Business Lending Programs Disincentivize Growth? Evidence from India's Priority Sector Lending Program, *SSRN*, https://ssrn.com/abstract=2960598

Bigsten, A., Collier, P., Dercon, S., Fafchamps, M., Gauthier, B., Gunning, J. W., Oduro, A., Oostendorf, R., Patillo, C., Soderbom, M., Teal, F. and Zeufack, A. (2003). Credit Constraints in Manufacturing Enterprises in Africa, *Journal of African Economies*, 12(1): 104–125.

Binks M. R. and Ennew, C. T. (1996). Growing Firms and the Credit Constraint, *Small Business Economics*, 8(1): 17–25.

Blanchard, L., Zhao, B. and Yinger, J. (2008). Do Lenders Discriminate against Minority and Women Entrepreneurs? *Journal of Urban Economics*, 63(2): 467–497.

Blanchflower, D. G., Levine, P. B. and Zimmerman, D. J. (2003). Discrimination in the Small-Business Credit Market, *Review of Economics and Statistics*, 85(4): 930–943.

Blinder, A. S. (1973). Wage Discrimination: Reduced Form and Structural Estimates, *Journal of Human Resources*, 8(4): 436–455.

Bostic, R. W. and Lampani, K. P. (1999). Racial Differences in Patterns of Small Business Finance, in Blanton, J., Williams, A. and Rhine, S. (eds.), *Business Access to Capital and Credit*, Washington, DC: Federal Reserve System, pp. 253–276.

Brunell, T. L. and DiNardo, J. (2004). A Propensity Score Reweighting Approach to Estimating the Partisan Effects of Full Turnout in American Presidential Elections, *Political Analysis*, 12: 28–45.

Burgess, R. and Pande, R. (2005). Do Rural Banks Matter? Evidence from the Indian Social Banking Experiment, *American Economic Review*, 95(3): 780–795.

Burgess, R., Pande, R. and Wong, G. (2005). Banking for the Poor: Evidence from India, *Journal of the European Economic Association*, 3(2–3): 268–278.

Cabral, M. B. and Mata, J. (2003). On the Evolution of the Firm Size Distribution: Facts and Theory, *American Economic Review*, 93(4): 1075–1090.

Cameron, A. C. and Trivedi, P. K. (2009). *Microeconometrics Using Stata*, College Station, TX: Stata Press and Lakeway Drive.

Carpenter, R. E. and Petersen, B. C. (2002). Is the Growth of Small Firms Constrained by Internal Finance? *The Review of Economics and Statistics*, 84(2): 298–309.

Carter, S. and Rosa, P. (1998). The Financing of Male and Female Owned-Business, *Entrepreneurship and Regional Development*, 10(3): 225–241.

Cavalluzzo, K. S. and Cavalluzzo, L. C. (1998). Market Structure and Discrimination: The Case of Small Businesses, *Journal of Money, Credit and Banking*, 30(4): 771–792.

Chaudhuri, K. and Cherical, M. M. (2012). Credit Rationing in Rural Credit Markets of India, *Applied Economics*, 44(7): 803–812.

Chen, M. (2013). The Impact of Firm Productivity on External Finance, Conference Paper, Paper presented at *the AIDEA Bicentenary Conference*, Lecce, Italy.

Cheng, S. (2015). Potential Lending Discrimination? Insights from Small Business Financing and New Venture Survival, *Journal of Small Business Management*, 53(4): 905–923.

Claessens, S. (2006). Access to Financial Services: A Review of the Issues and Public Policy Objectives, *The World Bank Research Observer*, 21(2): 207–240.

Coad, A. and Rao, R. (2008). Innovation and Firm Growth in High-Tech Sectors: A Quantile Regression Approach, *Research Policy*, 37: 633–648.

Coad, A. and Tamvada, J. P. (2012). Firm Growth and Barriers to Growth among Small Firms in India, *Small Business Economics*, 39(2): 383–400.

Coate, S. and Loury, G. C. (1993). Will Affirmative-Action Policies Eliminate Negative Stereotypes? *American Economic Review*, 83(5): 1220–1240.

Cole, S. (2009). Financial Development, Bank Ownership, and Growth: Or, Does Quantity Imply Quality? *The Review of Economics and Statistics*, 91: 33–51.

Coleman, S. (2002). The Borrowing Experience of Black and Hispanic-Owned Small Firms: Evidence from the 1998 Survey of Small Business Finances, *Academy of Entrepreneurship Journal*, 8(1): 1–20.

Coleman, S. (2007). The Role of Human and Financial Capital in the Profitability and Growth of Women-Owned Small Firms, *Journal of Small Business Management*, 45(3): 303–319.

Cooley, T. F. and Quadrini, V. (2001). Financial Markets and Firm Dynamics, *American Economic Review*, 91: 1286–1310.

Cowling, M., Liu, W. and Zhang, N. (2018). Did Firm Age, Experience, and Access to Finance Count? SME Performance after the Global Financial Crisis, *Journal of Evolutionary Economics*, 28: 77–100.

Cragg, J. G. (1971). Some Statistical Models for Limited Dependent Variables with Application to the Demand for Durable Goods, *Econometrica*, 39(5): 829–844.

Das, K. (2008). SMEs in India: Issues and Possibilities in Times of Globalisation, in Lim, H. (ed.), *SME in Asia and Globalization*, ERIA Research Project Report 2007–5, Economic Research Institute for ASEAN and East Asia (ERIA), Jakarta, Indonesia.

Das, M. B. and Dutta, P. (2007). *Does Caste Matter for Wages in the Indian Labour Market?* Washington, DC: The World Bank.

Das, S. K. (1995). Size, Age and Firm Growth in an Infant Industry: The Computer Hardware Industry in India, *International Journal of Industrial Organization*, 13: 111±126.

Das, S. K. (2015). *Industrial Finance in the Era of Financial Liberalisation in India: Exploring Some Structural Issues*, Working Paper No. 186, Institute for Studies in Industrial Development, New Delhi, India.

Davidson, P., Achtenhagen, L. and Naldi, L. (2005). Research on Small Firm Growth: A Review, in Prats, J. and Velamuri, R. (eds.), *35th EISB Conference: Sustaining the Entrepreneurial Spirit over Time: Implications for Young Companies, Family Businesses, and Established Companies*, Spain: IESE Business School, pp. 1–27.

De, P. K. and Nagaraj, P. (2014). Productivity and Firm Size in India, *Small Business Economics*, 42(4): 891–907.

Degryse, H., Lu, L. and Ongena, S. (2016). Informal or Formal Financing? Evidence on the Co-Funding of Chinese Firms, *Journal of Financial Intermediation*, 27: 31–50.

De Mel, S., McKenzie, D. and Woodruff, C. (2009). Are Women More Credit Constrained? Experimental Evidence on Gender and Microenterprise Returns, *American Economic Journal: Applied Economics*, 1(3): 1–32.

De Mel, S., McKenzie, D. and Woodruff, C. (2012). One-Time Transfers of Cash or Capital Have Long-Lasting Effects on Microenterprises in Sri Lanka, *Science*, 335: 962–966.

Demirgüc-Kunt, A., Klapper, L. F. and Panos, G. A. (2011). Entrepreneurship in Post-Conflict Transition, *Economics of Transition*, 19(1): 27–78.

Derera, E., Chitakunye, P. and O'Neill, C. (2014). The Impact of Gender on Start-Up Capital: A Case of Women Entrepreneurs in South Africa, *Journal of Entrepreneurship*, 23(1): 95–114.

Deshpande, A. (2017). *The Grammar of Caste: Economic Discrimination in Contemporary India*, New Delhi, India: Oxford University Press.

Deshpande, A. and Sharma, S. (2013). Entrepreneurship or Survival? Caste and Gender of Small Business in India, *Economic and Political Weekly*, 48(28): 38–49.

Deshpande, A. and Sharma, S. (2016). Disadvantage and Discrimination in Self-Employment: Caste Gaps in Earnings in Indian Small Businesses, *Small Business Economics*, 46(2): 325–346.

Dinh, H. T., Mavridis, D. A. and Nguyen, H. B. (2012). The Binding Constraint on the Growth of Firms in Developing Countries, in Dinh, H. T. and Clarke, G. R. G. (eds.), *Performance of Manufacturing Firms in Africa: An Empirical Analysis*, Washington, DC: World Bank, pp. 87–137.

Dohmen, T., Falk, A., Huffman, D., Sunde, U., Schupp, J. and Wagner, G. G. (2005). Individual Risk Attitudes: New Evidence from a Large, Representative, Experimentally-Validated Survey, IZA Discussion Paper No. 1730, Institute for Study of Labour, Bonn.

Donati, C. (2016). Firm Growth and Liquidity Constraints: Evidence from the Manufacturing and Service Sectors in Italy, *Applied Economics*, 48(20): 1881–1892.

Ebben, J. and Johnson, A. (2006). Bootstrapping in Small Firms: An Empirical Analysis of Change over Time, *Journal of Business Venturing*, 21(6): 851–865.

Eddleston, K. A., Ladge, J. J., Mitteness, C. and Balachandra, L. (2016). Do You See What I See? Signaling Effects of Gender and Firm Characteristics on Financing Entrepreneurial Ventures, *Entrepreneurship Theory and Practice*, 40(3): 489–514.

Engel, C. and Moffatt, P. G. (2014). Dhreg, Xtdhreg, and Bootdhreg: Commands to Implement Double-Hurdle Regression, *Stata Journal*, 14(4): 778–797.

Fafchamps, M., McKenzie, D., Quinn, S. R. and Woodruff, C. (2014). Female Microenterprises and the Fly-Paper Effect: Evidence from a Randomized Experiment in Ghana, *Journal of Development Economics*, 106(1): 211–226.

Fairlie, R. W. (2005). An Extension of the Blinder-Oaxaca Decomposition Technique to Logit and Probit Models, *Journal of Economic and Social Measurement*, 30(4): 305–316.

Fairlie, R. W. (2006). Entrepreneurship Among Disadvantaged Groups: Women, Minorities and the Less Educated, in Parker, S. C., Zoltan, J. and Audretsch, D. R. (eds.), *International Handbook Series on Entrepreneurship*, vol. 2, New York: Springer, pp. 437–475.

Fang, H. (2001). Social Culture and Economic Performance, *American Economic Review*, 91(4): 924–937.

Fang, H. and Moro, A. (2011). Theories of Statistical Discrimination and Affirmative Action: A Survey, in Benhabib, J., Jackson, M. O. and Bisin, A. (eds.), *Handbook of Social Economics*, vol. 1A, Elsevier: Amsterdam.

Fanta, A. B., Mutsonziwa, K., Berkowitz, B., Maposa, O., Motsomi, A. and Khumalo, J. (2017). *Small Business Performance: Does Access to Finance Matter? Evidence from SADC Using FinScope Surveys*, Policy Research Paper No. 05/2017, FinMark Trust, South Africa.

Fazzari, S., Hubbard, R. G. and Petersen, B. C. (1988). Financing Constraints and Corporate Investment, *Brookings Papers on Economic Activity*, 19(1): 141–195.

Fernandes, A. M. (2008). Firm Productivity in Bangladesh Manufacturing Industries, *World Development*, 36(10): 1725–1744.

Ferrando, A. and Ruggieri, A. (2018). Financial Constraints and Productivity: Evidence from Euro Area Companies, *International Journal of Finance & Economics*, 23(3): 257–282.

Fisman, R. J., Paravisini, D. and Vig, V. (2017). Cultural Proximity and Loan Outcomes, *American Economic Review*, 107(2): 457–492.

Fowowe, B. (2017). Access to Finance and Firm Performance: Evidence from African Countries, *Review of Development Finance*, 7: 6–17.

Galli, E., Mascia, D. V. and Rossi, S. P. S. (2020). Bank Credit Constraints for Women-Led SMEs: Self-Restraint or Lender Bias? *European Financial Management*, 26(4): 1147–1188.

Gang, I. N., Sen, K. and Yun, M. (2017). Is Caste Destiny? Occupational Diversification Among Dalits in Rural India, *European Journal of Development Research*, 29(2): 476–492.

Garcia-Santana, M. and Pijoan-Mas, J. (2014). The Reservation Laws in India and the Misallocation of Production Factors, *Journal of Monetary Economics*, 66: 193–209.

GEM (Global Entrepreneurship Monitor GEM) (2015). *Women's Entrepreneurship*, London: Global Entrepreneurship Research Association, London Business School.

Gertler, M. and Gilchrist, S. (1994). Monetary Policy, Business Cycles, and the Behavior of Small Manufacturing Firms, *Quarterly Journal of Economics*, 109(2): 309–340.

Ghosh, S. (2006). Did Financial Liberalization Ease Financing Constraints? Evidence from Indian Firm-Level Data, *Emerging Markets Review*, 7: 176–190.

Gibrat, R. (1931). *Les inégalités économiques*, Paris: Librairie du Receuil Sirey.

Giddens, A., Duneier, M., Appelbaum, R. P. and Carr, D. (2009). *Introduction to Sociology*, 7th edn, New York: W.W. Norton & Company, Inc.

Giovanni, J. D., Levchenko, G. and Rancière, R. (2011). Power Laws in Firm Size and Openness to Trade: Measurement and Implications, *Journal of International Economics*, 85(1): 42–52.

Girma, S. and Vencappa, D. (2015). Financing Sources and Firm Level Productivity Growth: Evidence from Indian Manufacturing, *Journal of Productivity Analysis*, 44(3): 283–292.

GOI (Government of India) (1991). *Report of the Narsimhan Committee on the Financial Sector*, Ministry of Finance, New Delhi, India.

GOI (Government of India) (2012). *Report of the Sub-Group on Flow of Private Sector Investments for MSME Sector*, Planning Commission, New Delhi, India.

GOI (Government of India) (2016). *All India Report of the Sixth Economic Census*, Ministry of Statistics and Programme Implementation, Central Statistics Office, New Delhi, India.

GOI (Government of India) (2018). Annual Report 2017–2018, *New Delhi Ministry of Micro, Small and Medium Enterprises*, https://msme.gov.in/sites/default/files/MSME-AR-2017-18-Eng.pdf

Gollin, D. (2008). Nobody's Business But My Own: Self-Employment and Small Enterprise in Economic Development, *Journal of Monetary Economics*, 55(2): 219–233.

Goraya, S. S. (2019). *How Does Caste Affect Entrepreneurship? Birth vs Worth*, Working Paper No. 1104, GSE, Barcelona.

Greene, W. H. (2003). *Econometric Analysis*, 5th edn, Upper Saddle River, NJ: Prentice Hall.

Guariglia, A., Liu, X. and Song, L. (2011). Internal Finance and Growth: Microeconometric Evidence from Chinese Firms, *Journal of Development Economics*, 96: 79–94.

Haltiwanger, J., Jarmin, R. S. and Miranda, J. (2013). Who Creates Jobs? Small versus Large versus Young, *Review of Economics and Statistics*, 95(2): 347–361.

Hansen, H. and Rand, J. (2014). The Myth of Female Credit Discrimination in African Manufacturing, *Journal of Development Studies*, 50(1): 81–96.

Harvie, C. (2011). Framework Chapter: SME Access to Finance in Selected East Asian Economies, in Harvie, C., Oum, S. and Narjoko, D. (eds.), *Small and Medium Enterprises (SMEs) Access to Finance in Selected East Asian Economies*, ERIA Research Project Report 2010–14, Jakarta, pp. 17–40.

Heckman, J. and Robb, R. (1985). Alternative Methods for Evaluating the Impact of Interventions, in Heckman, J. and Singer, B. (eds.), *Longitudinal Analysis of Labor Market Data*, New York: Cambridge University Press pp. 156-245.

Heckman, J. J. (1979). Sample Selection Bias as a Specification Error, *Econometrica*, 47(1): 151–161.

Heckman, J. J., LaLonde, R. J. and Smith, J. A. (1999). The Economics and Econometrics of Active Labor Market Programs, in Ashenfelter, O. and Card, D. (eds.), *Handbook of Labor Economics*, vol. 3A, Elsevier, New York..

Hellerstein, J. K. and Neumark, D. (1999). Sex, Wages, and Productivity: An Empirical Analysis of Israeli Firm-Level Data, *International Economic Review*, 40(1): 95–123.

Hsieh, C. and Klenow, P. J. (2009). Misallocation and Manufacturing TFP in China and India, *The Quarterly Journal of Economics*, 124(4): 1403–1448.

Hsieh, C. and Klenow, P. J. (2014). The Life Cycle of Plants in India and Mexico, *The Quarterly Journal of Economics*, 129(3): 1035–1084.

Hurst, E. and Lusardi, A. (2004). Liquidity Constraints, Household Wealth and Entrepreneurship, *Journal of Political Economy*, 112: 319–347.

Huynh, K. P. and Petrunia, R. J. (2010). Age Effects, Leverage and Firm Growth, *Journal of Economic Dynamics and Control*, 34(5): 1003–1013.

International Finance Corporation (IFC) (2017a). *Closing the Credit Gap for Formal and Informal Micro, Small, and Medium Enterprises*, International Finance Corporation, Washington, DC.

International Finance Corporation (IFC) (2017b). *MSME Finance Gap: Assessment of the Shortfalls and Opportunities in Financing Micro, Small, and Medium Enterprises in Emerging Markets*, International Finance Corporation, Washington, DC.

Irwin, D. and Scott, J. M. (2010). Barriers Faced by SMEs in Raising Bank Finance, *International Journal of Entrepreneurial Behaviour & Research*, 16(3): 245–259.

Iyer, L., Khanna, T. and Varshney, A. (2013). Caste and Entrepreneurship in India, *Economic and Political Weekly*, 48(6): 52–60.

Jann, B. (2006). *FAIRLIE: Stata Module to Generate Nonlinear Decomposition of Binary Outcome Differentials*, Statistical Software Components, Boston College Department of Economics, Boston, MA.

Jann, B. (2008). The Blinder-Oaxaca Decomposition for Linear Regression Models, *Stata Journal*, 8(4): 453–479.

Jensen, B., McGuckin, R. H. and Stiroh, K. J. (2001). The Impact of Vintage and Survival on Productivity: Evidence from Cohorts of U.S. Manufacturing Plants, *The Review of Economics and Statistics*, 83(2): 323–332.

Jodhka, S. (2010). *Dalits in Business: Self-Employed Scheduled Castes in North-West India*, Working Paper, Indian Institute of Dalit Studies, New Delhi, India.

Johnson, S. (1997). An Empirical Analysis of the Determinants of Corporate Debt Ownership Structure, *Journal of Financial and Quantitative Analysis*, 32: 47–69.

Johnson, S., McMillan, J. and Woodruff, C. M. (1999). Property Rights, Finance and Entrepreneurship, Conference Paper, *the Nobel Symposium in Economics-the Economics of Transition*, Stockholm.

Jones, A. M. (1989). A Double-Hurdle Model of Cigarette Consumption, *Journal of Applied Econometrics*, 4(1): 23–39.

Jovanovic, B. (1982). Selection and the Evolution of Industry, *Econometrica*, 50(3): 649–670.

Kale, D. (2016). *The Impact of Directed Lending Programs on the Credit Access of Small Businesses in India: A Firm-Level Study*, MPRA Paper 72510, University Library of Munich, Germany.

Kapur, D., Prasad, C. B., Pritchett, L. and Shyam Babu, D. (2010). Rethinking Inequality in Uttar Pradesh in the Market Reform Era, *Economic and Political Weekly*, 46(35): 39–49.

Kasseeah, H. and Thoplan, R. (2012). Access to Financing in a Small Island Economy: Evidence from Mauritius, *Journal of African Business*, 13(3): 221–231.

Katrak, H. (1999). Small Scale Enterprise Policy in Developing Countries: An Analysis of India's Reservation Policy, *Journal of International Development*, 11: 701–715.

Kauffmann, C. (2005). Financing SMEs in Africa, *Policy Insights* 7, May, Paris: OECD.

Khera, P. (2018). *Closing Gender Gaps in India: Does Increasing Women's Access to Finance Help?* IMF Working Paper 18/212, International Monetary Fund, Washington, DC.

Klapper, L. F. and Parker, S. C. (2011). Gender and the Business Environment for New Firm Creation, *The World Bank Research Observer*, 26: 237–257.

Koenker, R. and Bassett, G. S. (1978). Regression Quantiles, *Econometrica*, 46: 33–50.

Korreck, S. (2019). *Women Entrepreneurs in India: What Is Holding Them Back?* ORF Issue Brief No. 317, September, Observer Research Foundation, New Delhi.

Kumar, A., Mishra, A. K., Saraoj, S. and Joshi, P. K. (2017). Institutional vs Non-Institutional Credit to Agricultural Households in India: Evidence on Impact from a National Farmers' Survey, *Economic Systems*, Forthcoming, https://doi.org/10.1016/j.ecosys.2016.10.005

Kumar, S. M. (2013). Does Access to Formal Agricultural Credit Depend on Caste? *World Development*, 43(3): 315–328.

Kumar, S. M. (2016). *Why Does Caste Still Influence Access to Agricultural Credit?* Working Paper 2016/86, UNU-WIDER, Helsinki.

Kumar, S. M. and Venkatachalam, R. (2016). *Caste and Credit: A Woeful Tale?* Working Paper, King's College, London.

Kumar, S. M. and Venkatachalam, R. (2018). Caste and Credit: A Woeful Tale?, *Journal of Development Studies*, 55(8): 1816–1833.

Kuntchev, V., Ramalho, R., Rodriguez-Meza, J. and Yang, J. S. (2012). *What Have We Learned from the Enterprise Surveys Regarding Access to Finance by SMEs?* Mimeo and World Bank, Washington, DC.

Kwong, C. C. Y., Jones-Evans, D. and Thompson, P. (2012). Differences in Perceptions of Access to Finance Between Potential Male and Female Entrepreneurs:

Evidence from the UK, *International Journal of Entrepreneurial Behaviour & Research*, 18(1), 75–97.

Lewbel, A. (2012). Using Heteroscedasticity to Identify and Estimate Mismeasured and Endogenous Regressor Models, *Journal of Business & Economic Statistics*, 30(1): 67–80.

Lin, F. (2017). Credit Constraints, Export Mode and Firm Performance: An Investigation of China's Private Enterprises, *Pacific Economic Review*, 22(1): 123–143.

Little, I. M. D., Dipak, M. and Page, J. M. (1987). *Small Manufacturing Enterprises: A Comparative Analysis of India and Other Economies*, Oxford: Oxford University Press.

Long, T. Q. (2019). Becoming a High-Growth Firm in a Developing Country: The Role of Co-Funding, *Finance Research Letters*, 29: 330–335.

Macpherson, A. and Holt, R. (2007). Knowledge, Learning and Small Firm Growth: A Systematic Review of the Evidence, *Research Policy*, 36: 172–192.

Madestam, A. (2014). Informal Finance: A Theory of Moneylenders, *Journal of Development Economics*, 107: 157–174.

Madheswaran, S. and Attewell, P. (2007). Caste Discrimination in the Indian Urban Labour Market: Evidence from the National Sample Survey, *Economic and Political Weekly*, 42(41): 4146–4153.

Madill, J., Riding, A. L. and Haines, G. H. (2006). Women Entrepreneurs: Debt Financing and Banking Relationships, *Journal of Small Business and Entrepreneurship*, 19(2), 121–142.

Majumdar, S. K. (1997). The Impact of Size and Age on Firm-Level Performance: Some Evidence from India, *Review of Industrial Organization*, 12(2): 231–241.

Marques, H. (2015). Does the Gender of Top Managers and Owners Matter for Firm Exports?, *Feminist Economics*, 21(4): 89–117.

Martin, L. A., Nataraj, S. and Harrison, A. E. (2017). In with the Big, Out with the Small: Removing Small-Scale Reservations in India, *American Economic Review*, 107(2): 354–386.

Mastercard (2018). *Mastercard Index of Women Entrepreneurs (MIWE) 2018*, https://newsroom.mastercard.com/wp-content/uploads/2018/03/MIWE_2018_Final_Report.pdf

Mathenge, N. and Nikolaidou, E. (2018). *Financial Structure and Economic Growth: Evidence from Sub-Saharan Africa*, ERSA Working Paper 732, Economic Research Southern Africa, South Africa.

Mathew, A. (2019). Making It in India, *Finance and Development*, 56(1): 14–17.

McGahan, A. M. (1999). The Performance of US Corporations: 1981–1994, *Journal of Industrial Economics*, 47: 373–398.

Meyer, L. H. (1998). The Present and Future Roles of Banks in Small Business Finance, *Journal of Banking and Finance*, 22(6–8): 1109–1116.

Mijid, N. and Bernasek. A. (2013). Gender and Credit Rationing of Small Businesses, *The Social Science Journal*, 50(1): 55–65.

Minard, P. (2016). Signalling through the Noise: Private Certification, Information Asymmetry and Chinese SMEs' Access to Finance, *Journal of Asian Public Policy*, 9(3): 243–256.

Ministry of MSME (2009). *Quick Results of the Fourth All India Census of the MSME 2006–2007*, Office of the Development Commissioner, New Delhi, India.

Ministry of MSME (2011). *Annual Report 2010–11*, New Delhi: Government of India.

Ministry of MSME (2018). *Annual Report 2017–18*, New Delhi: Government of India, https://msme.gov.in/sites/default/files/MSME-AR-2017-18-Eng.pdf

Moffatt, P. G. (2005). Hurdle Models of Loan Default, *Journal of the Operational Research Society*, 56: 1063–1071.

Mohamed, K. S. and Temu, A. E. (2009). Gender Characteristics of the Determinants of Access to Formal Credit in Rural Zanzibar, *Savings and Development*, 33(2): 95–111.

Mohan, R. (2002). Small-Scale Industry Policy in India: A Critical Evaluation, in Krueger, A. (ed.), *Economic Policy Reforms and the Indian Economy*, Chicago and London: University of Chicago Press.

Moro, A. and Norman, P. (2003). Affirmative Action in a Competitive Economy, *Journal of Public Economics*, 87(3): 567–594.

Moro, A. and Norman, P. (2004). A General Equilibrium Model of Statistical Discrimination, *Journal of Economic Theory*, 114(1): 1–30.

Morris, S., Basant, R., Das, K., Ramachandran, K. and Koshy, A. (2001). *The Growth and Transformation of Small Firms in India*, New Delhi: Oxford University Press.

Mukherjee, S. (2018). Challenges to Indian Micro Small Scale and Medium Enterprises in the Era of Globalization, *Journal of Global Entrepreneurship Research*, 8: 1–19.

Munnell, A. H., Tootell, G. M., Browne, L. E. and McEneaney, J. (1996). Mortgage Lending in Boston: Interpreting HMDA Data, *American Economic Review*, 86(1): 25–53.

Munshi, K. (2019). Caste and the Indian Economy, *Journal of Economic Literature*, 57(4): 781–834.

Muravyev, A., Talavera, O. and Schäfer, T. (2009). Entrepreneurs' Gender and Financial Constraints: Evidence from International Data, *Journal of Comparative Economics*, 37(2): 270–286.

Nagaraj, P. (2012). Essays on Firm Behavior, *CUNY Academic Works*, https://academicworks.cuny.edu/gc_etds/2219

Nair, T. and Das, K. (2019). Financing the Micro and Small Enterprises in India: Antecedents and Emerging Challenges, *Economic and Political Weekly*, 54(3): 37–43.

Nichter, S. and Goldmark, L. (2009). Small Firm Growth in Developing Countries, *World Development*, 37(9): 1453–1464.

Nikaido, Y., Pais, J. and Sarma, M. (2015). What Hinders and What Enhances Small Enterprises' Access to Formal Credit in India?, *Review of Development Finance*, 5(1): 43–52.

Nikaido, Y., Pais, J. and Sarma, M. (2012). Determinants of access to institutional credit for small enterprises, S. Takahiro (Ed.), The BRICs as Regional Economic Powers in the Global Economy, Hokkaido University, Sapporo. http://src-h.slav.hokudai.ac.jp/rp/publications/no10/10-10_Nakaido.pdf.

Oaxaca, R. L. and Ransom, M. (1998). Calculation of Approximate Variances for Wage Decomposition Differentials, *Journal of Economic and Social Measurement*, 24(1): 55–61.

Oliveira, B. and Fortunato, A. (2006). Firm Growth and Liquidity Constraints: A Dynamic Analysis, *Small Business Economics*, 27: 139–156.

Pan, E. Y. (2014). *Discrimination in Access to Finance: Evidence from the United States Small Business Credit Market*, Senior Thesis, Haverford College, USA, https://scholarship.tricolib.brynmawr.edu/handle/10066/14567

Phelps, E. S. (1972). The Statistical Theory of Racism and Sexism. *American Economic Review*, 62(4): 659–661.

Prakash, A. (2010). Dalit Entrepreneurs in Middle India, in Harriss-White, B. and Heyer, J. (eds.), *The Comparative Political Economy of Development Africa and South Asia*, London: Routledge.

Presbitero, A. F. and Rabellotti, R. (2016). The Determinants of Firm Access to Credit in Latin America: Micro Characteristics and Market Structure, *Economic Notes*, 45(3): 445–472.

Presbitero, A. F., Rabellotti, R. and Piras, C. (2014). Barking Up the Wrong Tree? Measuring Gender Gaps in Firm's Access to Finance, *Journal of Development Studies*, 50: 1430–1444.

Rahaman, M. M. (2011). Access to Financing and Firm Growth, *Journal of Banking and Finance*, 35(3): 709–723.

Raj, R. S. N. and Sen, K. (2015). Finance Constraints and Firm Transition in the Informal Sector: Evidence from Indian Manufacturing, *Oxford Development Studies*, 43(1): 123–143.

Raj, R. S. N. and Sen, K. (2016). *Out of the Shadows? The Informal Sector in Post-Reform India*, New Delhi: Oxford University Press.

Rajan, R. G. and Zingales, L. (1998). Financial Dependence and Growth, *American Economic Review*, 88(3): 559–586.

Rao, C. B. (2014). *An Appraisal of the Priority Sector Lending by Commercial Banks in India*, Monograph 27/2014, Madras School of Economics, Chennai, https://www.mse.ac.in/wp-content/uploads/2016/09/Monograph-for-web-27.pdf

Regasa, D., Fielding, D. and Roberts, H. (2019). Sources of Financing and Firm Growth: Evidence from Ethiopia, *Journal of African Economies*, doi:10.1093/jae/ejz012

Reserve Bank of India (RBI) (2009). *Report of the High Level Committee to Review Lead Bank Scheme*, https://rbidocs.rbi.org.in/rdocs/PublicationReport/Pdfs/LBSR240809.pdf

Reserve Bank of India (RBI) (2015). *Master Circular – Priority Sector Lending – Targets and Classification*, https://rbidocs.rbi.org.in/rdocs/notification/PDFs/53MN7BF63B7F465A4A2F9341D423B5773C5A.PDF

Reserve Bank of India (RBI) (2019). *The Report of the Expert Committee on Micro, Small and Medium Enterprises*, https://rbidocs.rbi.org.in/rdocs//PublicationReport/Pdfs/MSMES24062019465CF8CB30594AC29A7A010E8A2A034C.PDF

Rietz, D. A. and Henrekson, M. (2000). Testing the Female Underperformance Hypothesis, *Small Business Economics*, 14(2): 1–10.

Robb, A. M. and Fairlie, R. (2007). Access to Financial Capital among U.S. Businesses: The Case of African American Firms, *Annals of the American Academy of Political and Social Science*, 613: 4–72.

Robb, A. M. and Fairlie, R. (2009). Gender Differences in Business Performance: Evidence from the Characteristics of Business Owners Survey, *Small Business Economics*, 33(4): 375–395.

Robb, A. M. and Watson, J. (2012). Gender Differences in Firm Performance: Evidence from New Ventures in the United States, *Journal of Business Venturing*, 27: 544–558.

Robins, J. M., Hernan, M. A. and Brumback, B. A. (2000). Marginal Structural Models and Causal Inference in Epidemiology, *Epidemiology*, 11: 550–560.

Rosenbaum, P. and Rubin, D. (1983). The Central Role of the Propensity Score in Observational Studies for Causal Effects, *Biometrika*, 70(1): 41–55.

Rosenthal, S. S. and Strange, W. C. (2004). Evidence on the Nature and Sources of Agglomeration Economies, in Henderson, J. V. and Thisse, J. F. (eds.), *Handbook of Urban and Regional Economics*, vol. 4. Amsterdam: Elsevier, pp. 2119–2172.

Rubin, D. (1973). Matching to Remove Bias in Observational Studies, *Biometrics*, 29(3): 159–183.

Rubini, L., Piguillem, F. and Crespo, A. (2012). Breaking Down the Barriers to Firm Growth in Europe, *Bruegel Blueprint 18*, http://faculty.smu.edu/kdesmet/papers/efigefirmgrowth.pdf

Sabarwal, S. and Terrell, K. (2008). *Does Gender Matter for Firm Performance? Evidence from Eastern Europe and Central Asia*, IZA Discussion Papers 3758, Institute for Study of Labour, Bonn.

Sacerdoti, E. (2005). *Access to Bank Credit in Sub-Saharan Africa: Key Issues and Reform Strategies*, Working Paper WP/05/166, International Monetary Fund, Washington, DC.

Saini, P. (2014). *Study of Micro, Small and Medium Enterprises*, Working Paper 319, Centre for Civil Society, India.

Sarap, K. (1990). Factors Affecting Small Farmers Access to Institutional Credit in Rural Orissa, India, *Development and Change*, 21(2): 281–307.

Schmitz, H. (1982). Growth Constraints on Small-Scale Manufacturing in Developing Countries: A Critical Review, *World Development*, 10(6): 429–450.

Sen, K. and Vaidya, R. R. (1997). *The Process of Financial Liberalization in India*, New Delhi: Oxford University Press.

Shah, M., Rao, R. and Vijay Shankar, P. S. (2007). Rural Credit in 20th Century India: Overview of History and Perspective, *Economic and Political Weekly*, 42(15): 1351–1364.

Shankar, S. (2019). *The Role of Credit Rating Agencies in Addressing Gaps in Micro and Small Enterprise Financing: The Case of India*, ADBI Working Paper Series No. 931, Asian Development Bank Institute, Tokyo.

Shanmugam, K. R. and Bhaduri, S. N. (2002). Size, Age and Firm Growth in the Indian Manufacturing Sector, *Applied Economics Letters*, 9(9): 607–613.

Sharma, S. (2014). Benefits of a Registration Policy for Microenterprise Performance in India, *Small Business Economics*, 42(1): 153–164.

SIDBI (2010). *Report on Micro, Small and Medium Enterprises Sector*, Small Industries Development Bank of India, New Delhi, India.

Singh, C. and Wasdani, K. P. (2016). *Finance for Micro, Small, and Medium-Sized Enterprises in India: Sources and Challenges*, Working Paper No. 525, ADBI Working Paper Series, Asian Development Bank Institute, Tokyo, Japan.

Sleuwaegen, L. and Goedhuys, M. (2002). Growth of Firms in Developing Countries: Evidence from Côte d'Ivoire, *Journal of Development Economics*, 68(1): 117–135.

Snodgrass, D. R. and Biggs, T. (1996). *Industrialization and the Small Firm: Patterns and Policies*, San Francisco: ICS Press.

Stiglitz, J. E. (1973). Approaches to the Economics of Discrimination, *American Economic Review*, 62(2): 287–295.

Stiglitz, J. E. and Weiss, A. (1981). Credit Rationing in Markets with Imperfect Information, *American Economic Review*, 71(3): 393–410.

Storey, D. J. (1994). *Understanding the Small Business Sector*, London: Thomson Learning.

Storey, D. J. and Thompson, J. (1995). *The Financing of New and Small Enterprises in OECD Countries*, Paris: OECD.

Tendulkar, S. and Bhavani, T. A. (1997). Policy on Modern Small Scale Industries: A Case of Government Failure, *Indian Economic Review*, 32(1): 39–64.

Thorat, S. K. and Neuman, K. S. (eds.) (2012). *Blocked by Caste: Economic Discrimination in Modern India*, Oxford and New Delhi: Oxford University Press.

Thorat, S. K. and Sadana, N. (2009). Caste and Social Ownership of Private Capital, *Economic and Political Weekly*, 44(23): 13–16.

Tlaiss, H. A. (2014). Women's Entrepreneurship, Barriers and Culture: Insights from the United Arab Emirates, *The Journal of Entrepreneurship*, 23(2): 289–320.

Tobin, J. (1958). Estimation of Relationships for Limited Dependent Variables, *Econometrica*, 26(1): 24–36.

Topalova, P. and Khandelwal, A. (2011). Trade Liberalization and Firm Productivity: The Case of India, *Review of Economics and Statistics*, 93(3): 995–1009.

Treichel, M. Z. and Scott, J. A. (2006). Women-Owned Businesses and Access to Bank Credit: Evidence from Three Surveys Since 1987, *Venture Capital*, 8(1): 51–67.

Tsai, K. S. (2004). Imperfect Substitutes: The Local Political Economy of Informal Finance and Microfinance in Rural China and India, *World Development*, 32(9): 1487–1507.

Van Biesebroeck, J. (2005). Firm Size Matters: Growth and Productivity Growth in African Manufacturing, *Economic Development and Cultural Change*, 53(3): 545–583.

Van de Ven, W. P. M. M. and Van Praag, B. M. S. (1981). The Demand for Deductibles in Private Health Insurance: A Probit Model with Sample Selection, *Journal of Econometrics*, 17(2): 229–252.

Verheul, I. and Thurik, R. (2001). Start-Up Capital: Does Gender Matter? *Small Business Economics*, 16(4): 329–345.

Watson, J. (2002). Comparing the Performance of Male- and Female-Controlled Businesses: Relating Outputs to Inputs, *Entrepreneurship Theory and Practice*, 26(3): 91–100.

WEF (World Economic Forum) (2018). *Global Gender Gap Report*, World Economic Forum, Geneva, Switzerland.

WEF (World Economic Forum) (2020). *Global Gender Gap Index 2020*, World Economic Forum, Geneva, Switzerland, www3.weforum.org/docs/WEF_GGGR_2020.pdf

Wolfolds, S. E. and Siegel, J. (2019). Misaccounting for Endogeneity: The Peril of Relying on the Heckman Two-Step Method without a Valid Instrument, *Strategic Management Journal*, 40(3): 432–462.

World Bank (2008). *Finance for All? Policies and Pitfalls in Expanding Access*, Washington, DC: World Bank.

INDEX

Page numbers in **bold** and *italics* refer to figures and tables respectively.

For Product Safety Concerns and Information please contact our EU representative GPSR@taylorandfrancis.com
Taylor & Francis Verlag GmbH, Kaufingerstraße 24, 80331 München, Germany

www.ingramcontent.com/pod-product-compliance
Lightning Source LLC
LaVergne TN
LVHW021127300926
849160LV00010B/894

* 9 7 8 0 3 6 7 6 9 3 0 1 5 *